W9-BVW-686

Contents

Part II
Yoga: Prayer of the Body

Part III
Praying with Heart and Body

Acknowledgments

This book is a community effort, reflecting in its different stages the support and assistance of friends and colleagues.

Though he is now deceased, I would like to pay tribute to Dom John Main who served me as a spiritual guide and whose teaching is at the root of Part I on Meditation. God's providence seems intent to keep me in the footsteps of my teacher as I become co-director of Unitas, formerly the Benedictine Priory founded by John Main, and now an ecumenical center for spirituality and Christian meditation. It is a grace and a privilege to be one of many who carry the work forward.

The training program leading to certification as a yoga instructor, and thus Parts II and III of this manuscript, were made possible by a grant from the Graymoor Friars of the Atonement as well as by a generous contribution from friends of the Canadian Centre for Ecumenism who wish to remain anonymous.

The helpful comments of several friends and colleagues—Carolyn Cronk, Margaret O'Donnell, Francis McKee, Pat O'Rourke, Philip St. Romain, Tom Gillette—resulted in improvements in the presentation and content. Sharon Smith's meticulous proofreading helped me clean up the final text.

Were it not for the technical expertise of computer wiz Ann Herbert and the redrafting assistance of Eliane Massoud, this book would very likely still be "in the oven" instead of being laid on the table for general consumption.

I owe a very special thanks to Elizabeth Pascal for her wonderful illustrations. "Yoga books tend to feature perfect bodies," I said. "Give me real, ordinary people. That's who this book is for." And she did.

Finally, I am grateful to my editor, Fr. Larry Boadt, CSP, for his editorial comments, intuitions, suggestions, and the dialogical style in which he expresses them.

To each and every one of you: heartfelt thanks for your appreciated contribution!

Dedication

To all those friends and teachers who are
bringing their own creativity and dedication to
helping Christians make the points of
connection between the practice
of meditation and yoga
and their faith.

Foreword

In this book Thomas Ryan is underlining a truly good news for us: it is possible for all of us to enter into a loving communion with God; it is possible for us all to become fire. The experience of God is not reserved for a few strong people, capable of great ascetism, men and women called into total abnegation in the desert. If Father Ryan has offered me the privilege of writing this Foreword it is precisely because he knows I am living in l'Arche with people who have a mental handicap. These wonderful men and women unable to fully develop their intellect have nevertheless "mystical hearts": they are able to live a real experience of love with God in Jesus. They have revealed to me clearly the meaning of the words of Jesus: to enter into the Kingdom of God, which is the Kingdom of love, we must become like little children. We must all rediscover our mystical hearts.

So this book is good news for us all, but especially for those who are tempted to seek God in Eastern spiritualities, "mystical" techniques, or in movements akin to the "new age," and who have felt disappointed, even cheated, by the Christian churches. These churches have seemed to many to be closed 'n in moral laws or turned outward in social justice. They

enc.

trary, we find God as we find our true roots and our own mystical hearts.

However if this gift is offered to us all, it requires nevertheless a certain discipline. Quoting extensively both classical and contemporary authors, Fr. Tom helps us to discover a

1

simple yet concrete way to enter into relationship with God. It is the way of the heart or the way of the *mantra*. Repeating slowly and lovingly a sacred word, a word of love, we are as if led into the presence of God. And then we can be still, and listen, in love. Open. Quiet.

Tom has had the opportunity to place himself at the feet of spiritual leaders of the East. He has experienced in his own prayer life the value of the "ways" taught in India and in Buddhist monasteries. In his previous book, *Disciplines for Christian Living: Interfaith Perspectives*, he showed the value that can come from contacts with other religions.

Fr. Ryan is rooted in his own Christian background and Catholic tradition. He is able to integrate all that is beautiful, wise and holy in other traditions. This is of great value. His book is pacifying and unifying. It can help us all to understand the need for disciplines such as yoga and meditation with their accent on posture, breathing, and focused awareness to assist us in entering the path of union with God. At the same time, as he stresses, this union is not the fruit of a technique. It is the gift of love of a loving person, Jesus, who is in love with each one of us and offers us the joy of a relationship which takes us into the very mystery of God.

Jean Vanier
L'Arche
Trosly-Breuil, France

Introduction

This book is for several kinds of people:

1) Practicing Christians who are going to church but who feel that their present routine still leaves them far from the vitality and inner peace in Christ which they seek.

2) Christians who meditate and/or do yoga and who experience real benefit from it but who find little or no support for it in their church community.

3) Christians who are are somewhat unclear in their own minds what the points of connection are between practices like imageless, non-verbal prayer, yoga and their Christian faith.

4) Christians who practice meditation or centering prayer, who are clear about how it relates to their faith, but who would like to come to deeper centeredness and awareness. For those who find themselves described here, Part I on Meditation will serve as a good review of the historic roots and the practical aspects of meditation in a Christian context. Part II on Yoga may open new doors for those who have no idea that yoga was essentially designed as a series of postures and breathing methods to quiet the body and focus the mind so as to meditate with greater clarity of consciousness.

5) Those of no church background, or whose Christian faith is no longer active, or those who may be members of

other religions and are simply curious as to what Christian faith has to say about meditation and yoga.

About this last group I would like to say a special word. Isaac Thomas Hecker, the founder of my religious community, the Paulists, was a nineteenth century New Yorker who for several years was in the thick of the Transcendentalist movement and its utopian communitarian experiments at Fruitlands and Brook Farm in Massachusetts. It was a movement in which some of the brightest and most zealous young people of the time turned their backs on the "cold corpse" of established religion, moving from the "world of creeds and rituals to the temple of the Living God in the soul."[1]

God was within, readily available, and anxious to perfect the human soul. Ralph Waldo Emerson, the most brilliant among the proponents of Transcendentalism, told a Harvard Divinity School audience to "go alone, refuse the good models, even those most sacred in the imagination of men, and dare to love God without mediator or veil."[2] Liberated from a pervasive sense of their own sinfulness, from old worries about human pride and divine judgment, the Transcendentalists— so called because they believed in an order of truths which transcends the sphere of the external senses—read their "soul hunger" and yearning for God as sure signs that union with God was possible. They maintained that the truth of religion did not depend on tradition, nor on historical facts, but has an infallible witness in the soul. Hecker spent the better part of his life, after his own spiritual journey led to the church, trying to demonstrate to that stratum of society he regarded as "earnest seekers" how Catholicism responded to its aspirations.

In my own perception, the twentieth century parallel of the nineteenth century Transcendentalists are those spiritual seekers pilgrimaging to meditation centers and yoga ashrams, here and abroad, looking for teachers, masters, and gurus who will speak to them of that "light in the soul" and provide them with reliable methods and techniques to make it grow until it sets their hearts ablaze. In most cases, these spiritual technologies come out of a Hindu or Buddhist context. The increasing availability of such centers of instruction here in the West is a logical outgrowth of the immigration influx from Eastern countries. According to a recent newspaper article, the largest Buddhist monastery in the world is soon to be built in the Eastern Townships outside of Montreal.

In ages past, the West was identified as Christian and the East as Hindu, Buddhist, Taoist, and Muslim. The one knew precious little about the others. All that is changing. The once clearly demarcated lines are blurring as Middle and Far Easterners come to the West, and Westerners routinely travel in the East. The old stereotype of Westerners being outer-directed (e.g. studying nature and controlling it for their own purposes) and of Easterners being inner-directed (concerned simply with how to live in harmony with nature) no longer holds. Fr. Bede Griffiths told the story of a Hindu who express-ed genuine surprise upon learning that her Christian friends meditated: "You mean you Christians pray? I thought you just ran schools, hospitals and orphanages!" The age of Christian meditation, yoga and Zen, as well as of Buddhist and Hindu social action consciousness, is upon us. We are sharing our insights regarding the human project with one another.

I participated in the teacher-training program in yoga at a large center in North America, Kripalu (a Sanskrit word meaning "compassion"), set in the Berkshire mountains near Lenox, Massachusetts. There are two observations for our present purposes that I would like to make about this ashram.

First, it is located in a large building which, until 1985, served as a Jesuit novitiate. The Jesuits sold it because they didn't have enough recruits seeking to join their ranks for a life of church service. Today, there is a residential community of three hundred, most of whom accept celibacy, all of whom accept simplicity of lifestyle and obedience to their teacher, Yogi Amrit Desai. Add to that another three hundred pro-gram participants who swell the ranks to six hundred in any given week or month of the year. Nowadays, every available inch of space is needed to accommodate those who want to come. During my several weeks there, I occupied one among twenty-four bunk beds in a basement room probably designed for storage in the original seminary plans.

There is a further irony. In the main chapel one can still see a beautiful mosaic of St. Ignatius of Loyola, the founder of the Jesuits, looking up with hands outstretched toward the spot where the crucifix once hung behind the main altar. That spot is now occupied by a large framed picture of the guru at the head of this ashram's lineage. Ignatius' uplifted hands toward the guru might well be captioned, "Where did we go wrong?" The organ still sits in the choir loft with a dust cover over it. The pews, with crosses carved on the ends of them, line the hallways and continue to give rest to spiritual seekers. Though the proprietorship changes hands, God is a permanent tenant. The spiritual work of healing, calling people to selfless service, and bringing them into contact with the divinity that inhabits us goes on.

The second thing I observed is that the vast majority of those who are responding to what Kripalu is offering are between 20 and 45 years of age. One Sunday I looked around me at the congregation gathered for Mass at the nearby Catholic church in Lenox and observed that the vast majority of them were between 50 and 75. I do not know of a mainline church pastor who does not worry about the graying trend of his or her congregation, nor bemoan the absence of the young. On that score, one of the most impressive program components at Kripalu is called Spiritual Life Training (SLT). Most of its participants are young people.

In the SLT brochure, one finds that it offers "a chance to see for yourself what total immersion in a spiritual lifestyle can mean." Participants commit to celibacy for the 3-4 month program and serve forty hours per week without pay with two half days off per week. The ways in which they serve are not at all glamorous: washing dishes, cleaning bathrooms, vacuuming carpets, preparing food, serving in the dining room, and so forth. They are invited to discover the "deep joy and satisfaction that fills you when you are giving of yourself fully," for "when you serve others, your own life is enriched." The emphasis is on "discovering yourself and your true potential through selfless service and self-awareness," "growing through service to others" and "letting go of habitual concerns about recognition, compensation, perfection, and competition."

By and large, the churches have yet to find similar ways of making service roles in the church attractive to the energetic, idealistic young.

Obviously, there are some things to be learned from the places that are drawing young adults, young and middle-aged parents and singles. In looking at the broad range of programming at Kripalu, one of my own conclusions about what draws people and brings them back again and again is that here is a place that helps them get out of their heads and into their bodies and feel comfortable there. Getting in touch with their embodied self and its innate wisdom can be an inner experience of coming home for people, many of whom have absorbed negative messages about their bodies in early childhood and have never had a positive experience of "being in their bodies."

Christianity, by contrast, is in the awkward position of trying to affirm the goodness of creation without ever having delighted in human bodiliness. One would think that between our two central doctrines of the Incarnation and the Resurrection—the one, in which God chose to call human bodiliness "home," and the other, in which that broken, weary body is not discarded but re-embraced and taken into the very life of the Trinity for all eternity—we could do better at helping people to embrace and relate positively to their enspirited flesh as a joyful mode of existence!

On one level, as expressed in the hospitals, orphanages, soup kitchens and the like, Christianity has been very incarnational. However, I would submit that the church is not yet incarnational enough in its healing ministry to people in all respects. When people come with problems for counseling, our inclination is to sit them down in chairs and let them talk it out. That surely has its place. Yet if it stays just at the level of the "head," then once again we have denied our body and its role in things. Many people in our Western world do precious little with their bodies. They sit at a desk all day at work, sit during their lunch break, sit behind the wheel of a car commuting, and sit in front of a television at night to try to relax. Yoga is a gentle way to get people back in touch with their bodies. While it has the benefit of being a full-body muscular and skeletal strengthening exercise, it is, as I hope to show in these pages, a profound spiritual discipline as well. It is still in its infancy in the West but there is one thing about it that particularly recommends it for Westerners: it provides fidgety activists with something to do. One of its sterling values is that it gives them a taste of inner stillness.

In his book *Healing and the Mind*, Bill Moyers interviews Jon Kabat-Zinn, the founder of a stress reduction clinic at the University of Massachusetts.[3] Kabat-Zinn speaks about meditation and yoga as "consciousness disciplines." Their essence has to do with cultivating awareness and a deeper understanding of what it means to be human. In our culture we are busy doing, doing, doing all the time, but much of it is distracted. Are there any among us who could not benefit from greater awareness? If we were more in touch with the present moment, almost everything would become more vivid and alive. Meditation has to do with being fully here, now. Yoga provides the opportunity to reestablish contact not only with our body but with our feeling and mood states. After one has put one's body in various positions, then one simply experiences the feelings and sensations that emerge as one relaxes into the posture. Thus, yoga serves basically as a doorway into awareness. In meditation, one passes through that doorway and becomes aware of the Mystery at the root of one's being.

Stress and tension have become societal and cultural plagues in the Western world. In a 1992 survey of how Canadians spend their time, Statistics Canada discovered that one in three felt they were "constantly under stress"—"Too much to do, too little time to do it."[4] Job stress is a worldwide plague that afflicts British miners and Swedish waitresses just as it burns out Japanese schoolteachers and American executives. The 1993 World Labor Report by the International Labor Organization said that "stress has become one of the most serious health issues of the twentieth century. The Japanese have even coined a term for death by overwork: *karoshi*."[5] The report indicated that stress has become a global phenomenon. In Australia, stress claims by government workers have increased 90 percent in three years. A French survey showed that 64 percent of nurses and 61 percent of school teachers were upset over stressful working conditions. Another study said stress-related diseases such as ulcers, high blood pressure and heart attacks cost the U.S. economy $200 billion a year.

Says Kabat-Zinn: "When people develop the capacity to relax deeply, to stablize the mind, to become aware of what's going on within them and around them, oftentimes what's wrong with them will take care of itself or they'll become clear what corrective steps need to be made . . . . Meditation and yoga invite the stressed-out citizen of the 1990s not to all of a sudden do nothing, but to practice creative non-doing. Doing so brings us to focused, conscious awareness and begins to transform the quality of our experiencing and the quality of our living."[6]

Prayer of Heart and Body is intended as a companion volume to *Disciplines for Christian Living*[7] which developed a positive content for the notion of discipline: that which disposes and liberates us to realize, through the working of the Holy Spirit, what is deepest and best in us. The subjects treated in *Disciplines* surprised some people who were not expecting to find friendship and family life, taking a day off regularly, exercise and play alongside of more traditional topics like fasting and service. But each of them fulfills the notion of discipline set forth in that book and carried forward in this one.

In our desire to fully appreciate what it means to be human, we are foolish if we do not take seriously the efforts made by people over thousands of years to look inward. Some of these efforts come from the East, some from the West, some from Christians, some from members of other living faiths. In our era, thanks to the technological advances that have reduced the distances between us, we have come to realize that we are not so far from one another in the things we yearn for and the responses we develop to those yearnings. As we move ahead in the cozy confines of our spaceship earth, it seems fully time that the various traditions of human consciousness share their accumulated wisdom with one another.

Part I
Meditation: Prayer of the Heart

1

Meditation: Breaking Through to the Real

Once upon a time there was a man who cultivated the skill of reproducing very authentically the sounds of various animals. He became so good at it that people would gather in crowds to listen to his performances, at the end of which he would pass the hat and collect a small fee. By moving around in the region, he earned more than he needed to live on and enjoyed a comfortable existence. One day as he was performing in a town park, a sage passed by with his disciples. The sage watched the man grunt like a pig, whinny like a horse, and cock-a-doodle-do like a rooster. He decided he would teach his disciples one of life's important lessons.

The following day the sage put up a small platform and advertised that there would be a better performance and no fees. A big crowd gathered. The sage brought out a pig, a horse, and a rooster and squeezed each until it made its characteristic sound. Though their sounds were authentic and real, the people booed and cat-called, shouting that he had tricked them.

When the crowd had dispersed, the sage turned to his disciples and said, "You see, people are so stimulated by appearances that they do not care about reality."

In a television special entitled "The Image and America," Bill Moyers analyzed the methods of the advertising industry and concluded: "We have more ways than ever now of presenting forms of unreality." We are caught up in the world of appearances. The real in oneself and in the external world is not the object of concern for the majority of people. Those who focus upon the real and speak about it to others are often looked at askance, as though they are drawing people away from what is useful and productive in society. The American writer and philosopher Henry David Thoreau spoke about his desire to get beyond appearances to touch what was deepest and best in life when he wrote:

> *Most of the luxuries, and many of the so-called comforts in life, are not only not indispensable, but positive hindrances to the elevation of humankind. I went to the woods because I wished to live deliberately, to front only the essential facts of life, and see if I could learn what it had to teach, and not, when I came to die, discover that I had not lived. I did not wish to live what was not life; living is so dear, I wanted to live deep, and suck out all the marrow of life, to live so sturdily and Spartan-like as to put to rout all that was not life.[1]*

More and more people today are realizing that the human spirit cannot find fulfillment in mere material success or material prosperity. It isn't that material success and prosperity are bad in themselves; rather, they are simply not adequate as a final, ultimate answer to the human situation. In order to know and understand ourselves, to get our problems into perspective, we simply must make contact with our spirit. At a conference Fr. Bede Griffiths was giving at his ashram in South India, he was asked, "What advice would you give to those seeking to achieve a greater harmony of spirit, mind and body?"

"My answer," he replied, "is meditation. I do not know any other way of discovering this inner harmony. If a person learned to sit and meditate and allowed the body and mind to become calm, then the deeper level of the spirit would emerge." All self-understanding arises from understanding ourselves as spiritual beings, and it is only contact with the universal Holy Spirit that can give us the depth and the breadth to understand our own experience. Meditation is the way most commonly employed by seekers throughout history in their quest to penetrate surface appearances and come to grips with the Real.

Meditation is not merely the intellectual effort to master certain ideas about God, or even to impress upon our minds the mysteries of the Christian faith. Conceptual knowledge of religious truth has an important place in our lives. The spiritual life needs strong intellectual foundations, and reading theology helps us understand faith experience. But meditation itself is neither study nor intellectual activity as such. Its purpose is not to acquire or to deepen our speculative knowledge of God or of revelation. Rather than seeking to know *about* God, we are seeking to *know God directly*, beyond all the objects which God has made. We are seeking to *experience* God's presence with the awareness of loving faith.[2]

What Do We Mean by Meditation?

Unfortunately, the term "meditation" does not always have a clear and distinctive meaning because in the history of spirituality the word is used to refer to very different kinds of prayer. In many Western schools of spirituality—the Ignatian and Carmelite schools, for example—meditation most often refers to a mentally discursive form of prayer which employs rational thought and imagination. Texts like those of Reginald Garrigou-Legrange, in vogue up to the middle of this century, speak of meditation as a form of mental prayer in which the *mind thinks* about God and divine things. The stress is on the intellect and will in the employment of reflections, affections and holy resolutions.

Other schools of Christian spirituality, as well as other religions like Hinduism and Buddhism and movements like Transcendental Meditation, use the word meditation when they want to speak about focusing the awareness in ways which use no thoughts or images. Such is generally referred to in the Christian manuals on prayer as "contemplation." A recent and widespread movement among Christians which teaches imageless prayer attempted to avoid this confusion of terminology by adopting the name Centering Prayer. A similar international movement promoting the imageless method uses the identifying tag Christian Meditation.

Meditation falls into two basic types: concentrative meditation, and uncovering or awareness meditation. In concentrative meditation, you focus attention upon a single object to the exclusion of everything else. As soon as you become aware that you are thinking, you bring your attention back to the single object—an image, a word, a candle flame. In the second kind of meditation, uncovering or awareness meditation, you try to be aware of all that you are experiencing. So the attention is constantly directed to different objects of awareness—emotions, body sensations, noises. Neither one employs thinking and analyzing. Both employ simple awareness in surrendered openness. In the first case, the field of awareness is restricted and concentrated; in the second, it is open and receptive to everything that is happening in one's body and mind.[3]

There are many different useful techniques for accomplishing both forms of meditation. In learning to meditate, it is advisable to work with only one method and become solidly grounded in it. It is better to dig a deep well and strike water than to dig several shallow holes.

The particular type of meditation set forth in these pages is concentrative. It is drawn from Christian writings relating to contemplation or contemplative prayer. We appear consigned to a certain degree of terminological ambiguity where these words—meditation and contemplation—are concerned, so it becomes all the more important in talking or writing about meditation to establish the meaning the word carries for the user. The particular way of prayer indicated should become clearer in the following general description of it.

The form of prayer referred to here by the term "meditation" is based upon the conviction that, in addition to the mind and heart with which we ordinarily communicate with

God, we are endowed with a mystical heart, a faculty which makes it possible for us to know God directly, to grasp and intuit God's very presence and being, though in a dark manner, apart from all images and concepts. Anthony de Mello[4] speaks of it in the following terms.

Ordinarily, all our contact with God is indirect—through images and concepts that necessarily distort God's reality. To be able to grasp God beyond these thoughts and images is the privilege of this faculty of the "mystical heart." In most of us, this heart lies dormant and undeveloped. If it were to be awakened, it would be constantly straining toward God. It is like a magnet filing covered over with obstructive matter. In order to allow its natural property to come forth, the dross covering it must be removed so that it can be attracted to the Eternal Magnet. We might be inclined to think of such dross only in terms of selfishness and sin, but the dross might also be the vast number of thoughts and words and images that we constantly interpose between ourselves and God in our efforts to communicate with God. Words sometimes serve to impede rather than to foster communication and intimacy. As spouses know, silence can be a very powerful form of communication and union when hearts are full of love. As long as our mind machine keeps spinning out millions of thoughts and words, our mystical heart remains undeveloped.

Development of this faculty, however, takes place in relation to the shutting down of certain other faculties on which we normally rely. It is like the development of sharper visual perception in a deaf person; because she cannot hear, she learns to watch the movement of lips very closely and to read them. A blind person develops his sense of hearing and touch to compensate for sight. What is called for in our meditation might be thought of as a "mental blindness." If we could put a bandage over our mind while we are communicating with God, we would likewise be forced to develop some other faculty for communicating—that faculty which is already straining to move out to God anyway if it were given a chance to develop: the mystical heart.

It is one thing, however, to look lovingly into the eyes of an intimate friend and communicate beyond words, but what do we look at when we simply seek to gaze upon God? At first, it seems like nothing more than staring into an empty, blank void. Nothing seems to happen. It feels as if we're wasting our time. To escape from this uncomfortable and seemingly unnatural state, we take the bandage off our minds and begin to think and speak with God. But eventually we may find that this well of words and thoughts dries up every time we try to communicate with God. Then we may feel inclined to abandon prayer altogether because we find ourselves forced to choose between the frustration of not being able to use our minds and the hollow feeling of wasting our time and doing nothing in the darkness that meets us when we silence our minds.

But if we avoid this trap and persevere in imageless meditation and expose ourselves, in blind faith, to the emptiness, the darkness, the idleness, the nothingness, we will gradually discover, at first in small flashes, later in a more permanent fashion, that there is a glow in the darkness, that the emptiness mysteriously fills our hearts, that the idleness is full of God's activity, that in the nothingness our being is recreated and shaped anew—and all of this in a way that we just cannot describe either to ourselves or to others. We only know that something mysterious has been working within us, bringing refreshment and nourishment and well-being with it. We will notice that we have a yearning hunger to return to this dark contemplation that seems to make no sense and yet fills us with life. An example of the directives given for meditating in this way is as follows:

Seek out a quiet place. Find a comfortable, upright position in which you are relaxed but alert, with your eyes lightly closed. Remain as still as possible.

Silently, begin to say interiorly a single word or phrase selected from the context of Christian faith. Listen to it as you say it gently but continuously with faith and love. Do not think or imagine anything, spiritual or otherwise. If thoughts and images come and your attention strays, as soon as you become aware of this, return to saying your word.

Meditate each morning and evening for between twenty and thirty minutes.

This form of prayer, so simple in its instructions yet so fulfilling in its practice, may strike many as unlike any of the ways in which they were taught to pray. In the chapters that follow, the rationale for the use of a sacred word, for frequency and length of time in reciting it and so forth, will all be carefully explained. It suffices for the moment to acknowledge that this way of praying has its own rich history in both Eastern and Western Christianity. The purpose of Part I of this book is to help those of Christian background who meditate to consciously root their practice in the soil of Christian faith.

2

What Makes for Christian *Meditation?*

There are similarities among the world religions in methods of meditating. This is not surprising, since all people, including the Zen masters, the yogis, the monks of Tibet and Christian meditators, have the same kind of mental faculties and nervous system. Historical studies in various meditation techniques indicate that the practice of meditation has never been confined to any one religion or culture. Though its methods of practice vary, meditation has been known worldwide, in every religion and culture from ancient Egypt to the Inuit (Eskimo) and native North American Indians.[1]

It is only in more recent times that methods of meditation have been recorded in books which explain what it is, what it does, and how it works. Some say it is a way to evoke the relaxation response. Others say it is a way to train and strengthen awareness; a method for centering and focusing the self; a way to halt constant verbal thinking; a technique for calming the central nervous system; a way to relieve stress, bolster self-esteem, reduce anxiety and alleviate depression. And, in fact, meditation has been clinically demonstrated to do all of these things.

But meditation is, and always has been, a *spiritual* practice. Meditation, whether Christian, Hindu, or Muslim, was invented as a way for the soul to venture inward and to find there an experience of union with the Godhead. Whatever else it does, meditation is first and foremost a search for the God within. It has to do with awakening to one's true Self, with Spirit found in one's heart. As such, meditation is part of the universal spiritual culture of humankind. It is part of what has been called the "perennial philosophy."[2]

The perennial philosophy is the worldview that has been espoused by the vast majority of the world's greatest spiritual teachers, philosophers, theologians and scientists. It is called "perennial" or "universal" because it shows up in virtually all cultures across the globe and across the ages. One finds it in India, China, Egypt, Japan, Tibet, Greece, Ireland and so on. And wherever it is found the world over, it has essentially similar features. Whether they lived five thousand years ago or are living today, men and women report the same insights and teach the same essential doctrine from Mexico in the West to Cambodia in the East. This remarkable convergence of experience testifies to the universal nature of these truths, to the universal experience of a collective humanity that has everywhere agreed to certain profound truths about the human condition and its access to the Divine.

The existence of different human cultures does not negate these similar conclusions when one allows for the important distinction made by anthropology between "deep structures" and "surface structures." "Deep structures" refer to the universal features of the human person which are everywhere essentially the same. The human body, for example, has the same number of bones and internal organs everywhere in the world. And every human mind has the capacity to form images, symbols, concepts and rules. Just as the human body universally grows hair and the human mind universally grows ideas, so the human spirit universally grows intuitions of the Divine. Those intuitions and insights form the core of the world's great spiritual traditions. It is on this level of the deep structures that the perennial philosophy emerges; and it is the human encounter with the Divine in which it is particularly interested.

The variants from one culture to another relate to the "surface structures." Thus, different cultures use the deep structures in different ways, from Chinese footbinding to Ubangi lipstretching and body painting to clothing styles. Similarly, the mental surface structures vary considerably, but the mental deep structures are virtually identical. Just as you don't have a Scandinavian physics versus a Canadian physics, you don't have a Christian mystical science versus a Muslim mystical science. Rather, they are in fundamental agreement as to the nature of the soul, the nature of Spirit, and the nature of their supreme identity, among many other things. This is what the scholars refer to as "the transcendental unity of the world's religions." When you find a truth that the Taoists and Buddhists and Hindus and Christians and Muslims all agree on, then you have likely found something that is profoundly important, something that touches the very core of the human condition.

According to the perennial philosophy, reality consists of several different levels, from the least real to the most real, going from matter to body, to mind, to soul, to spirit. In human growth and development, the real Self starts out identified with the material self, then the bodily self, then the mental self, then the soul self, and finally awakens to its own true nature as spirit. Each stage includes the previous stage, and then adds its own unique aspects in order to form a larger union until all the dimensions of reality are integrated one with another but obedient to spirit. Meditation is simply a way to carry forward this ongoing development beyond the mind into the levels of soul and spirit. The experience of timeless unity of spirit with Spirit is not an idea or a wish, but a direct apprehension on the part of seekers across the ages.

The laboratory in which seekers in different cultures carried out their experiments was the human mind, and the method used was meditation. People today who try it for themselves and compare their "test results" continue to affirm the validity of this consensually validated pool of experiential knowledge. Through meditation, they arrive at certain laws of the spirit, at certain profound truths which, in the perennial philosophy, have been summarized as follows: 1) Spirit exists. 2) Spirit is found within. 3) Most of us don't realize this Spirit within because we are living in a fallen, illusory state of sin. 4) There is a way out of this fallen state, a path to our liberation. 5) If we follow this path to its conclusion, there is a direct experience of Spirit within, a Supreme Liberation which 6) marks the end of sin and suffering and 7) ushers in mercy and compassion on behalf of all. [3]

In the wisdom of these great traditions of spirituality expressed in the perennial philosophy, it is our ego which blocks our realization of our supreme identity, our realization of the deepest or highest part of ourselves which transcends our mortal ego and directly partakes of the Divine. The distinction between a person's immortal spirit and a person's ego is a fundamental tenet of the perennial philosophy. The ego is a conglomeration of identifications (Canadian, Catholic, Québecois), roles (son, brother, priest), values, goals, and judgmental convictions (athletic, intelligent, sensitive) that we have been socialized into or programmed with through our upbringing and with which we have identified. The culture provides many identifications, roles, and judgmental convictions for the ego to choose from and identify with.

However, the ego is not the true Self. It is a stage in our growth and our awareness. It is not false in the sense of *unreal*; our sense of *I* is real enough. What is false about it is that the *I* is totally identified with roles and judgmental convictions which it in fact believes itself to be. The goal of the spiritual journey is to shift our point of identification from this conditioning which represents our personal ego, our self (small s), to our real Self, capital S, that is one with God, one with Spirit. Thus did St. Augustine say in a succinct Latin phrase, *Noverim te, noverim me*: "May I know You, may I know myself!"

Is God Identical with or Distinct from the Self?

This kind of language necessitates dealing with the ongoing dialectic between theologies of transcendence and theologies of incarnation. In other words: is God identical with, or distinct from, the Self?

It is tempting to contrast the great world religions, placing Hinduism, for example, in the monistic camp, and Christianity in the dualistic. Hinduism, for example, has shown a monistic face to the West in the form of the *advaita* (non-dualistic) Vedanta school of Hindu thought, with the central insight that *Atman* (Self) is *Brahman* (God). And conversely Christianity, rejecting pantheism, is at pains to keep a firm distinction between God the creator, on the one hand, and humans who are part of God's creation, on the other.

The great world religions however, know we must speak of God in metaphors since the reality of God transcends our ordinary experience and images. So beliefs about God are expressed in paradoxical ways that fall far short of embodying ultimate truth. Traditional Christian theology for example, speaks of God as infinite being. Nothing, including creation, can be outside of God. But in the same breath, it says that creation is distinct from God, and not part of God. So creation is at the same time not outside of God and not part of God. How can this be?

The answer lies in an appeal to the metaphor of "sharing" in the divine being. This is the doctrine of "participation." The Self participates in the being of God, while at the same time remaining distinct from God. The Self has no reality apart from God and yet is not identical with God. Thus, the metaphor of participation in the life of God allows Christians to say that the Self shares in the divine being which is all-embracing, but that the Self is not God.[4]

Another alternative is apophatic (Greek: *apophasis*, negation) or negative theology, which says that we can know what God is not, but we cannot know what God is. God, for example, has the qualities of goodness and love that we observe in ourselves, but without the limitations we experience. So we know what God is not: God is *not* limited. Since such qualities taken to their infinite expression exceed the capacity of our minds to understand, we end up saying: "We do not know what God is." Attempts to describe God in positive experiential terms leave us speechless.

Thus, there are different answers to the question, "Is God identical with or distinct from the Self?" The monist will say: "The Self is identical with God." The dualist will say: "The Self is distinct from God." The person sensitive to the paradoxes of human efforts to grasp transcendence will answer: "Both." The person who approaches the question from the apophatic perspective will answer: "Neither."[5]

The mystics say that there is only one God, one Self, one Spirit. Sin is the separate-self sense, the self-contraction in each of us. "Sin," "suffering," and "self" are so many names for the same contraction or fragmentation of awareness that results when we split ourselves off from each other and fail to see our deep unity. Since we are all one in the same Self, then in serving others I am serving my own Self. The process of turning from the self to the Self is known in Christianity as *metanoia*, conversion, implying both repentance and transformation until we are able to say with Paul, "It is no longer I who live, but Christ who lives in me" (Gal. 2:20).

Hindus, Buddhists, and Muslims also have their death, transformation and resurrection imageries. In both Hinduism and Buddhism, one speaks in terms of the death of the individual soul and the reawakening of one's true nature, which metaphorically the Hindus describe as All Being and the Buddhists as Pure Openness. But in the end, the paths of all the religions break down into just two major paths: a) expand your ego to infinity ("I am God") or b) reduce it to nothing ("I am nothing, O God, You are everything").

And in conjunction with these two major paths are two basic types of meditation: "self-power" versus "other-power." Some would see self-power as epitomized by Zen, *vipassana*, and jnana (enlightenment through knowledge) yoga. In these forms of meditation, one relies on one's own power of concentration and awareness in order to break through the ego to a larger identity. In other-power, one relies on the power of God, or the guru, or simply on complete surrender.

Where does Christian practice fit in? Is there anything to

be said about the distinctive characteristics of Christian meditation? It is to these questions that we now turn our attention.

Distinguishing Characteristics
of Christian Meditation

The renewal of contemplative prayer in the life of the churches at large is so recent that there has as yet not been a concerted effort on the part of the churches to speak to the distinctiveness of meditation in the Christian faith experience vis-à-vis the practice of other living faiths. Thus it is difficult to find authoritative statements issued from the teaching offices in the different churches for the reflection of their members. The only recent document that takes up these questions comes from a Roman Catholic agency. The Letter provides some valuable points of reference for all Christians who practice meditation.

On October 15, 1989, the Vatican's office of the Congregation for the Doctrine of the Faith published a "Letter to the bishops of the Catholic Church on some aspects of Christian meditation."[6] The letter was intended to serve as a reference point for the different forms of prayer practiced today. As an official acknowledgment and sanction for the use of non-Christian methods and ways by Christians, it is a landmark declaration. Yet it is careful to note that Christian prayer is always determined by the structure of the Christian faith, and identifies several characteristics.

Christian prayer expresses the communion of redeemed creatures, based on baptism and the eucharist, with the intimate life of the Trinity. It implies an attitude of conversion, a flight from the "Self" to the "You" of God. It is at one and the same time authentically personal and communitarian (even when one is praying alone, one is conscious of praying for the good of the church in union with Christ, the Holy Spirit, and together with all the saints). It is the meeting of two freedoms, the infinite freedom of God with finite human freedom.

It is related to Revelation; hence everything converges on Christ and the gifts of the Holy Spirit. Finally, the authentic sign of Christian prayer is love.

Meditation practice often strikes people as excessively introvertive, and indeed, it is not difficult to find in various books on meditation references to "turning off the outside world." The Letter speaks about how God's creation can also lead one to an encounter with the Divine, lest we become too "other-worldly." It recognizes that many today have a keen desire to learn how to experience a deeper and authentic prayer life despite the difficulties which modern culture places in the way of the need for silence, recollection and meditation. It sees the awakened interest among many Christians in forms of meditation associated with Eastern religions as a sign of a pronounced desire for deep contact with the divine Mystery everywhere present to us. What most Christians do not realize is that there is a rich tradition of meditation within Christianity itself.

The Letter affirms the Christian's experience of this desire for union with God which the Greek Fathers of the Church spoke of as divinization. But it is careful to respect the "otherness" or difference in nature existing between God and ourselves as finite creatures. That said, it recognizes the mystery that, though we are not God, God and our true Self are joined. They are not separate. Yet our fulfillment in God does not come at the loss of our personal identity, nor is our nature as a creature dissolved, only to disappear into the sea of the Absolute.

As to our participation in the very life of God, the Letter is unambiguous: "The Fathers are perfectly correct in speaking of the divinization of man who, having been incorporated into Christ, the Son of God by nature, may by his grace share in the divine nature and become a 'son in the Son.' Receiving the Holy Spirit, the Christian glorifies the Father and really shares in the Trinitarian life of God."[7] It is through incorporation into the Incarnate Son that we participate by pure grace under the action of the Holy Spirit in the interior life of God.

Given our character as creatures who know that only in

grace are we secure, we do not invest all our hopes of getting close to God in any technique. The love of God is a reality which cannot be mastered by any method or technique; it remains a gift of faith to which we dispose ourselves in confidence through the practice of the disciplines of the spiritual life.[8] God is always free to empty us of all that holds us back and to draw us more completely into the Trinitarian life of love by means of God's, rather than our own, choosing.

While documents destined for the guidance of Christians taking up a host of meditation practices may be in short supply, the central convictions of Christian faith expressed in the broad tradition offer direction for those who seek it.

The Cross as a Critical Difference in Christian Practice

In the practice of meditation outside the context of Christian faith, one habitually encounters what the history of Christian doctrine calls Pelagianism. Pelagius was a sixth century Christian monk in Britain who essentially taught that we achieve our purification and salvation through our own good efforts. Adam and Eve gave us a bad example, Jesus a good example. Since even after the Fall we are in possession of our full integrity, we need no other support than that of our own freedom and courage, so follow Jesus' example—that's all there is to it. The Council of Orange in 529 discerned that Pelagius' view of reality (subsequently called "Pelagianism") represented a serious variance from Christian faith regarding the meaning of Jesus' atoning death for us on the cross. We do not, for example, achieve a God-centered life by meditating twice a day, but by the saving work of Christ. The Holy Spirit responds to the invitation represented by meditation to enter in and accomplish the work of God in us.

Similarly, we do not win the victory over the forces of sin, evil and death; that victory is given to us as a free gift. Jesus won the combat by his total obedience to God. He so identified himself with the design of God that he embraced the weapon of death, the cross, and made it totally his own.[9] The instrument of death became an instrument of life; the powers of the reign of darkness were broken by the cross and defeated. In the power of that cross, we can be free of domination by the forces of evil. We need no longer be held in bondage (Eph. 2:7; Gal. 5:1). We can and do experience freedom from Satan's bondage when we affirm in faith that through the cross Jesus triumphed. Countless saints testify to this freedom. It can be ours as well. But the basis of our salvation (the root meaning of which is liberation) is not a human work (e.g. meditation), but a divine work, the work of God in Christ.

In 1991, I was on a study sabbatical in India participating in an intensive course on Buddhist doctrine and meditation practice at a Tibetan Buddhist retreat center in the Himalayas. One evening after our meditation period, one of the instructors approached me with some questions about Christian faith. "How do you explain suffering in the world?" she wanted to know. "For us it is explained by karma. If something happens to you, it is because you merited it either in this or a former life. Reincarnation provides you with repeated opportunities to work off the negative karmic imprints on your soul."

I did my best to explain that in Christian faith there is no need for the doctrine of reincarnation which is made necessary by karma. We have been set free from our karmic debt of sin and death by Christ's atoning death on the cross. She listened intently, and struggling to understand what I was saying, asked: "But how could it be that one man could atone for everyone's sins, even those who have not yet been born?" Indeed, how could it be? The Good News of what God has done for us in Jesus seems at times simply too good to be true. But let us state the astonishing claims of Christian faith without wavering.

Before time began, it was God's plan that the Second Person of the Trinity should take on human nature and give his life for humanity. It was God's will that Jesus be the new Adam, representing all humanity. Consequently, when Jesus died on the cross, he represented every human being throughout time.

Because he lived in complete purity of heart, obeying the Father in everything he said and did, Jesus could offer his life for everyone. Because he was faithful unto death, he has won for us an everlasting covenant of grace and mercy. As St. Paul wrote: "We are convinced that one has died for all; therefore all have died" (2 Cor. 5:14). By divine intention, we were in Christ when he was crucified and when he was raised from the dead.

This grace and mercy come to us through faith in his blood and in baptismal union with his death on the cross. At our baptism, this divine intention became a reality in our lives: "All of us who have been baptized into Christ Jesus were baptized into his death . . . . We know that our old self was crucified with him so that the sinful body might be destroyed, and we might no longer be enslaved to sin" (Rom. 6:3,6). Most of us, however, were baptized as infants, and it may never have occurred to us that in baptism we were crucified with Christ. We may have been marked outwardly with the sign of Christ's death, but we have never consciously appropriated the inward reality expressed by this outward sign. The sign of baptism must be followed by a progressive, inward dying to our old, fallen nature. In this way, the objective reality becomes our subjective experience.

When we are baptized and regenerated, we receive a whole new life. This is the life of grace, of the indwelling Holy Spirit. But this new life can only come about through a death. If we want to know a new life centered on God, we must accept the death of the old life that is centered on self. When we try to make ourselves better by dint of our own will power and moral exertion alone, we haven't yet understood the meaning of the cross of Christ. This death to self is only possible through faith in the cross of Jesus—through the realization that in his death, we too were crucified.

To the Galatians, Paul wrote: "I have been crucified with Christ; and it is no longer I who live, but it is Christ who lives in me. And the life I now live in the flesh I live by faith in the Son of God, who loved me and gave himself for me" (Gal. 2:19-20). A Christian has not only a new life, but a new life with a new center and identity. The old I, the ego, has been crucified with Christ and is now dead. Now, because the ego is crucified, it is possible for Jesus himself to indwell and to be the center of my life.

Some might say, "How can I claim to be dead to sin when I know that every day I continue to sin? My experience shows me something very different from what Paul wrote!" We need to be clear on this point. Our sins are paid for—*all* of them— but this does not mean that we are *sinless*. Christ died for all our sins, even those that we will commit years from now.

But we no longer live under the *reign* of sin; we now live under the reign of grace. We are out from under sin's rule, but it is a difficult and complex matter for us to understand our new status as sons and daughters of God. While we are no longer slaves to sin, a force of darkness and evil is still around and hard at work, calling us and tempting us, even though we are living under the reign of grace. It is as if we live in the household of God, but Satan lives across the road and can still invite us to sin.

Let's use another analogy. Suppose that a long-time prisoner is finally released from captivity. While this person is truly and legally free, in reality old habits, ways of thinking and attitudes may take years to change and be healed. This person will have to *learn* how to be free again. He or she will have to use this new freedom in acceptable ways—if only to avoid ending up in prison again. To be legally free and to enjoy the fruit of that freedom can be two distinct things!

So it is with us. It may take countless daily experiences over a period of years for us to know fully what it means to be dead to sin and alive in Christ. Nevertheless, we can begin here and now to learn to cooperate with the daily work of the cross within us.

For the new life of the Holy Spirit to grow within us, we have to die to the old life centered on self. We die to self as we hold in faith that we are united with Christ in his death on the cross. Every day, through faith in the cross of Christ, we can know victory over patterns of sin. Every day, we can overcome temptations to give in to anger, fear, bitterness, lust.

Whenever we are tempted to think or act in a way that is unfaithful to God's word, we can say, "No, I have been crucified with Christ. I have been given a new life in Jesus Christ, and I do not have to submit to these temptations. Jesus, by the power of your cross, give me the strength to withstand these trials. Increase my faith in your victory on Calvary so that I may live in peace and confidence."

These perspectives and convictions of Christian faith provide the context in which a Christian comes to the practice of meditation. In meditating, we dispose and open ourselves to the work of the Holy Spirit. We have no illusion that we will attain union with God or a transformed life by our own virtue or diligence. The human heart is deformed and needs to be reconstructed by a divine work of grace. Many times we are satisfied with a patch-up job, propping up our lives so that they aren't too bad or bring us a little more happiness and peace. But God wants much more than that for us. God wants us to be made *new*, to become a reflection of God's own Self. If we're only looking for a patch-up job, we will never taste the fullness of the life God offers us. But if we are willing to die with Christ on the cross so that we might rise with him to new life, then we will begin to share in the life God intends for us.

This letting go of self—of our ideas, our desires, our cherished ways—to make way for new life is truly a death. Pain is involved in allowing these attachments to be cut away from our hearts, even as it gives way to a new and more elevated joy in the Spirit. Consider but one scenario of the ways that meditation requires this letting go in order to make way for new life. Some people have become accustomed to disorganized ways of living—always improvising, never planning in advance, simply doing what comes to them at the moment. They have to change this style of living when they commit themselves to meditation. Being faithful to two periods of contemplative prayer each day requires planning, prioritizing, and perseverance. They can no longer just go with the flow of things. They have to take responsibility for what is important to them, for thinking and planning ahead so they can be faithful to their rendezvous with the Lord. They will constantly have to let go of other things in order to be faithful; they will constantly have to die to their old self.

When people who meditate regularly cannot live or work peaceably together, it may be because they have slipped into pursuing a model of "human salvation" based on their own efforts. The signposts on their path to union with God may be inscribed more according to human criteria than marked with the sign of the cross. Authentic Christian meditation will be marked by a spirit of compunction, an awareness of our contingency before God which frees us from any false self-illusions. To walk toward the inner light of the Trinity is to become acutely aware of the darkness within ourselves, of our own need for repentance and reconciliation because we become aware of our sin. The light of God shining on the soul is like bright sunlight in a diseased eye. We could only recoil at our own inadequacy, at our unhealthy state, were it not for the healing and restoration offered to us in the cross of Christ. It is by no means just a coincidence that many of the sacred words and phrases recommended for use in Christian contemplative prayer throughout the centuries ask for mercy and help, i.e. "Jesus, Mercy"; "O God, come to my assistance, O Lord, make haste to help me"; "Holy God, Holy Mighty, Holy Immortal, have mercy on us."

In giving talks on Christian meditation I occasionally encounter someone who says, "I get turned off by all this sin stuff. I'm much more inclined to just focus on the light within." I understand that the person who says this may be reacting to an early, negative emphasis on sin and punishment in his or her upbringing. And there *is* a light within. But there is also darkness. And the light does not overcome the darkness until we have recognized that there is a darkness and that we are in need of a light to dispel it. There is no getting around the fact that Christianity is a religion for those who are aware that there is a deep wound, a fissure of sin that strikes down to the very heart of our being. It is a spiritual path for those who have tasted the sickness that is present in the inmost human heart estranged from God by guilt, suspicion and self-seeking. If that sickness is an illusion, then there is no need for the cross, the church, and the sacraments.

When we speak of the cross, we are speaking of God's plan for our salvation: Jesus' sacrifice of atonement for our sins. When we speak of the cross, we are talking about the power and the wisdom of God. When we speak about the cross, we are acknowledging that our salvation is in that sign of divine liberation, in *his* effort, and in none other.

With these reflections as a backdrop, we now turn our attention to the particular forms of Christian contemplative prayer from the earliest centuries onward.

3

Historical Highlights in the Practice of Christian Meditation

Christian monasticism was founded in Egypt in the early fourth century. Since the earliest days of the desert monastic communities, the Jesus Prayer has been in use in the Christian East. It is the endless repetition of the holy name of the Savior in a long or short formula derived from two passages of the New Testament, that of Jesus' encounter with the blind man Bartimeus who cried out to him as he passed by the city of Jericho: "Jesus, Son of David, have mercy on me" (Lk. 18:38), and that of the publican, "O God, be merciful to me a sinner." The Jesus Prayer combines elements from both in its longer formula: "Lord Jesus Christ, Son of God, have mercy on me a sinner" (Lk. 9:13). In the shorter version, one simply says "Jesus, mercy."

St. Macarius of Egypt and Diadochus of Photice in the fifth century, and St. John Climacus in the sixth century, are among those who recommend the constant repetition of the name of Jesus. The prayer spread beyond the monasteries and penetrated into the daily lives of believers, eventually becoming a cornerstone of Eastern Christian spirituality.

This prayer has been widely practiced in the monasteries of Mount Athos, a famous peninsula in northern Greece inhabited only by monks since the seventh century. They sought to encounter God through Jesus Christ and his indwelling Spirit in an interior movement that they described

35

as "the prayer of the heart" which is, strictly speaking, more
extensive than the Jesus prayer, often thought to be its synopsis in verbal form. The "prayer of the heart" consisted in
invoking the name of Christ with profound attention in the
deepest psychological ground of one's being, that is to say, "in
the heart," considered as the root and source of all one's own
inner truth. To invoke the name of Christ "in one's heart"
was equivalent to calling upon him with the deepest and
most earnest intensity of faith, concentrating one's entire
being on a prayer stripped of all non-essentials and reduced
to nothing but the invocation of his name with the simple
petition for help.

The practice of keeping the name of Jesus ever present in
the heart was, for the ancient monks, the secret of the "control of thoughts," and of victory over temptation. It accompanied all the other activities of the monastic life, imbuing
them with prayer. It was the essence of monastic meditation.
St. Gregory of Sinai says, "God is gained either by activity
and work, or by the art of invoking the Name of Jesus." He
adds that the first way is longer than the second, the second
being quicker and more effective. For this reason, some of the
holy Fathers gave prime importance to the Jesus Prayer
among all the different kinds of spiritual exercises.[1]

It is one of the most popular prayer forms in the Eastern
churches, suitable for monks and beginners alike. As a form
of prayer that seeks its roots in the very ground of our being,
not merely in our mind or affections, it leads us to meet God
in our depths by invoking the name of Jesus in faith, wonder
and love. The climate of this prayer is one of awareness, gratitude and a totally obedient love which seeks nothing but to
please God. "Prayer of the heart" is the active effort we make
to keep our hearts open so that we may be enlightened by the
Lord and filled with the realization of our true relation to
him. The whole purpose of this prayer as a form of meditation is to deepen our consciousness of this basic relationship
of creature to Creator, sinner to Savior.

The letters of the Apostle Paul provide ample encouragement for this form of meditational practice: Christians are

those who invoke the name of Jesus Christ (1 Cor. 1:2), a name in which divine power rests, "a name that is above every name so that at the name of Jesus every knee should bend, in heaven and on earth and under the earth and every tongue should confess that Jesus Christ is Lord to the glory of God the Father" (Phil. 2:10-11).

A rich literature on the use of this prayer is found in *The Philokalia*[2] (Greek, meaning "the love of the good"), an eighteenth century compilation of the writings of the traditional hesychastic Fathers. The Jesus Prayer also formed the soul of the Hesychast movement, a spiritual movement which developed in the Eastern Church during the medieval period in close connection with the contemplative tradition of the Fathers of the Desert. The name comes from the Greek *hesuchia*, which means quietness, silence, solitude. Among its promoters were two of the Christian East's most revered divines, Symeon the New Theologian and Gregory Palamas. In succeeding centuries it spread to Russia, from which came *The Way of a Pilgrim*,[3] a simple and unpretentious introduction to the workings and nature of the Jesus Prayer in the account of one man's experience of it.

Other prayer words or phrases were certainly used in the same repetitive manner. Some made constant use of the first verse of Psalm 70: "O God, come to my assistance; O Lord, make haste to help me!" For others, the common invocation was the Trisagion, in either of its forms: the "Holy, holy, holy is the Lord" of the vision of Isaiah (6:3), or the "Holy God! Holy Mighty! Holy Immortal One! Have mercy on us!" of the Oriental liturgical tradition. Many have also used the sacred invocation which St. Paul reminds us is constantly whispered in the depths of our hearts by the Holy Spirit: "Abba, Father" (Rom. 8:15; Gal. 4:5). Another popular scriptural prayer is the cry of the early church, which closes Paul's First Letter to the Corinthians (16:22), as well as the book of Revelation (22:20)—Maranatha (Come, Lord!). But all these prayers were fundamentally used in the same way, as a sacred word or phrase continuously repeated to fix one's mind on God and to offer God the homage of one's love. The rosary, too, could be considered a form of mantric prayer in Christian faith. It repeats over and over a composite of the biblical words of the angel Gabriel's and Elizabeth's salutations to Mary: "Hail, Mary, full of grace! The Lord is with you" (Lk. 1:28). "Blessed are you among women, and blessed is the fruit of your womb" (Lk. 1:42).

By the fifth century, Christian monasticism was beginning to flourish in the West, as well as in the East. The tradition of meditative prayer was transported to the Christian West by St. John Cassian who went to live for over seven years with the monks in the Egyptian desert to learn from their experience in the spiritual life. He eventually established two monasteries in Marseilles, France, one for women and one for men. In his *Institutes*, he recounted the practices of the monks in Egypt and adapted them for use in the West. In his *Conferences*, presented in the form of conferences given by various great Desert Fathers, he shared with his monks the most significant teachings he had received. In the "Second Conference of Abba Isaac on Prayer," we find the first written expression in the West on this way of praying:

> *I must give you a formula for contemplation. If you carefully keep this formula before you, and learn to recollect it at all times, it will help you to mount to contemplation of high truth. Everyone who seeks for continual recollection of God uses this formula for meditation, intent upon driving every other sort of thought from his heart . . . . The formula is this: "O God, come to my assistance; O Lord, make haste to help me."*
>
> *The mind should . . . restrict itself to the poverty of this single word . . . and thus it attains to that purest of pure prayers . . . the prayer which looks for no visual image, uses neither thoughts nor words; the prayer wherein, like a spark leaping up from a fire, the mind is rapt upward, and destitute of the aid of the senses or of anything visible or material, pours out its prayer to God.[4]*

St. Benedict made extensive use of John Cassian's collection of teachings, and thus Cassian had a far-flung influence on monastic life in the West where this tradition of prayer remained strong until it was lost at the time of the Reformation with the suppression of the monasteries in many countries and the prosecution by the Inquisition of forms of quiet prayer associated with suspicious illuminating experiences. Caught between these two hostile forces, contemplative life in the West went into hiding.

One of the finest examples to come down to us today of a teaching on contemplative prayer slightly predates this development. Titled *The Cloud of Unknowing*, it was written by an unknown English Catholic writer of the fourteenth century. It represents advice given by a spiritual father addressed to a particular disciple. Because it presupposes the oral instruction that has already been given, simply reading the treatise does not yield a clear, systematic presentation of the method. But those who practice the method will undoubtedly draw encouragement and understanding from reading passages like the following:

> *If you want to gather all your desire into one simple word that the mind can easily retain, choose a short word rather than a long one . . . . But choose one that is meaningful to you. Then fix it in your mind so that it will remain there come what may. Fasten this word in your heart so that it never leaves you, come what may. This word is to be your shield and your spear, whether in peace or in war. With this word you are to beat upon the cloud and the darkness above you. With it you are to smite down every manner of thought under the cloud of forgetting. So much so that if any thought should press upon you to ask you what you would have, answer it with no other words but this little word (chapter 7).[5]*

The author of *The Cloud*, receiving a way of prayer that had developed in the monastic tradition, passed it on with wisdom and discretion to those living busy lives in the home and marketplace. Each age needs spiritual teachers and guides who will take what is ancient and time-tested and package it anew for modern usage.

Contemporary Teachers

Among those who have served in this way in our time are three Trappists—Thomas Merton, M. Basil Pennington, Thomas Keating—and two Benedictines—John Main and Laurence Freeman—who have all made significant contributions to the recovery and promotion of meditation in Christian life in our time. Between them, they have given us, newly wrapped and packaged, the gift of this valuable prayer tradition either under the name of Centering Prayer (Merton, Pennington, Keating) or Christian Meditation (Main, Freeman).

Fr. Louis (Thomas) Merton will be recognized by most as one of the most eminent spiritual guides the West has known in this century. His many books on contemplation continue to engender life in the hearts of men and women throughout the Christian world and beyond. He spoke frequently of attaining the experience of God by going to one's center and passing through it into the center of God. Thus the expression "centering prayer" derived from his teaching. The subtle symbol of the "center" has proved to be an effective moniker and has stuck, making centering prayer a popular name used by many for this particular method of entering into contemplative prayer as drawn from our Christian tradition and taught by those mentioned above. While the Christian East prefers to use the more specifically human and sensible image of the heart (calling the Jesus Prayer the "prayer of the heart"), the analogy of the center as an almost imageless image serves many Westerners.

Pennington observes that the term "meditation" is used to refer to such different kinds of prayer, e.g., use of rational thought and imagination as in the Ignatian method, as well as imageless prayer which uses no thoughts, that it does not always have a clear and distinctive meaning. "However," he writes, "I think it might at times be advantageous, when presenting this form of prayer in a popular context, such as a college campus, to speak of it as 'Christian meditation' . . . . "[6]

Two of Merton's Cistercian brothers, Thomas Keating at St. Benedict's Monastery in Snowmass, Colorado, and M. Basil Pennington at St. Joseph's Abbey in Spencer, Massachusetts, could be rightly called the founders of the centering prayer movement. Their writings[7] and talks have served to take contemplative prayer out of the monastery and set it forth as a challenge addressed to all Christians.

This is a message which is certainly not original to them, but which needs to be regularly repeated. St. Teresa of Avila taught that those who were faithful to prayer could expect in a relatively short time—six months to a year—to be led into a prayer of quiet. One of the signs that St. John of the Cross pointed to as an indication that one is ready for this is that prayer using thoughts and images no longer works.[8] Certainly, those who might recognize themselves in either of these descriptions are not all in monasteries!

When Fr. Keating moved to Snowmass, Colorado, in 1981, he had no intention of traveling. Today, his travel schedule is booked a year in advance and he offers fifteen 10-day retreats a year at Snowmass to meet the demand. In 1984-1985, he was invited to give centering prayer instruction in two New York city parishes, which in turn spawned a nationwide "contemplative outreach." Since 1987, contemplative outreach has spread to twenty-six states. The network draws together small groups who practice centering prayer for mutual support.[9]

Two other teachers brought to Canada and beyond their vision of a contemplative renewal at every level of the church's membership. John Main and Laurence Freeman came to Montreal, Canada, from England in 1977 to found a house of prayer from which they would teach Christian meditation, based upon the teachings of John Cassian. John Main died in 1982,[10] but his colleague Fr. Freeman carried on the work of teaching and writing[11] which fostered the foundation of sixteen other Christian meditation centers and more than 900 meditation groups in some thirty-five countries, with 95 percent of the groups and centers led and staffed by lay people.[12] There is no way of knowing how many are practicing centering prayer and Christian meditation today without any relation to a known group or network, but there is reason to believe that they are legion. The tradition of Christian contemplative prayer has been effectively crystallized and made available to laity and clergy alike and is enjoying an unprecedented period of flowering throughout the Church.

In the writings of many Christian holy men and women like Teresa of Avila, John of the Cross, the author of *The Cloud*, and others, we find teachings that reflect this tradition, but nowhere do we find the "how to" addressed in simple, straightforward terms. That is the invaluable contribution of contemporary teachers. They have brought the scattered elements of the tradition together from the yellowed pages of tomes on the spiritual life into regularized and synthesized presentations for modern men and women. They have put order in it with an eye toward our contemporary inclination for simple "how-to" instructions. For the Christian who is seeking guidance in meditation today, there are more resources readily available than has been the case at any time in twenty centuries of Christianity. There is a new spirituality emerging, combining the wisdom of the East and West.

4

Is Contemplative Prayer for Everyone?

Contemplation has to do with ways of making oneself aware of the presence of God who is always there. Awareness is central to contemplation because it reduces the distance between us and that of which we are aware. A very deep sense of awareness further reduces the gap between us and brings us together into unity.

Etymologically, the word *contemplation* derives from the Latin *templum*. Among the Romans, the *templum* was a space in the sky or on the earth sectioned off for the augurs to read the omens. This area, marked off from other space, was considered sacred. In this space, for example, the augurs would examine the entrails of birds for portentious signs. Thus, the *temple* was the sacred space where certain designated persons looked at the *insides of things* (animals) to discover divine meanings and purposes. Contemplation referred not so much to the place, but to the actual *looking* at the *insides of reality*.[1]

This is the basis for William McNamara's definition of contemplation as *a long, loving look at the real*,[2] or for George Maloney's language of *inscape*.[3] When we look deeply at the insides of reality, we discover that things of themselves are nothing. They *are* only because at the level where we discover their nothingness, we discover at the same time a source that is their origin and the ground in which they find their identity. In *looking* at that source, we are *looking at* God. Therefore, contemplation puts us in touch with the innermost reality of everything. It is the inbuilt capacity of our everyday mind to explore the *inscape* of things, to look at our present reality with loving awareness and see God there.

Origen (ca. 185-255) and Gregory of Nyssa (ca. 335-395), two Eastern Fathers, represent two ways of understanding contemplation and two trends that influenced the subsequent history of spirituality. The ways they represent are what we have earlier discussed as the *kataphatic way*, the way of affirmation (in Greek: *kataphasis*), and the *apophatic way*, the way of negation or denial (in Greek: *apophasis*).

Origen uses the *kataphatic* way which talks about God by affirming of God all the perfections seen in creatures. We look at our human experiences of justice, mercy, compassion, generosity, love, and affirm their full and perfect realization in God. While these affirmations tell us about God, they are limited in that they never reach God's inmost reality. That is why there is another way of talking about God, represented by Gregory of Nyssa: the *apophatic* way of negation. No thoughts, ideas, words, images or symbols can express God's innermost reality. To attain that reality, one must go barehanded, with all conceptual gloves removed, into the darkness. One puts out the lights of the mind and enters the darkness through love.[4]

Both Origen and Gregory also described three stages of spiritual progress which have found their place in the tradition of spirituality, stylized as the purgative, illuminative, and unitive ways. Similarly, two images they used to describe the path of ascent involved in these three stages have had an enduring influence: the mountain (used later by Dante, John of the Cross, and Thomas Merton), and the ladder, based on Jacob's dream at Bethel (Gen. 28:10-15).[5] Today, the image which is often used in spiritual direction is the image of journey. On a journey, one follows a path, and that path can lead through many different kinds of terrain and subject one to all kinds of weather. As one looks at the innermost reality of things along the way and there encounters God, the way of *looking at* may be dominantly affirmative or negative, dominantly kataphatic or apophatic. But it will always be an admixture of both, as the affirmative way is inextricably linked to the negative way because God is always ineffable and incomprehensible.

Is *everyone* called to look at *the insides of things*, and most of all, at the *insides* of one's self and others and find God there? Certain teachers in Christian history are distinguished by the unrelenting passion with which they have answered this question.

One such is another Eastern Father, Symeon the New Theologian (949-1022), who lived in Macedonia. Symeon burned with a holy zeal to call Christians back to the mystical core of their faith, which he considered available to all baptized Christians. He is one of the great charismatic figures in Christian spirituality, one of three whom the Christian East honors with the formal title of *theologian*. He felt that the Christian religion of his day had degraded into a static formalism that had stifled for the masses of Christians the real message of Jesus Christ and his Gospel.

Symeon's teaching is solidly rooted in the traditional teaching of the Fathers, but he accentuates with great originality the need for a stage in the Christian life beyond baptism, where the individual Christian comes to a deeper conversion to and consciousness of Jesus Christ as Lord and Savior. He represents the first Byzantine mystic who speaks so freely about his own experiences of contemplation. He strongly believed that the Holy Spirit wanted him to speak of his experiences to show people in his day that they too could reach such intimacy and transformation in Christ if they followed the same teachings of Holy Scripture and the Fathers as he had. His language is sincere, simple, yet full of fire and persuasion as he attempts to bring his listeners to a greater sensitivity to and awareness of the indwelling Trinity. To his mind, the great blasphemy against the Holy Spirit is to deny that the Spirit can be experienced today and divinize contemporary Christians the same way as in the early Church.

Symeon's *Discourses* are marked by two main themes. The

first is the field of positive practices one must undertake to open oneself to true contemplation: repentance, renunciation, charity, the works of mercy, and the practice of the commandments. The second theme is the operations of the Holy Spirit who, taking full advantage of the opening, effects the end of the spiritual life in the Christian: union with the indwelling Trinity. The foundational stone for the building of contemplation is the stirring of the Christian to true repentance.

Symeon insists that the ordinary Christian should tend toward contemplative experience for of such is every Christian life necessarily made up. He continually comes back to the theme that the divine life, the indwelling of the Trinity, is what Jesus Christ merited for all of us and that this is a reality that should become a living, conscious experience within our hearts. He wishes to move Christians into a deeper person-to-person relationship with God, to invite them to go beyond words and ideas and live in the awesome darkness of the Mystery that becomes a light to those who have become purified. Symeon challenges us in the words of St. Paul, "Awake, you that sleep, and Christ will give you light" (Eph. 5:14). "How is it," he wants to know, "that one who has put on the Son of God, who has been made god by grace and by adoption, will not be god in awareness and knowledge and contemplation?"[6]

Rahner and Merton on Contemplation and Mysticism

In the history of spirituality, the term *contemplation* is often used interchangeably with *mysticism*. This association is unfortunate to the extent that, in our time, mysticism connotes extraordinary phenomena like visions, ecstasies, locutions, and levitation. But the fundamental nature of Christian mysticism as originally understood in the Church is far from an understanding based on such phenomena. The meaning of *mystical* in early Christian literature cannot be understood apart from the New Testament term *mystery*, which conveys a sense of something hidden or secret, an inner meaning. Paul's letters refer to the "mystery of Christ" (Eph. 3:4), "the mystery hidden throughout the ages and generations" which is said to be "Christ in you, the hope for glory" (Col. 1:26,27). The aspect of Christian mysticism that could be considered the most central of all is the conviction expressed by Paul that "it is no longer I who live, but it is Christ who lives in me" (Gal. 2:20). The truly important thing is to be deeply convinced that Christ lives within us, and to act in accordance with that conviction. In the experience of most, this is not accompanied by palpable feelings and extraordinary phenomena, but it nonetheless fully qualifies as mysticism.[7]

One can say, therefore, that "a mystic is not a special kind of human being; rather, every human being is a special kind of mystic."[8] This assertion has been developed with great theological precision by the German Jesuit Karl Rahner (1904-1984), widely considered the most important Catholic theologian of the twentieth century. Rahner developed an organic and comprehensive theology that flowed from his central insight that we human beings, in all our acts of knowing and loving, are positively oriented to the Holy Mystery we call God. All authentic experiences of faith, hope, and love contain at least an anonymous experience of God. Rahner speaks freely of the "mysticism of ordinary life" and of normal Christians as "anonymous mystics." His ideas have filtered down through insightful interpreters and numerous popularizers to help many ordinary Christians reject a sharp dichotomy between the sacred and the secular in favor of a more integrated, incarnational spirituality which helps them find and serve God in all aspects of human existence, even the most routine.[9]

We are naturally and basically oriented toward God. This dynamic movement of our being has to be recognized and put into action by an intelligent and enlightened faith expressed through worship, education, and regular practice of the Christian disciplines. If experiencing the immediacy of God is fairly rare in our experience, it is not due to the parsimony of grace but to the smallness of the opening in our lives to the action of God. Faith is the free consent to God in me. And the life of faith becomes a conscious communion with that Presence. In every activity, circumstance, and state of mind, I can freely consent to and communicate with God in me and become a contemplative in action. Contemplation and mysticism are in very close relationship. Contemplation relates to the *looking at*, and mysticism refers to the mystery hidden there which one *sees*.

Another twentieth century figure who has contributed significantly to refocusing the contemplative calling of all Christians is Thomas Merton (1915-1968). If Rahner is the most important Catholic theologian of this century, to many, Merton is its most important spiritual writer both in volume and content, an estimation supported by his continuing popularity and the ever-increasing corpus of writings concerning him. One writer surmised that when the people "of the twenty-fifth and fiftieth centuries read the spiritual literature of the twentieth century, they will judge the age by Merton."[10]

When Merton died in 1968 he left a large amount of literature, much of which was concerned with the nature and function of prayer. In his early writings he draws generously from John of the Cross and Teresa of Avila. In later years, as his horizon widens, his net brings in an ever-expanding circle of Christian mystics: John Ruysbroeck, Henry Suso, Johan Tauler, Meister Eckhart. He does not so much describe techniques and methods of meditation in his writings as writes down his own experiences in prayer, so that what we are left with is a map of his own journey. He believed that "the only way to find out anything about the joys of contemplation is by experience."[11]

In Merton's view, there is a variety of forms of prayer, but the ultimate end of these forms is contemplative prayer as "contemplation is the highest expression of a person's intellectual and spiritual life."[12] He sought to rescue contemplation from specialists and return it to all those to whom it belongs as their birthright.[13] He saw contemplative prayer

not so much as a method but as an "outlook of faith, openness, reverence, expectation, supplication, trust, joy," because
it "is not so much a way to find God as a way of resting in
him whom we have found."[14]

One might understand contemplative prayer, then, as a
certain at-easeness in relationship to God. It might be compared to the relationship of an elderly couple who don't have
to talk all the time but sometimes like to sit and watch the
sunset together. In such a relationship, one moves beyond
conversation into moments of simply enjoying each other's
presence. Contemplation is an initiation into the fact that
God is not only close or present, but is intimately present
within us as the source of our being, speaking to us not only
with words, but also with the secret inspirations of grace
through which one is intuitively aware of the presence of
God. Merton believed that such meditative awareness was
the best method of prayer for the greatest number of people.[15]

In *New Seeds of Contemplation* Merton proposes a twofold
function for meditation. First, it teaches "a person how to
work themself [sic] free of created things and temporal concerns," and secondly it instructs one "how to become aware of
the presence of God" and bring oneself to "a state of almost
constant loving attention to God, and dependence on him."[16]
Hence the aim of meditation, in the context of Christian
faith, is not to arrive at an objective and apparently "scientific" knowledge about God, but to come to know God through
the realization that our very being is penetrated with God's
knowledge and love for us.[17]

In talking about contemplation, Merton distinguishes
between the two forms of it found in Christian mysticism:
active contemplation and passive, or infused contemplation.
Active contemplation prepares a person for the possibility of
occasions of infused contemplation by teaching one how to see
God's presence in one's life and in the world. In *The Waters of
Siloe* he defines infused contemplation as "a simple intuition
of God, produced immediately in the soul by God and giving
the soul a direct but obscure and mysterious experiential
appreciation of God . . . . "[18]

Merton believed that since all people are called to infused contemplation, it must therefore be attainable by all. As the basis of this conviction, he pointed to the Last Supper Discourses in John's gospel where Jesus promises union with God through the Holy Spirit to his followers who obey in love. While contemplation is a gift infused by God into the soul, it is also a gift of God for which one can work and pray. It is only given in proportion as one has emptied oneself of false concerns by meditation.

This process of emptying ourselves of our feelings, images, and ideas leads us beyond the level of our understanding into darkness where we can no longer think of God, but are forced to reach out to God by blind faith and hope and love. As we descend to the center of our own nothingness, it is then possible for the Spirit to lead us to find God, for whom we have been searching. We then confront "the Abyss of the unknown yet present-one who is more intimate to us than we are to ourselves."[19]

While Rahner is more affirmative or kataphatic in his approach to the mysticism of ordinary life, Merton's writings consistently express his firm preference for the apophatic way. Thus he writes:

Now, while the Christian contemplative must certainly develop by study the theological understanding of concepts about God, he is called mainly to penetrate the wordless darkness and apophatic light of an experience beyond concepts . . . . Relinquishing every attempt to grasp God in limited human concepts, the contemplative's act of submission and faith attains to His presence as the ground of every human experience and His reality as the ground of being itself.[20]

Thus far we have looked at the fundamental meaning of contemplation and mysticism, and listened to three important teachers—Symeon the New Theologian, Karl Rahner, and Thomas Merton—share their common conviction that contemplative prayer is for everyone. The witness of Origen and Gregory of Nyssa is that there are two paths: the way of affirmation and the way of denial. In order to make it unmistakably clear that both pathways have produced great contemplatives and mystics, we will now look at the lives and teachings of two saints, one of whom espouses the apophatic way and the other the kataphatic. Both of them lived in sixteenth century Spain.

Ignatius of Loyola and John of the Cross

Ignatius of Loyola (1491-1556) began his career as a courtier, a gentleman, and a soldier. When he was 30 he suffered a severe leg wound while defending a fortress against French forces at Pamplona, Spain. During his recuperation he experienced a profound religious conversion. Through his contemplative and mystical experiences God purified, illuminated, and transformed Ignatius from a knight in the service of a temporal lord to a knight under Christ's banner in the service of the Trinity. Ignatius gathered together a group of companions in Christ, the Society of Jesus, which became a renowned religious community better known today as the Jesuits.[21]

Because Ignatius' spirituality is so clearly affirmative or kataphatic, a consideration of it next to the apophatic way of John of the Cross illustrates that there are different ways in which a person can be purified, illuminated by and united to God. Ignatian spirituality and mysticism finds God in all things in order to love and serve God in all things. It is a mysticism of joy in the world which serves God in and through this world. It is an Easter spirituality that loves the earth because the Trinitarian God creates, redeems and loves it. Ignatian mysticism is not a mysticism absorbed in God's activity at the center of the soul. His mystical union with the Trinity did not incline him away from the senses and the world. He did not see mystical prayer as an end in itself, as the summit of earthly life, but only as a means to service.[22]

In an experience he had in prayer at La Storta near Rome,

the Father placed Ignatius under Christ's banner and Christ engraved in Ignatius' heart the words, "I want you to serve us." The *Constitutions* which Ignatius wrote for the Society of Jesus underscore this service orientation. In the *Constitutions*, one finds the expression "the service of God" or its equivalent over 140 times.[23] Ignatian spirituality is incarnated in a community for effective apostolic service that includes social and political dimensions.

The Ignatian *Spiritual Exercises* offer one of the clearest and most influential expositions of the affirmative way. The exercises are essentially meditations and contemplations on Christ's life, death, and resurrection to aid one to become free of all disordered loves in order to restore a person's right relationship with God, and after accomplishing this, to seek and to discover "the divine will regarding the dispositions of one's life" (Ex., no. 1). Instead of calling upon persons to forget everything for the sake of the love of God, Ignatius guides persons in the progressive simplification of their prayer through meditation upon and contemplation of Christ's life, death and resurrection. The result is an increasing transparency of the images, symbols, and mysteries of salvation history to the mystery of God's self-communicating love.

The apophatic way recommends that a person use a sacred word in prayer to control distractions of the mind while emptying it of all created things. For Ignatius, however, the Christian mystery itself becomes a highly concentrated *word*. It is a word that draws attention not to itself, but to what it is in its essence: a sacrament of the healing, transforming presence of God. St. Teresa of Avila teaches the same when she exhorts her nuns to turn to the risen Lord within themselves and to use the mysteries of Christ's life, death and resurrection as "sparks" to enkindle love.[24]

The power of this form of prayer comes from its ability to initiate the whole body-person in the Christian mysteries. The directives in the *Spiritual Exercises* are meant to ensure that the exercitant fully utilizes his or her senses, emotions, passions, fantasy, memory, reason, intellect, heart and will, in order to interiorize the material of the exercise. In praying with a biblical passage presenting Christ on the cross, for example, the person is instructed to make a "mental image of the place" (Ex., nos. 47, 65, 91), and to see, hear, taste, smell, and touch in imagination what is occurring in that particular Christian mystery (Ex., nos. 66-71). Ignatius' *Autobiography* and *Spiritual Diary* reveal a mystic who knew the importance of religious emotions. One should give vent to spontaneous feelings and desires and ask for tears, shame, sorrow, affectionate love, joy, gladness, peace and tranquillity.[25]

Ignatian spirituality is versatile. The *Exercises* are open to every method of examination of conscience, of meditation, of contemplation, of vocal and mental prayer, and to every way that removes disordered loves and attachments, thus enabling one to seek and find God's will. Ignatius, in fact, urged that the exercises "be adapted to the requirements of the persons who wish to make them . . . according to their age, their education, and their aptitudes" (Ex., nos. 18, 72). The *Exercises* teach nearly twenty different ways of praying. Thus, they can lead persons at any level of spiritual development into ever-deeper realms of the spiritual life. The link between prayer, reformation of life, and seeking, finding and executing God's will is a distinctive feature of Ignatian spirituality. The purpose Ignatius sees for our lives is to praise, reverence and serve God in all things. For this reason, commentators have distinguished his *service* mysticism from the *bridal* mysticism of John of the Cross in which the divine-human intercourse at the soul's center is accentuated.[26]

John of the Cross (1542-1591) was a profound contemplative, theologian, and poet at the same time as he was a co-founder, reformer and busy administrator in the Carmelite order in sixteenth century Spain. In the 1926 bull proclaming him a Doctor of the Church, placing the Church's highest approval upon his teachings on the spiritual life, Pope Pius XI declared his writings so "full of such sound spiritual doctrine . . . that they are rightly looked upon as a code and guide for the faithful soul endeavoring to embrace a more perfect life."[27]

In John's pastoral work, his deepest concern was for those who in their spiritual lives were undergoing interior trials, those for whom "mental prayer," consisting of logical, discursive reasoning, active imagining, and the deliberate stirring up of the affections, was not working. Their needs prompted him to write *The Ascent of Mount Carmel* and *The Dark Night*, in which he shows that this kind of mental prayer tends to conflict with our silent and receptive attention to the inner working of the Holy Spirit, especially if we attempt to carry on with it once its usefulness has come to an end. Misplaced effort in the spiritual life often consists in stubbornly insisting upon compulsive routines which, while seeming important in our limited view of things, actually block the work of the Spirit in us. John shows that it is precisely this attachment to our own ways of prayer that hinders our growth in the spiritual life. This stubborn insistence cannot be cured by our own activity, and needs to be purified by God in the "night" of contemplation.

In *The Ascent*, John explains how God moves us from discursive, mental prayer built upon forms, figures and images (the imagining of Christ crucified, of the glory of God as a beautiful light, or the picturing of any other human or divine object) to a form of prayer empty of images and ideas. We must begin with forms and images of created things because this is the order followed in the process of knowing. Knowledge is acquired through the senses. God brings us along according to our nature, proceeding from the lowest and most exterior ways of knowing to the highest and most interior. God gently weans the soul from the level of the senses to bring it to spiritual wisdom, which is incomprehensible to the senses.[28]

Not surprisingly, while this weaning process is taking place, a person will sometimes practice forms of personal prayer using images and ideas and words, and sometimes a form of contemplative prayer which uses none.[29] Just as it is important that the former be surrendered at the proper time so as not to be a hindrance to God's work, so it is also important not to abandon the imaginative, verbal form of prayer before the due time. Imaginative prayer has an important contribution to make; it disposes our spirit and develops in us a taste for spiritual things. John delineates four signs by which one can judge whether or not it is the opportune time to discontinue mental prayer.

1. You don't receive satisfaction from it as before. Dryness is now the outcome of fixing the senses upon subjects which formerly provided satisfaction.

2. You become aware that you have little or no inclination to fix your mind, imagination, or senses upon extraneous things.

3. You become aware of a growing contentment to remain alone in loving awareness of God, in interior peace, quiet and repose, without the kind of prayer exercises in which one progresses mentally from point to point. You prefer to remain only in general loving awareness, without particular knowledge or understanding.

4. You must observe within yourself the preceding three signs together, e.g. the presence of the first without the second does not suffice.[30]

When one judges that one can no longer do verbal or imaging prayer, John's counsel is that such a person should learn to remain in God's presence with a loving attention and a tranquil intellect, even though one seems to oneself to be idle. "For little by little and very soon the divine calm and peace with a wondrous, sublime knowledge of God, enveloped in divine love, will be infused into his soul. He should not interfere with forms or discursive meditations and imaginings. Otherwise his soul will be disquieted and drawn out of its peaceful contentment to distaste and repugnance. And if scruples about his inactivity arise, he should remember that pacification of the soul (making it calm and peaceful, inactive and desireless) is no small accomplishment. This, indeed, is what our Lord asks of us . . . : Learn to be empty of all things—interiorly and exteriorly—and you will behold that I am God" (Ps. 45:11).[31]

If those who assume this posture before God learn how to remain quiet, John assures that they will soon delicately experience the interior nourishment that, like air, escapes when one tries to grasp it in one's hand. For John, "contemplation is nothing else than a secret and peaceful and loving inflow of God which, if not hampered, fires the soul in the spirit of love."[32] It is a ray of darkness, for it bestows knowledge or light, but the knowledge is not understood clearly, is darkness to the intellect, and remains a hidden, secret, mystical knowledge of God. At the same time, it is a knowledge that is experienced: "Since the soul experiencing this is aware that what she has so sublimely experienced remains beyond her understanding, she calls it 'I don't know what' . . . although, as I say, one may know what the experience of it is."[33]

The mind must advance by unknowing, by blinding itself and remaining in darkness rather than by opening its eyes. The reason for this is simple: nothing which could possibly be imagined or comprehended in this life can be a proximate means of union with God. Everything the intellect can understand, the will experience, and the imagination picture is most unlike and disproportioned to God. All created things can serve as a remote means to union with God, but they are like the steps on a flight of stairs, having no resemblance to the goal at the top toward which they are the means.

> If a man in climbing them does not leave each one behind until there are no more, or if he should want to stay on one of them, he would never reach the level and peaceful room at the top. Consequently, a man who wants to arrive at union with the Supreme Repose and Good in this life must climb all the steps, which are considerations, forms, concepts, and leave them behind, since they are dissimilar and unproportioned to the goal toward which they lead. And this goal is God.[34]

Once we are introduced to the calm and repose of inner quietude, we may imagine ourselves to be idle and to be doing nothing and thus we return to a more mentally active form of prayer. Then we may become filled with aridity and trial because of efforts to get satisfaction by means no longer apt. The more intense our efforts, the less our gain. We have abandoned the greater for the lesser, turned back down stairs already climbed. We are "like someone who turns from what has already been done in order to do it again, or one who leaves a city only to re-enter it, or like the hunter who abandons his prey to go on hunting again."[35] This is the context for John's counsel that, if you find the orange peeled, eat it!

All that has been said above from John of the Cross about "dark contemplation" and "the night of the senses" must not be misinterpreted to mean that the normal culture of the senses, of artistic taste, of imagination and of intelligence is to be renounced by anyone interested in meditation. On the contrary, such culture is presupposed. One cannot go beyond what one has not yet attained. Normally, the realization that God is "beyond images, symbols and ideas" dawns only on one who has already made good use of all these things and, having reached their limit, is able from time to time to go beyond them. These things still have their legitimate place in the everyday life even of the most thoroughly contemplative, forming part of the environment and cultural atmosphere in which he or she lives. Merton elaborates on the role of the aesthetic and the sensory in our prayer:

> *The function of image, symbol, poetry, music, chant, and of ritual (remotely related to sacred dance) is to open up the inner self of the contemplative, to incorporate the senses and the body in the totality of the self-orientation to God that is necessary for worship and for meditation. Simply to neglect the senses and body altogether, and merely to let the imagination go its own way, while attempting to plunge into a deeply abstracted interior prayer, will end in no result even for one who is proficient in meditation.[36]*

All religious traditions have ways of integrating the senses into higher levels of prayer. The greatest mystical literature, generously contributed to by St. John of the Cross himself, speaks not only of "darkness" and "unknowing," but also of an extraordinary flowering of the "spiritual senses and aesthetic awareness" underlying and interpreting the more direct union with God "beyond experience."[37] In *The Spiritual Canticle* he tells in lyric verse of the loving exchange which takes place between a soul and Christ. In the commentary on one of the verses he writes:

> *Oh, then, soul . . . , so anxious to know the dwelling place of your Beloved that you may go in quest of Him and be united with Him, now we are telling you that you yourself are His dwelling and His secret chamber and hiding place. This is something of immense gladness for you, to see that all your good and hope is so close to you as to be within you . . . .*
>
> *. . . What more do you want, O Soul! And what else do you search for outside, when within yourself you possess your riches, delights, satisfactions, fullness, and kingdom— your Beloved whom you desire and seek? Be joyful and gladdened in your interior recollection with Him, for you have Him so close to you. Desire Him there, adore Him there. Do not go in pursuit of Him outside yourself. You will only become distracted and wearied thereby, and you shall not find Him, or enjoy Him more securely, or sooner, or more intimately than by seeking Him within you.[38]*

This may conjure up a kind of passive quietism which thumbs its nose at financial, political, familial and environmental concerns, but such is not the case when the whole teaching is considered.

One of the distinguishing traits of the Christian mystics, in fact, is their ready passage from the Infinite to the definite, from vision to action. Both the lives of Ignatius of Loyola and John of the Cross clearly reveal it. During the years in which John did his writing, he served as Rector, Prior, and Vicar Provincial, a post which made him responsi-

ble for monasteries of the friars in seven cities. He also had in
his charge all the houses of nuns in that part of Spain. He
was much sought out as a spiritual director and was liberal
with his time in guiding the many friars, nuns, and lay persons who came to him.

He held a special concern for the poor and the sick. If any
of his friars were ill, he made a point to spend time at their
bedside and would often himself prepare special food for
them. Nor was he a stranger to manual labor. When the
monasteries were being built at Granada and at Segovia, he
went out to help the workmen in quarrying stone for the construction. At Beas he helped the nuns put up partition walls,
lay bricks, and scrub the floors.

Integral to people's discovery of God at their center is the
simultaneous discovery that the God they have discovered is
love. So their life of union with God through contemplation
demands a life of more loving actions. As well as loving the
God whom they cannot see, they must love the brothers and
sisters whom they can see. Action and contemplation grow
together into two aspects of the same thing, Merton wrote.
"Action is charity looking outward to other people, and contemplation is charity drawn inward to its own divine
source."[39] In *No Man Is an Island*, he compares action to a
stream and contemplation to the spring. The spring is essential, and from it flows the stream. Thus should contemplation
penetrate and enliven all the areas of a person's life, including temporal concerns.

A New Era

The long period dating from the sixteenth century Reformation up until recent times has been, with a few exceptions and
apart from monastic life, an arid period for contemplation in
general and a risky time for espousing the apophatic tradition
in particular. This was due largely to the condemnation of a
seventeenth-century contemplative movement called Quietism,

found mainly in Italy and France. It encouraged complete passivity and abandonment to God through an attitude of surrender in obscure faith. It discouraged all other forms of prayer
and spiritual practice, including acts of virtue and devotion, as
obstacles to remaining absolutely passive in a spirit of interior
annihilation. Even temptations were not to be resisted, since
objectively evil actions were thought not to be sinful as long as
the soul remained passive and resigned. It is not difficult to
see how the moral implications of such behavior would incur a
condemnatory assessment. Quietism is a persistent danger
whenever contemplation is disengaged from virtuous action.[40]

The spectre of Quietism hung uneasily over the lives of
people of prayer from the Council of Trent (convened in 1545)
to the Second Vatican Council (1962-1965). Even contemplatives like Ignatius of Loyola, John of the Cross, and Teresa of
Avila had to at times tone down what they wanted to say for
fear of incurring the ire of the Inquisition, which seemed to
sniff the scent of Quietism everywhere.[41] Thus, theologians in
the seventeenth and eighteenth centuries considered contemplation a rare gift; it was not the call of most Christians, they
believed. They therefore divided the study of spirituality into
ascetical theology, which dealt with virtuous human striving
under grace for perfection, and mystical theology, which was
concerned with the extraordinary graces by which God brings
the passive soul to mystical union. This division was consecrated by the rigidly intellectualistic manuals published before Vatican II.[42]

Today the contemporary term "spirituality" overcomes the
dichotomies and conflicts implicit in the distinction between
ascetical and mystical theology. But just a generation ago
people were customarily told that contemplative prayer was
probably for monastics and certainly for later in life in any
case. Those who wanted to learn to pray were counseled to
begin by using their imagination, memory, understanding
and will (traditionally called discursive meditation). Spiritual
directors were advised not to talk much about contemplative
prayer, though if people arrived there by themselves through
the work of the Spirit, that would be fine.

Now we are in a new age, one that is manifesting a hunger for and seeking out contemplative practices. The new perspective is that the more active one is, the more one needs this experience of "inscape," of looking at the deep-down reality of things and finding God there as their source and ground of being. In the past 400 years, laity as well as priests and sisters from the active orders were often discouraged from reading books about contemplation. They were even taught that it was contrary to humility to aspire to it. This misrepresentation of the mainstream tradition deprived those who needed it most of a deeper life of prayer to sustain them.

Today young and middle-aged adults in particular seem to be looking for this deeper meaning and sustenance. They are traveling to the East in order to learn how to sit, how to breathe, how to use a sacred word, how to do walking meditation, and so forth. They want to learn how to "be still and know that God is God," how to look at the "insides of things" and find the Mystery hidden there through the ages. And they will learn it, if not from us in Christian practice, then from others who will happily teach them according to their own methods.

The plain fact is that contemplative prayer is available and recommended to everyone. Contemplative experience in fact, is at the heart of Christian faith. It could hardly be otherwise, for the core experience of Christian life is a heart-to-heart relationship with the person of Christ and the indwelling Trinity who have come to make their home with us.

5

A Method for the Journey: The Use of a Sacred Word

The form of contemplative prayer that is taught in the remaining chapters of Part I on Meditation is apophatic in nature. One eventually comes to the practical question: how does one pray in this way? It is natural for people to assert the impossibility of voiding the mind and imagination of all ideas and forms. John of the Cross anticipated these objections:

In your view there will be two difficulties insurmountable by human strength and capacity: the banishment of the natural through one's natural strength, and contact and union with the supernatural (which is far more difficult, and, to be truthful, impossible by one's natural ability alone).

I reply that, indeed, God must place the soul in the supernatural state. Nevertheless, an individual must insofar as possible prepare himself. This he can do naturally with God's help. In the measure that he embarks through his own efforts upon this negation and emptiness of forms, he will receive from God the possession of union . . . . God will give the . . . union when He is pleased to do so and in accordance with the individual's preparation.[1]

John is emphatic on two key points: union is God's gift, but we have to earnestly solicit God's divine cure. In this cure God will heal us of what through our own efforts we are unable to remedy. "No matter how much an individual does through his own efforts, he cannot actively purify himself enough to be disposed in the least degree for the divine union of the perfection of love. God must take over and purge him . . . ."[2]

So, while disposing ourselves does not do everything, without it God may do nothing. How, exactly, does one dispose oneself for what God seeks to do?

We have seen in the brief historical survey of key teachings in the practice of Christian contemplative prayer a recurring method for quieting the mind. This method involves the use of a short word or phrase to reduce the number of thoughts and dissolve them into the single thought or intention of opening to God. The Jesus Prayer, the Trisagion ("Holy God, Holy Mighty, Holy Immortal One"), "O God, come to my assistance, O Lord, make haste to help me," "Maranatha," are all examples of a sacred "word" used in the history of Christian spirituality to dispose oneself for contemplative prayer. This method in itself is not unique to Christianity; one finds it as well in other religions.

In the history of religions, the term used for this sacred word is *mantra*. The term itself bears looking at etymologically because its meaning suggests why people of many religions have evolved to a similar practice in their quest for union with God. It is derived from the Sanskrit root *man* which relates to the mind, and the ending *-tra* which indicates a tool or instrument. *Mantra* is thus a "mental tool," an instrument used to modify the thought process itself. It contributes to an alteration of consciousness by breaking down the ordinary connection between speech and thought. Speech is normally used to express thought, but here it is not so used. In the poetic phrase of T.S. Eliot, a mantra is a "raid on the ineffable," and breaks the bond that ties human language to the everyday levels of consciousness.

Examples in Christian experience are the invocation of the name of Jesus and prayer in tongues in which phrases, syllables, or even a single vowel-sound, without concrete signification for the one who utters them, lifts prayer upward beyond the limits of language and conceptual thought.[3]

The use of a mantra in meditation is a consciousness instrument, a technique of spiritual development. I will use the terms "sacred word" and "mantra" interchangeably in these pages. It is essentially an expression of one's intent to encounter God, a gesture, a pointer. It has more to do with intent than content. Thus, its meaning and emotional resonance are not of the essence, but play a supporting role.

The less mental associations and images which attach to the word the better. Its function is to establish an inner climate which facilitates the movement toward God in faith. Oftentimes people who have a relationship with the Lord will already have a word which they use habitually and which sums up for them their whole movement to God in faith and love.

We noted above how this ancient Christian prayer form has been renewed through two contemporary "schools," centering prayer and Christian meditation. Both use the same source material as their reference points, but there is a difference in emphasis on the importance attributed to saying one's word from the beginning to the end of the meditation. The centering prayer school says, "We use the prayer word to the extent that it is useful and helps us to abide with the Lord. If that means using it constantly, fine; we use it constantly. If we do not need to use it, fine; we can let it go. We do not concern ourselves with whether or not we are using the word. It matters little. Our attention is to the Lord."[4]

The Christian meditation school attaches more importance to the repetition of the mantra from the beginning to the end of the time of meditation. Many people follow each school of teaching and testify to its fruitfulness in their lives. The difference in emphasis is pointed out here for two reasons: first, to alert to this variation those who may avail themselves of literature from both schools; and second, to encourage each one to follow the way that seems most persuasive and to remain consistent with it in one's practice. "Where the Spirit is, there is freedom" (2 Cor. 3:17). In my own journey in this way of prayer, I was blessed to have Fr. Main as a guide, so in my exposition here I will abide by my own counsel and remain consistent with his teaching on this particular point. Apart from this difference in emphasis surrounding the use of the word, both schools reflect each other's instruction on the other points.

It may be useful to state once again the "how-to" in its essential core.

Sit still and upright, relaxed but alert, with your eyes lightly closed. Silently, interiorly begin to say a single word or phrase selected from the context of Christian faith. Listen to it as you say it gently but continuously with faith and love. Do not think or imagine anything, spiritual or otherwise. If thoughts or images come and your attention strays, as soon as you become aware of this, return to saying your word. Meditate each morning and evening for between twenty to thirty minutes.

Those few phrases represent the eminent simplicity of the method, a simplicity which I do not wish to befuddle with a lot of "rules." Various questions inevitably arise, however, concerning the application of this method, and it is with those queries in mind that the following elaborations of an explanatory and interpretive nature are offered. The reader should understand that they are not rules, but recommendations and suggestions based upon experience.

In the teaching of the Christian meditation school of thought, the essence and the art of meditation is simply learning to say your word from the beginning to the end of the meditation. Once you have settled upon a particular word or phrase, it should not be changed but for a very good reason. Through repeated use of the word one seeks to root it in one's consciousness to the point where it becomes automatic, reflex, like the beating of one's heart. Switching from one to another works against this process.

For the sake of our exercise, then, let us work with the word proposed by Frs. Main and Freeman and widely used

throughout the international network of Christian meditators: *Maranatha* (Come, Lord!). Because it is an Aramaic
word, we do not have a lot of mental associations or images
attached to it and consequently are less inclined to think
about its meaning while saying it. At the same time, its relationship to faith and scripture are clear and provide it with
an inherent "lean" toward opening oneself to God.

The word is to be said slowly, distinctly, rhythmically in
four equally stressed syllables: Ma-ra-na-tha. It is silently
articulated in the mind. For beginners who may have difficulty moving immediately to a silent articulation in the mind, it
is quite acceptable to begin repeating the word inaudibly (or
if one is alone, audibly) with the lips. The utterance will do
its work in its own time and become rooted in the mind
where, with the lips silent now, one recites it interiorly.[5]

The purpose of repeating the word from the beginning to
the end of one's meditation is twofold; one theological, the
other psychological. The first purpose of repeating the word
is to lead you gently away from your own thoughts, your own
ideas, your own desire, your own sin and to lead you into the
presence of God by turning you around, away from yourself,
toward God. The second purpose relates to the active nature
of the mind; it must have something to occupy it. The mind is
like the trunk of an elephant leading a procession through a
narrow street lined by vendors' kiosks. As long as the trunk
is unengaged, it is exploring in all directions and into everything. But if the trainer gives the elephant something like a
simple stick of bamboo to hold in its trunk, it leads the way
with trunk held aloft steady and stable. We cannot expect the
mind to remain perfectly still; it is its nature to be active. So
we give it one simple word or phrase to occupy it—a word
which, by virtue of the love and faith with which it is uttered,
inclines our hearts toward God.

The continuous repetition eventually unhooks our minds
from that amalgam of images, ideas, concepts, words and
thoughts which normally occupy us mentally. Meditation is
learning to look out beyond ourselves, to break out of the
closed system of self-consciousness and self-concern, to liber-

ate ourselves from the prison of the ego. When we are saying the word, we are not thinking our own thoughts. We are not analyzing what is happening to us. We are letting go and launching out into the deep. It requires an act of faith to leave oneself behind. "To remain in oneself: this is the real danger," St. Augustine said, instructing us to transcend the self (ego) which is not God in order to encounter our real Self, "who is deeper than my inmost being and higher than my greatest height" yet who is in us and with us, but transcends us in mystery.

Sometimes in praying the word, we may feel a certain peacefulness and calm and feel tempted to say to ourselves, "This is good. I think I'll let go of my mantra and just rest in this experience." We're like a rower who sets out from the bank of the river with the intention of getting to the other side. Once out in the water, she feels the warm sun on her back and says, "Oh, this feels good. I think I'll put down my oars and lie back in the boat and just relax out here awhile." So she dozes off and wakes up only to find that the current has carried her far off course.

The discipline of saying one's word from the beginning to the end of the meditation is designed to get us across the river, to move us from the shore of our own self-preoccupation toward union with the consciousness of Christ. The narcissistic traits of our culture insinuate themselves even into our spirituality, inviting us to keep our own feelings at the center of our experience, e.g. I'm watching what I'm feeling and as soon as my experience changes I will take up my word or start "rowing" again until I recover the experience of peace and tranquillity. Staying with the mantra is a divestment of self, an emptying, a leaving of myself behind and an entering into the prayer of Christ. So, in order to turn our attention increasingly away from ourselves and toward Christ, we say our word until we can no longer say it, and as soon as we have become aware that we have stopped saying it, we begin saying it again.

The Power in a Word

Particularly in the Eastern religions, there is an understanding of the sacred nature of the mantra. It is spoken of in terms of a divine energy encased in a sound structure, divine power manifested in a sound-body, a sound-key permitting one access to transcendental realms. One reads that the audible sound of a mantra has a necessary, mechanical connection with certain kinds of vibratory energy present in the universe or in the body. These pseudo-scientific explanations are not verifiable, and are at times even contradicted among the Eastern religions by the different pronunciations of the same mantric phrases and their application to different but supposedly corresponding cosmic elements.

One might find a rich devotional reflection, however, in the notion of divine power manifested in a sacred word, since a mantra is usually the name of or relates to the divinity. The one whose name is used or to whom the mantra is addressed might be envisioned as the informing power of the sound. For example, one might understand the Holy Spirit as the "breath" of God who informs my breathing, who in fact "breathes me" and "says" the word which I listen to within me.

Sounds are essentially energy vibrations. Just as the splitting of an atom in the physical world manifests the tremendous forces latent in it, so in the spiritual realm the repetition of the holy name invokes the mysterious power of God. There is nothing magical or superstitious here. It is clearly not the number of times the name is repeated, but the intentionality of faith and the love with which the name is said that opens the door to the action of God. It presupposes a personal relationship, a movement of self-surrender. When one says the name with love and faith, one generates the flow of love and faith in one's heart. Prayer's effect is in us. Thus, it is said that we become what we meditate on.

In a parable told by the Indian spiritual masters, a farmer decided to take up a spiritual discipline. He tried meditation but found himself constantly distracted by thoughts concerning his water buffalo. The man went to seek advice from his guru who told him that first he must learn to concentrate, after which meditation would come easily. The holy man suggested that the farmer use the image of one of his water buffalo to cultivate his powers of concentration. He gave him a hut near his own in which to practice for two weeks; then he should come and report on his progress. The two weeks passed, and the farmer did not come. So the sage decided to go to the farmer's hut to see what he was doing and why he had not come. Once arrived, he called out to the farmer to come out. In a humble voice, the farmer requested the guru to come in, saying, "My horns prevent me from getting out of the low, narrow entrance of the hut."[6]

The farmer's unbroken concentration on the buffalo had filled him with "buffalo consciousness," and when he came out of his meditation he behaved like a buffalo. Similarly, the person who becomes absorbed in God through repetition of the Holy Name is filled with God-consciousness and is transformed into God-likeness. Christian literature has its own, albeit less popularized, versions of the same truth:

The power of God is present in the name of Jesus, so that the invocation of the Divine Name acts as an effective sign of God's action, as a sort of sacrament. The name of Jesus, present in the human heart, communicates to it the power of deification . . . shining through the heart, the light of the Name of Jesus illuminates all the universe.[7]

The name is believed to contain in itself as in a nutshell the whole divine Mystery. It is understood to carry in a consecrated form everything that one can think or say of that Mystery. By the power it enfolds within itself, it leads the soul toward the very Center, the Origin, the unique Source and endows the mystical heart with a spiritual energy which will not stop short of divine union.

In our quest for communion with God, we oftentimes look outside ourselves to find God. God is always "at home"; it is we who are usually absent. God is constantly at work within, taking advantage of every opening we offer to draw us into deeper communion of life. It is a question for us of tuning in to who is there and the work in progress. The use of a sacred word has a focusing and penetrating effect relative to the journey within.

When thought-waves are directed toward diverse objects, each thought is quickly replaced by another and the energy in each is dissipated. But when all the thought-waves converge on the same point, then the energy amassed at that point begins to penetrate the image or its conceptualized quality and yield its true significance. An old newspaper can lie in the sun for years, and as long as the heat energy striking it is spread out and diffused, nothing happens to it but discoloration. But if the lens of a magnifying glass focuses the light, within minutes the paper will burst into flame.

Using the Word Through the Day

Though our sacred word serves to draw us into silence in focused awareness, many people employ it or use another, different phrase during the day while walking to work, standing at the bus stop, washing the dishes and so forth. When I was a boy I used to watch the men move the handcars up and down the railway line near our home. Two men pushed a lever back and forth a few times to get the handcar started. Then, once it picked up speed, it rolled effortlessly down the line. It's a convenient way to move something or someone from one place to another.

The prayer word or phrase acts in a similar way, bringing the resources we tap in meditation into play in our lives throughout the day. When we find ourselves provoked or worried or driven by some compulsive habit, the mantra handcar moves us into touch with the inner strength we glimpsed in that period of morning meditation. As we are able to extend its influence throughout our day by having recourse to it when we are walking or traveling, times imme-

diately before and after sleep, it becomes a lifeline maintaining in us the awareness of the indwelling presence of God.
Advertisers don't mind shocking us, or even offending us as
long as they can get the name of their product to stick in our
minds. They are using the power of the word to manipulate
us, to make us buy things that we don't need or that might
even be harmful to us. With the mantra, we are putting the
power of the word to positive use.

6

Practical Questions: Time, Place, Frequency, Posture, Breathing

There is a sense in which one cannot teach contemplative prayer; one can only teach another how to still the mind and enter into silence. Contemplation is a secret, loving inflow of God which, if not hampered, fires a spirit of love in the soul. As such, it is the work of God. Still, there are certain things one can do to dispose oneself. One's place of meditation, schedule, physical health and mental state should all reflect a readiness to enter into that encounter. One must be ready to accord it priority of time and to grant it a central position in one's life. One cannot live a double life and be moving toward depth, harmony and integration only in one half of one's life, as it were. Meditation is a process of "one-ing." Thomas Merton's words set the tone:

The great thing is prayer. Prayer itself. If you want a life of prayer, the way to get it is by praying . . . . In prayer we discover what we already have. You start where you are and you deepen what you already have. And you realize that you are already there. We already have everything, but we don't know it and we don't experience it. Everything has been given to us in Christ. All we need is to experience what we already possess. The trouble is we aren't taking the time to do so. If we really want prayer, we'll have to give it time. We must slow down to a human tempo and we'll begin to have time to listen . . . . This is what the Zen people do. They give a great deal of time to doing whatever they need to do. That's what we have to learn when it comes to prayer. We have to give it time.[1]

How Much Time Should Be Given?

The recommendation of twenty to thirty minutes is made with an eye to most people's rhythm of life. Busy people already have to stretch to make that much time available at the beginning and end of their day. Longer than that might discourage people from starting or continuing. The minimum time of about twenty minutes is also put forward out of a sense that it takes at least that long to establish interior silence. Early morning and late afternoon or early evening are the ideal times, before meals if at all possible. When the body is engaged in the processes of digestion and assimilation, it is more difficult to maintain a state of alert attentiveness.

Some may have both the time and the inclination to meditate for a longer period or a third time each day. With a little experience, meditators arrive at the amount of time which is most apt for them. If on occasion we have to compromise, we should accept that fifteen minutes is better than nothing and give to our prayer whatever time we have, avoiding an "all or nothing" approach. We're always dependent on the activity of God, and God is free to break through whenever God wants, so we should not underestimate the potential of whatever time we have. "I well understand that one must not put limits on God," Teresa of Avila wrote; "in a moment He can bring a soul to lofty experience . . . . His Majesty has the power to do whatever He wants and is eager to do many things for us."[2] A single moment of absorption in God is more valuable than a longer period of prayer during which we are constantly in and out of interior silence. It only takes a moment for God to enrich us.

We are essentially dealing with a prayer form that distills the essence of monastic life into two periods each day, so it is already a concentrated formula. That suggests by itself that one's efforts should not be in the direction of further reduction. One of my colleagues is diabetic and has to administer adequate dosages of insulin to herself each day in order to keep her system functioning the way it should. Meditation works similarly; our psyche and nervous system require a certain amount of inner silence and refreshment at regular intervals on a daily basis if we are to realize the positive effects that meditation offers. These two periods are like visits to the well for those working in the hot sun. Our spirits need resourcing at this deep level in the same way that our bodies need sleep and food.

We need to keep replenishing our reservoir of silence. Praying at the same time every day and for the same length of time does this. In addition, dividing the day between these two periods of prayer keeps us close to the well and enables its refreshing water to affect our whole day.

Place

Choose a quiet corner of your room. A space which you use only for meditation and which is free from other associations is ideal. Decorate it with an icon, a candle, or an open Bible. Many of the most difficult obstacles are eliminated just by creating an environment conducive to prayer. Regularity conditions the mind to slow down its activities with a minimum of delay. It will settle down more quickly when time and place are established. If there is no quiet place in the home, look for one along the way of your daily route. A friend of mine who is a district attorney with small children at home stops in a little church going to and coming from work each day and meditates there. Obviously, a place that is free from loud, distracting noises makes it easier to enter into an inner stillness, but that is not always possible. If your environment is noisy, try spending a few moments focusing on the sounds and becoming aware that the presence of God is holding them all in existence. Realize that the God you seek is there, all around you. Enter into conscious communion with this Presence by entering into the silent center within yourself and becoming a still point in the midst of all the noise.

As the ecumenical center where I work is national in its outreach, I am frequently faced with meditating on trains, planes or in waiting lounges. There are generally announcements in the background, children's voices and drifts of adult conversation all around me. I have learned that sounds are distracting only when you attempt to run away from them, when you attempt to push them out of your conscious, when you protest that they have no right to be there. If you just accept them as "what is," they can even be turned into a means for attaining interior silence.

Begin by listening to the sounds all around you, even the smallest ones. Let your mind alight for a moment on each sound you can pick up. Identify it, and notice the variations in pitch and intensity within each sound and among the different sounds. Now reflect that each one is made possible and sustained by God's presence. God is sounding all around you. Rest in this world of sounds. At the heart of it there is a silent center. Rest in God there, and begin to sound your word, listening to it deep within you.

Frequency

If you're meditating once a day, it's as though you're hopping. All the weight is on one foot. Adding the second meditation is like learning to walk with balance. There is a certain rhythm in two meditations a day that moves with the rhythm of nature; the traditional times are sunrise and sunset. We have to make time available each morning and each evening of our lives for this work of making contact with the Source of all life, for this work of creating inner space in our lives for the expansion of spirit. The "how-to" of meditation is simple. What is difficult is faithfulness to the discipline, to interrupt what you are doing in order to pray. We need to be convinced that our time of prayer is more important than any other activity apart from some urgent call of charity.

Fr. John Main and I both arrived in Montreal in the fall of 1977: I to serve as Director of the Chaplaincy Services Centre at McGill University, and he to open a house of prayer. Shortly thereafter, he became my teacher and guide in the way of meditation. I remember one communication in particular. I was pleading what I thought was a very convincing argument: the life of a campus minister is too hectic and unpredictable to maintain faithfulness to the second meditation each day. Students walked in unannounced, a church service preceded the supper hour, evening courses or visits in the dorms followed supper—there just wasn't time!

He listened patiently and attentively until I had said my piece. He knew I was applying pressure and hoping to extract an admission that, okay, in my case once a day would do. I was not, after all, living in a monastery where the whole day is structured around one's prayer times. He began sympathetically and I thought I could detect a verdict in my favor forthcoming. He granted that, yes, the life of an active pastor was considerably different from the more controlled world of the monastery, and he knew that a second meditation in the latter part of the day was like looking for stable footing on the high seas.

I began to feel a "But—" coming . . . and when it came, it had all the unflinching firmness of an uppercut to the jaw that stops the rude challenger dead in his tracks. "But if you wish to advance on this path," he said, "it is absolutely necessary that you be faithful to your second meditation. Look again where your time is going and make some decisions that reflect your priorities."

It was a showdown: the path of expediency versus the path of radical commitment. My own plea was sincere and in good faith. I was genuinely convinced that a second meditation in my schedule was unworkable. Anything less than his unblinking response would have left me secure in my own position of compromise. But the Gibraltar-like conviction of his words stood me up straight and sent me back home with the sense that I had to take another look at the pattern of my late-day activities and see if everything was as important and unmovable as I was making it out to be. When I sat down and really looked at it, I saw that he was right. We make time for what is important to us. Still, there may be some who, despite their best efforts and being as honest with themselves as they are able, simply cannot manage to squeeze out twenty quiet minutes at the back end of the day. For them, I simply repeat the axiom: "Pray as you can, not as you can't."

Most people find that protecting the place of the morning meditation period is much less of a challenge than doing so for the second one later in the day. During my study sabbatical in India, I stayed for a month at the Christian ashram of the Holy Trinity founded by two of the spiritual fathers of our century who served as pioneers in inter-faith dialogue in India, Fr. Henri Le Saux, O.S.B., and Fr. Jules Monchanin. Fr. Bede Griffith, their successor, carried forward the work of dialogue until his death in 1993.

There were some scenes in the daily life of this ashram, popularly known as Shantivanam (forest of peace), which spoke to me of the unique contribution the second meditation period makes to our lives each day.

One morning I watched a young woman arrive in the forest of eucalyptus trees with a large cloth folded over her shoulder. She took it off, unfolded it and laid it out on the ground. Then she began collecting dead strips of bark fallen from the trees. As she did so, she laid them in the cloth until she had accumulated a large pile. Then, with some struggle, she brought the four corners together and tied them at the top of the bundle. Straightening up, she took a firm grip on the knot and, much like a canoe camper grabbing the portage bar and giving the canoe a lift and flip onto her shoulders, she hoisted the bundle onto the top of her head. Then steadying it until

she had found the point of perfect balance, she walked gracefully away with her arms at her side.

Our field of consciousness is often like that cloth as we
head into the day after our morning meditation: unfolded and
open, ready to receive. Then the day loads it up with scattered pieces that come from everywhere: a discouraging
development at the office, gossip during the coffee break,
good news in the mail, bad news from the radio, the ups and
downs of the children. Toward the end of the day, the second
meditation gathers up all those pieces, ties the four corners
of the day together, lifts it all up, as it were, helps us find our
point of balance with all the little pieces of this and that
which the day has brought to our consciousness, and thus
carry it forward in a portable bundle which, while heavy, can
still be managed.

Each day in the ashram, the constant coming and going of
people, cows, carts, and water buffalo on the sandy paths creates a dusty, uneven terrain in which ruts and holes emerge
and dung collects. At the end of the day, the Indians take in
hand a broom of straw held together by a string. With long,
even, methodical strokes they brush the paths, leaving
behind them a smooth trail of sand.

The hours we live between our times of meditation are
generally like those paths. The dust gets kicked up, ruts and
holes emerge, waste matter accumulates. Our psychic state
at the end of the day is a grimy, dishevelled mess. Then we
restore the tranquillity of order to it with the slow, rhythmical strokes of the mantra. And when we are finished, we feel
as though we are renewed and our being reknit.

The Jungian psychological rationale for this is based on
the unity of our being, expressed in terms of the conscious
and unconscious which are in a hidden but dynamic process
of opening to one another. The night is the kingdom of the
unconscious, the day the kingdom of the conscious. Think of
your sleeping time (unconscious) as the unfettered inflow of
an ocean tide. Your sleep finished, you arise for your pre-
breakfast meditation in that transitional period of hours in
which body temperature, gravity and metabolism are in

shifting patterns. The tide is withdrawing. The morning meditation is a time in which the conscious blesses and loves the
unconscious which joins with, moves into, and surfaces
slightly in your rising daytime consciousness.

Your waking hours (conscious) may be compared with a
walk on the pebbles and rocks of a beach whose tide is out.
The day's "walk" brings numerous aches and pains, cuts and
stubbed toes, discoveries and reflections. Work over, you head
home, tired. Now temperature, gravity and metabolism are
again changing their patterns. This time, the unconscious
blesses and loves the conscious. In your pre-supper or evening
meditation, the active conscious gives over everything to the
unconscious without supervision, editing, suppression, or otherwise shaping it as is the case during the working hours. In
that deep-level exchange which meditation facilitates, the
unconscious gives understanding and tactical advice to the
conscious, strengthening it and enabling it to deal better with
problems and people.

We are creatures haunted by twoness, by a lack of the
unity for which we long. The two meditations, each in a different way, are instruments of letting both aspects of our
being—night/day, unconscious/conscious—interflow. They
thus complete each other, and in so doing advance the cause
of our healing and wholeness. One sees here the difference
between the morning and evening meditation, and their
mutual necessity if there is to be wholeness in one's meditation practice. For Jung the self embraces the conscious and
the unconscious. The self is not only the center, but the
whole. It is our genuine and complete personality which acts
to heal us, to reconcile opposites, to lead us to wholeness.[3]
How long will this take to be effected in us? It doesn't matter
how long it takes. All that matters is that we are truthfully
on the way, on the pilgrimage and that each day, if only by
one centimeter at a time, our commitment to truth and to
freedom grows.

"The truth will make you free," Jesus said. The freedom is
the freedom to be ourselves and to let others be themselves;
the freedom to love ourselves, to love others and to love God.

The Christian proclamation is that the Spirit of God is to be found in our own hearts. In its light we see light, and in that light we know ourselves to be free. The only way of arriving at that light, truth and freedom is by faith. If then our faith is tested by the struggle to be faithful to our daily rendezvous, it is by the same token also strengthened. "If you continue in my word, you are truly my disciples; and you will know the truth, and the truth will make you free. So if the Son makes you free, you will be free indeed" (John 8:31,36).

Posture

In C.S. Lewis' *The Screwtape Letters*, Uncle Screwtape reproaches his apprentice demon, Wormwood, for permitting his "patient" to become a Christian. Nevertheless, he says, there is no need to worry because "all the habits of the patient, both mental and bodily, are still in our favour." He advises Wormwood to have his man

> *remember, or to think he remembers, the parrotlike nature of his prayers in childhood. In reaction against that, he may be persuaded to aim at something entirely spontaneous, inward, informal, and unregularised; and what this will actually mean to a beginner will be an effort to produce in himself a vaguely devotional mood in which real concentration of will and intelligence have no part . . . . That is exactly the sort of prayer we want; and since it bears a superficial resemblance to the prayer of silence as practised by those who are very far advanced in the Enemy's service, clever and lazy patients can be taken in by it for quite some time. At the very least, they can be persuaded that the bodily position makes no difference to their prayers; for they constantly forget what you must always remember, that they are animals and that whatever their bodies do affects their souls.[4]*

Find a posture in which you can on the one hand be stable, settled in, and *still*, while on the other hand maintaining yourself *alert*. A posture that is relaxed, yet alert: that is the key. An erect but not rigid spine facilitates easeful breathing and alert wakefulness. The particular postures in which this may be carried out are several: sitting in a straight-backed chair (Figure 1); sitting with one's knees on the floor and one's seat on a prayer stool (Figure 2); sitting cross-legged on the floor with the buttocks slightly elevated by a cushion (Figure 3); or sitting with one's knees on the floor, astride a large cushion placed between the legs as though one were riding a horse (Figure 4).

Some further details may be helpful for those who wish to experiment with the posture shown in Figure 3. Use a firm cushion or folded blanket to elevate your buttocks a few inches off the floor. Take your right leg and fold it inward so that your right heel is just barely touching the area between your genitals and your anus. Now take your left leg and fold it inward, placing your left heel on your right calf. Give a slight forward tilt to your upper body to bring yourself to a point where you feel firmly and stably centered between your three points of contact: buttocks, right, and left knee. Finally, place your right hand in your left (or vice versa) with your thumbs slightly touching.

It is important to be comfortable so that bodily protest from any quarter not knock at the door of the mind asking for attention. When the mind goes to a belt or a strap that is too tight, to a crink in the back or the neck, it leaves the focused concentration on one's word behind. To this end, it is useful to wear loose clothing. Once one has settled into the chosen posture, one should remain as still as possible in it for the duration of the meditation. A quiet body disposes a quiet mind. This is the first discipline to be mastered: sitting perfectly still with an erect spine. We do not have to create silence; it is there within us. What we have to do is to let it emerge and enter into it, to become silence. Silence is the language of the Spirit.

Figure 1

Figure 2

Figure 3

Figure 4

Breathing

Deep, rhythmic, abdominal breathing brings oxygen to the brain. Many people use a brief breathing exercise when they come to their place of prayer to help them quiet their mind and body. It should be kept simple and unburdensome so that it may serve as an effective lead into a form of prayer which is eminently simple. For those who may not be familiar with such aids, and without wishing this or any other one to be taken as a "must," I offer this example of the genre. At the very beginning of your meditation period, focus your awareness by paying attention to your breathing. Keep the breathing regular. After several breaths taken in this manner, begin to count down, starting with ten: (inhale) ten, (exhale) ten; (inhale) nine, (exhale) nine, etc. At zero, begin to say your word.

Such relaxation and focusing exercises are particularly helpful prior to the second meditation because our mental processes have been in full gear all day long juggling a host of concerns. To expect the mind to come all of sudden to a screeching halt and be focused is unrealistic. A few minutes dedicated to transition time is equivalent to slowly applying pressure to the brake and bringing the car to a gradual stop.

Should the recitation of the mantra be coordinated with the breathing? Good authority can be found on both the "no" and the "yes" sides of this question. In the hesychastic tradition of the Christian East, the invocation of the name of Jesus is very quickly assimilated to breathing. At some period difficult to ascertain, but which cannot be any later than the eighth century, the association of the invocation with breathing was undertaken. Hesychius of Jerusalem makes the following promise: "If you wish to live in peace and ease and keep your heart watchful without difficulty, let the prayer of Jesus cleave to your breath and you shall succeed before long."[5] Theophan the Recluse (nineteenth century) adds: "It is important . . . to control your breathing a little so as to keep time with the words of the (Jesus) prayer. But the most important thing is to believe that God is near and hears."[6] Swami Satynananda Saraswati, a leader of the modern yogic renaissance, straightforwardly directs in his comprehensive book on meditation methods: "The mantra should be integrated with the breath."[7]

At the same time, Eknath Easwaren writes in his Mantram Handbook: "And let me urge you not to connect the repetition of the mantram with your breathing or heartbeat. There is no harm if this happens of its own accord, but in making a conscious effort to link the mantram with these rhythms, you may interfere with vital processes which the body, with its native wisdom, is already regulating at optimum efficiency."[8]

When all is said and done, there is a strong consensus among the spiritual fathers of the Christian East who recognize that

> *this teaching of the Fathers has created and continues to create many perplexities for its readers, although in fact there is really nothing difficult about it. We advise our beloved brethren not to try to practice this mechanical technique unless it establishes itself in them of its own accord . . . . The essential thing is for the mind to unite with the heart at prayer, and this is accomplished by divine grace, in its own time, determined by God . . . . All the mechanical methods of a material character are suggested by the Fathers solely as aids for a quicker and easier attainment of attention during prayer, and not as something essential. The essential, indispensable element in prayer is attention. Without attention there is no prayer . . . . Aids always remain no more than aids.*[9]

Contemporary teachers like John Main, Laurence Freeman and Basil Pennington recognize that most people say the word in conjunction with their breathing, but that it isn't of the essence. It is an external aid to inner work but is in no way essential. In a colloquium on Christian meditation, Fr. Freeman shared his view that "It is helpful to say the mantra in a way that synchronizes with natural body-rhythms, but if this makes it more complex, forget it, and just say your word."[10] Thus the sacred word may repeat itself, faster or slower, stronger or weaker. "It may take up the rhythm of our heart or of our breath, though we do not in any way seek to bring this about, or give any attention to either of these."[11]

Coming Out of Meditation

Hopefully, repetition of the word has served as a condition for deep, self-forgetful contemplation and brought one to silent awareness. Common sense, then, dictates that we give ourselves a few transitional moments before jumping back into the maelstrom of the day's activities. In preparing one-self for a dive into the waters of a swimming pool, showers are intended to acclimate the system and reduce the shock to the heart and nervous system of plunging into the water. Similarly, many meditators, before diving back into their work, take a few moments to savor the silence and the Presence, and to begin to say some vocal prayer quietly to themselves which expresses their attitude of self-surrender and of openness to God. Here are three such prayers:

Loving God, I abandon myself into your hands.
Do with me what you will.
Whatever you may do, I thank you.
Help me to be ready for all, to accept all.
Let only your will be done in me and in all your creatures.
I ask no more than this, O Lord.
Gracious God, into your hands, I commend my life.
I give it to you with all the love of my heart,
for I love you Lord,
and so need to give myself,
to surrender myself into your hands
without reserve and with complete confidence
for you are my Father.
                    (Prayer of Charles de Foucauld, slightly adapted)

Take, Lord, and receive all my liberty,
my memory, my understanding, and my entire will,
all that I have and call my own.
You have given it all to me.
To you, Lord, I return it.
Everything is yours;
do with it what you will.
Give me only your love and your grace.
That is enough for me.

(Prayer of Ignatius of Loyola)

Take my life and let it be
Consecrated, God, to thee;
Take my moments and my days,
Let them flow in ceaseless praise.

Take my hands and let them move
At the impulse of thy love;
Take my feet, and let them be
Swift and beautiful for thee.

Take my silver and my gold,
Not a mite would I withhold;
Take my intellect, and use
Every power as thou shalt choose.

Take my will, and make it thine;
It shall be no longer mine;
Take my heart, it is thine own;
It shall be thy royal throne.

Take my love; my God, I pour
At thy feet its treasure store:
Take myself, and I will be,
Ever, only, all, for thee. Amen.
(Prayer of Francis Ridley Havergol,
1874, slightly abbreviated and adapted)

In other words, one starts thinking thoughts again, looking ahead to the day and conversing with God about it. I went diving once off the Great Barrier Reef in Australia with a fellow who earned his living by catching tropical fish and then sending them to aquariums. He anchored a container in the deep, on the bottom, into which he put the fish he caught. When it came time for us to go, he brought the container up slowly, in stages, so as to give the fishes' air sacs time to adjust to the changing conditions of pressure. The same applies to us when we're coming out of the deep, interior silence of meditation. Like a person walking out of a room where the shades have been drawn, into the full light of day, our inner eyes and senses need time to adjust. A minute or two of transition time is all it takes to allow for such adjustment.

Physiological Benefits

Meditation-based medical programs have gained new momentum as part of a mushrooming movement within health care that tries to address the emotional distress of medical patients along with their medical care.

Meditation often offers people some relief from their symptoms in a wide range of health problems. Part of the relief is very likely psychological, but recent scientific work suggests the wide-spectrum impact of meditation on physical health may also be due to its effects on cortisol, a hormone released by the body in response to stress. Cortisol acts to increase available energy in the body, but at a price: tissue repair and the immune system work less effectively. This is a winning trade-off for the body in an emergency when intense activity might make the difference between survival or death. But if, as is the case in modern life, most days have minor crises and stresses, the secretion of cortisol takes a steady toll on health.

At the 1992 annual meeting of the Society for Neuroscience in Anaheim, California, neurochemist Kenneth G. Walton reported that people who were taught meditation had cortisol

levels 15 percent lower than before they had become meditators. An earlier study had found that long-term meditators
had a drop in their cortisol levels of nearly 25 percent during
a 40-minute meditation period. A colleague of Walton's who
studied more than six hundred men and women in Quebec
who meditate regularly reported that for three successive
years there was an average drop of 12 percent each year in
their need for medical services of all kinds.[12]

Although there remains some dispute in scientific circles
over precisely what the physiological effects of meditation are,
studies show that meditation reduces the body's response
(sweat) level, breath rate and blood measures. In short, the
calming of the mind in meditation triggers the physiological
opposite of the stress-induced fight-or-flight response.[13]

Physiological benefits aside, the lasting appeal of meditation for many remains spiritual. In an age of collapse of purpose, meditation stands as a classic pathway to the inner life
and deeper sources of meaning.

7

Dealing with Distractions

There is no more certain thing to say about the experience one will have in meditation than to say "There will be distractions." The key is not to invest any energy in fencing with the thoughts, images, and fantasies that surface and vie for our attention. Simply observe them and ignore them, channeling all your energy into a single course, doing what you came to do, which is simply to be before the One Who Is in full, loving attention. All meditation is, in essence, the systematic effort to retain attention.

One day as I was sitting with a group of people by the river at Shantivanam ashram, a tall, elderly woman with long white hair who was dressed in a bright red and yellow sari came down the path that led to the river from the village nearby. The villagers came regularly to wash their clothes and bathe and she had come down for her bath, only to find a group engaged in discussion near her preferred spot. Without any hint of consternation, she observed that we were there and then turned her back on us, loosening the tucks on her sari as she gracefully let herself down into the water. The sari floated to the surface while she discreetly bathed, then disappeared under the water again as she wrapped a couple of lengths around herself and stood up to hold the remainder of the cloth out in the wind and sun to dry (a sari is about fifteen feet long). When she had finished, she turned her steps back to the village with the same sense of self-possession and clarity of purpose that characterized her actions at the river. That is the way one should handle distractions: observe them, calmly turn one's back on them, and proceed to do what one came to do—in the case of meditation, to open oneself to God through the saying of one's word.

In practicing meditation, one must expect to come face-to-face with a constant flow of subtle distractions. To try to suppress all thoughts and feelings is both impossible and unhealthy. The object is neither to fight the mind nor to allow oneself to be preoccupied by its activities. Nor is it a question of not thinking. It is a question of *not entering into dialogue with thought*. One is aware of the thought in much the same way as one is aware of a sound during meditation. There is no identification with it; it's just another phenomenon. This simplifies the whole process by taking away the need for extra effort to "stop thinking." One doesn't dwell on it or try to get rid of it. It just passes by like a sound fading away; we are aware of it, but don't allow it to "hook" us and engage us.

Compare it to a man setting out to visit a friend. His destination is his friend's house; in meditating, our destination is the inner core of our being. If he allows himself to be engaged by everything he meets along the way—smelling the flowers, talking to passers-by—it will take a long time for him to arrive. Similarly, if we allow ourselves to be distracted by psychic scenery, it will take a long time to reach our destination. Yet the flowers and the passers-by are there; we cannot evacuate the sidewalks and uproot all the gardens just because we want to take a walk. The point is to make a bee-line for the goal and to hold oneself on course without stopping to dialogue all along the way.

Some people integrate the technique of "mental noting" from Buddhist *vipassana* meditation and find it very effective in disengaging from a passing thought which has "hooked" them. The method is easy to apply: when you observe that your mind is engaged in thought, you simply note it mentally with a concise generic word like "thinking," and then take up your mantra again.

There are different kinds of thoughts that come to us in the course of meditating: the phone rings ("I wonder who that could be?"); a brilliant idea for a project we're working on; an aware-ness of how wonderful this peacefulness feels; or emotionally charged thoughts and feelings may arise which signify the release of some deeply rooted tension. Any reflection, feeling, thought, perception or image should be treated in the same way.

We would be a lot kinder to ourselves and more realistic if we did not even *wish* to be completely free of potentially dis-tracting thoughts in meditation. Meditation and the subcon-scious mind are like a pail full of silty water. After it settles a while, the water on top will be pure because all the silt sinks to the bottom, the subconscious. It is relatively easy to make the "top" clear with prayer, good reading, and the like. But in order to make the whole of it pure, the drudge must be brought up from the bottom. Either one vacuums it out or pours it out through a filter; but it must come out through the top, i.e. pass through the conscious mind. This is what happens when medi-tation is deep. Subliminal thoughts and impressions come to the surface, purifying the mind. Hence, recitation of the mantra will be accompanied by thoughts and memories. This is natural and part of the inner process of emptying, purification, and liberation. When we accept this—that there are going to be a lot of thoughts and images which flicker by—we're much less likely to fall prey to discouragement. Nobody falls into a pool of peace for a blissful, distractionless half hour. It's not even the goal. The goal is surrender of one's whole being to God. And that means letting go even of our chagrin with these pesky thoughts and images. God may well be using them to do the work of healing and restoration within us.

Christian counselor and psychotherapist Philip St. Romain puts it this way:

All psychological experiences in this life take place in the body and affect the body in some manner. Psyche and body communicate through the medium of feelings. On the psychological side, thinking takes place; from the body's side chemical reactions take place; feelings are the consequences of thoughts in a chemical body.

All through the day, we have feelings about what is happening to us. If these feelings are painful and we fail to express them appropriately, then they are stored in some manner in the body and become physiological emotions. Feelings are the psycho-physiological responses to what is happening here now; emotions are feelings that happened long ago.[1]

As one meditates, emotional energy that has been stored in body tissues through repression becomes "shaken loose." This process might be thought of as analogous to the role of fever in fighting a bacterial infection. The purpose of the fever is to create an environment that is inhospitable to the bacteria. Likewise, the deep down "massage" of meditation creates an environment that is inhospitable to festering psychic wounds or emotional sores. The unconscious and bodily tissues are enticed to release their malevolent cargo. Meditation offers real potential for healing.

Again the Jungian perspective of the interplay between conscious and unconscious may be helpful. The mantra is a sound which resonates between the two, lessening ego control and allowing material from the unconscious to present itself. We don't engage with the images but at times they remain strongly in consciousness after meditation. This is material which we must deal with—and it can be troubling material like anger, anxiety, hints that we are not as pure as we think we are, images which are unexplainable to our current level of consciousness.

The name which Carl Jung gave to the dark and unwanted part of our personality is "the shadow," which he defined as "the sum of personal and collective psychic elements which because of their incompatibility with the chosen conscious attitude, are denied expression in life, and therefore coalesce into a relatively autonomous splinter personality with contrary tendencies in the unconscious. The shadow behaves compensatorily to consciousness, therefore its effect can be positive as well as negative."[2] We must include this unknown, rejected and strayed part of ourselves in order to be whole. No one is excluded from this effort. Even Jesus had to struggle with the powers of darkness, as well as undergo his own natural ego development. All parts of our being are to be brought toward the light of consciousness for unity to happen. We have to go through the struggle and work of opening to healing every part of ourselves before we are even somewhat in real unity within ourselves and with others. Meditation moves us to accept painful, unpleasant self-knowledge and gives us courage to change. Meditating with humility and openness to the inner realm facilitates the process of reconciliation and healing.[3]

In meditation, we essentially prostrate ourselves on the massage table and say, "Okay, God, do your work." So God starts kneading those unconscious knots and tension spots that are preventing us from being led to wholeness. When we open to God at the level of the unconscious, there may be light and airy moments and moments heavy with thoughts and emotion. Both experiences are part of a therapeutic massage. Since both are integral to the experience, both should be accepted with gratitude in the confidence that results are God's business. So we don't resist, retain or react to any thought or feeling. Regardless of whether you break out laughing, feel a tear trickle down your cheek, become aware that you're itching or twitching—treat it as you would any thought. Neither run from it nor embrace it. Let it sail on by. You can rest in it, reflect on it, allow it to engage you later. Stay gently with your word and know that God is slowly evacuating the undigested emotional material of a lifetime in as untraumatizing a way as possible. Wait it out.

Meditation, however, is not an uncovering technique, like psychoanalysis. The aims, goals, methods, and dynamics differ dramatically. Meditation's primary aim is not to lift the repression barrier and allow the shadow to surface, but to suspend mental-egoic activity in general and allow us to glimpse the Self beyond our ego. The repression barrier is often bypassed in this process, but it may be momentarily lifted upon occasion.

This release of energies from the unconscious takes the

form of either spiritual consolation or the experience of human weakness through humiliating self-knowledge. To protect ourselves from self-exaltation on the one hand or self-deprecation on the other, we need good habits of engaging in our spiritual practices to please God and not ourselves, and of serving others with compassion of heart. These habits of dedication to God and service to others form the two banks of a channel through which the energies of the unconscious may flow without submerging the psyche in the floodwaters of strong emotions.[4]

Sometimes when people get up from the massage table, they feel a transformation of mood has taken place. God is after much more than that in the opening we give in contemplative prayer: God is after transformation of personality, a restructuring of our consciousness, of our way of perceiving and responding to reality. The heart of the method doesn't consist in how we sit or in the length of time we give, but in how we handle the thoughts that arise and where we keep our attention focused. Contemplative prayer is characterized not so much by the *absence* of thoughts and feelings as by *detachment* from them. The essential point of all the spiritual disciplines that the world religions have evolved is the integration of the various levels of one's being and the surrender of that unified being to God.[5]

Evaluation of One's Meditation

Some forms of prayer call for frequent evaluation; Christian meditation is not one of them. The nature of this kind of prayer just doesn't lend itself to the usual kinds of questions like, "Did I have a lot of distractions? Did I experience any strong attractions or repulsions?" All those considerations are peripheral to and don't touch the essence of this prayer. It can't be judged on the basis of how much peace we had or how many thoughts or feelings came. It's like a river carving its way through the valley of a canyon; whether it's a sunny or rainy day, a slow, inevitable advance is registered. Advice to beginners is generally: "If you're serious about this, commit yourself to it for three months before you make any decision about continuing."

St. John of the Cross speaks of our "spiritual sweet tooth," our hankering for warm spiritual feelings, consolations and communications from God. These, he suggests, have all the nutritional value of a candy bar for our spiritual lives. And when God serves us up something substantive like dryness, distaste and trial leading to nakedness and poverty of spirit, we run from it as from death.[6] As we advance on the way of prayer, we are submitted more and more to a purifying action we cannot understand. We have to learn patience in wearying and arid periods. The dryness may grow more and more frequent, but aridity can almost be taken as a sign of progress in prayer, provided it is accompanied by serious efforts and self-discipline.[7]

This is the climate of serious meditation wherein, without light and consolation, we commit ourselves to an entire surrender to God. We begin to realize, at least obscurely, the truth of what the Desert Father St. Ammonas said: "If God did not love you he would not bring temptations upon you . . . . For the faithful, temptation is necessary, for all those who are free of temptation are not among the elect."[8] The purpose of difficulties is not to punish and afflict us, but to purify and liberate us from our own self-seeking. John of the Cross assures us that this way of the cross leads to perfect and lasting joy:

> O then, spiritual soul, when you see your appetites dark-ened, your inclinations dry and constrained, your facul-ties incapacitated for any interior exercise, do not be afflicted; think of this as a grace, since God is freeing you from yourself and taking from you your own activity. However well your actions may have succeeded you did not work so completely, perfectly, and securely—owing to their impurity and awkwardness—as you do now that God takes you by the hand and guides you in darkness,

as though you were blind, along a way and to a place
you know not. You would never have succeeded in reach-
ing this place no matter how good your eyes and your
feet.[9]

Yet, it is natural to reflect on one's experience and to evaluate it, even if only periodically. The kind of question to put
to oneself is along the lines of: "Do I find myself becoming
more peaceful and patient, more attentive to others' needs?
Do I experience a sharpened taste for the scriptures and the
eucharist?" The only way of evaluating is by looking at the
long-term fruits. It is in the effects and deeds following afterward that one discerns the true value of prayer; in fact, there
is no better crucible than this for testing prayer. "The important thing," said Teresa, "is not to think much but to love
much . . . . It doesn't consist of great delight but in desiring
with strong determination to please God in everything, in
striving, insofar as possible, not to offend Him, and in asking
Him for the advancement of the honor and glory of His son
. . . . These are the signs of love. Don't think . . . that if you
become a little distracted all is lost."[10]

The inclination to evaluate is perhaps stronger in the first
year when one continues to wonder whether this is just
another gimmick. Then comes a point when one is convinced
that this is authentic; observable benefits have emerged, the
fruits of the Spirit are present. It is at this point that the
decision to meditate moves to a deeper level. From then on
one just does it without regularly questioning whether or not
it's worth the time and the effort.

When my sister and her husband reached that point, they
rearranged their times of going to bed and getting up in order
to give themselves quiet time for meditating and good reading
before waking the children. Their alarm now goes off at 4:30
a.m., and they've discovered that the earlier morning hours
are one of the best-kept secrets in the world. They recently
went through a prolonged period of stress because of a situation that developed in my brother-in-law's job. Toward the
end of it, I received a letter from my sister in which she wrote:

"We've needed all the composure and clear thinking we could get. We've needed perspective on our life situation. Meditation has been the best thing we could have been doing. Nothing could have been more timely. And we stuck to it. It was our strength. As you well know, nothing else in life dropped off just because we had this new demand. The kids were still there with all their wants and needs and problems. Work was taking just as many hours as ever. Once again, if it hadn't been for meditation, I don't know how we could have dealt with this because just our regular schedule is emotionally draining and very time-consuming. One of my friends asked, 'How can you afford the time to meditate?' My response was, 'We can't afford not to.'"

The more active you are, the more you need this experience of deep prayer. And there will be periods in our lives, like the one my sister cites, when circumstances put us to the test and reveal whether we have unified our consciousness in God. Eknath Easwaren pictures God allowing a blow to be struck at us and when our whole being is agitated, saying:

"Now let me see you meditate." It is a stiff, honest test. The mind may rise in tides of turmoil and object, "How can I meditate when you have struck at me like this? I'm completely stunned." If that is so, you haven't passed the test. But if you have been meditating steadily and enthusiastically over a long period of time, your mind will remain centered on the Lord no matter what blows life deals you. Whatever reverse comes your way, your heart will be always filled with love. Then the Lord will say, "You pass."

Let your heart dwell on the Lord and let nothing else distract you.[11]

8

Learning To Let Go

The activity of the Holy Spirit within us becomes more and more important as we progress in the life of interior prayer. While our own efforts remain necessary, more and more they attain a new orientation. Instead of being directed toward ends we have chosen ourselves, they are more and more directed to an obedient and cooperative submission to grace—which implies an increasingly attentive and receptive attitude toward the hidden action of the Holy Spirit. It is precisely the function of meditation to bring us to this attitude of awareness and receptivity. If it is true that the deepest prayer is surrender to God, then all meditation and specific acts of prayer might be seen as preparations and purifications to ready us for this never-ending yielding.

There is a river of love that is continually flowing through us, the prayer of Christ animated by the Holy Spirit. To meditate is to enter into that stream and become aware of the prayer which the Spirit is ceaselessly praying within us. As we do so, our consciousness begins to merge with that of Christ so that it is not we who pray, but Christ who prays within us. We do not pray so much as we are prayed. It is something which is happening within us that we freely "let" happen the more we become conscious of it. It is a wave on which we are carried, to which we increasingly give ourselves over to take us where it will. We let go of our thoughts and feelings and join our wills and hearts with Christ's. Thus

Merton counseled that if saying your prayers is an obstacle to prayer, cut it out: "Let Jesus pray. Thank God Jesus is praying. Forget yourself. Enter into the prayer of Jesus. Let him pray in you . . . . This means a deep awareness of your true inner identity. By grace we are Christ. Our relationship with God is that of Christ to the Father in the Holy Spirit."[1]

"Meditation" comes from the Latin words *stare in medio* which mean "to stand in the center." In meditating we discover that when we are at one with our own center, we are at one with every center. To be in our center is to be in God, the center who is everywhere. The saints repeatedly witnessed to this: "God is the center of my soul," exclaimed St. John of the Cross. "My me is God, nor do I know myself save in him," testified St. Catherine of Genoa. Contemplation essentially means to look at the inside of something and see its deep-down reality. In contemplative prayer, one penetrates to one's own center and comes face-to-face with the reality of the indwelling Spirit.

In all nature, growth is from the center outward. Therefore the center is where we begin and where we return day after day. We seek to simply "stand in the center" awake and still, open and attentive to the Mystery at the root of our being. To return to this center and to live out of its depths is the first responsibility of every life. In living more and more out of this center, we come to realize that there is really only one prayer that is offered: the breath of love that flows constantly between Jesus and his Father. This breath, this stream of love is the Holy Spirit. Here we are at the heart of the distinctively Christian understanding of the nature of God as a communion of persons in love. The essence of Christian prayer is not therefore dialogue, but union. Meditation is the simplest way of entering into this experience of union that the tradition of Christian prayer offers.

John Main writes about meditation as a school of community and communion:

> *The great problems in life arise from the inability to communicate (to communicate even with ourselves) and meditation is a way into full communion, oneness of being.*

In meditation, and the life enriched by meditation, we are just fully ourselves, whoever we are. That is why meditation is a school of community because in discovering our own oneness, our own being and potential, we're aware that others possess being and potential, and their unique value is what leads us to service. So, meditation is a good school of community because by it we learn both to communicate and serve. The ultimate end of our meditation is communion. Not only do we discover our own oneness but we discover our oneness with the All and with all.[2]

Meditation as a Way of Poverty of Spirit

Meditation should begin with the realization of our nothingness and helplessness in the presence of God. This can be a deeply tranquil and even joyful experience as we let go of the burdens of trying to be more than we are. Our external, everyday self is to a certain extent a mask and a fabrication. We are not as secure as we present ourselves. Yet our true self, hidden in obscurity and nothingness at the center where we are in direct dependence on God, is not easy to find. But since the reality of all Christian meditation depends on this recognition, our attempt to meditate without it is in fact self-contradictory. It is like trying to walk without feet.[3]

Recognition of what? That, as we stand alone before God naked and defenseless, without explanation or theories, we are in dire need of the gift of grace and mercy. "The true contemplative," wrote Merton, "is not the one who prepares his mind for a particular message that he wants or expects to hear, but who remains empty because he knows that he can never expect or anticipate the word that will transform his darkness into light."[4]

Our task is to concentrate on the present moment as the place where the voice of God will fill our silence, if only by the silence revealing itself to us as a word of great power. It is here and here alone that time intersects with eternity. The great phases of transition from one epoch to the next will unfold as they are meant to, provided we surrender our possessive grasp of them and leave God free to act in us. What is clear from the New Testament is that Jesus achieved his mission by total abandonment of self, by handing over his life to the One whom he called *Abba*: "Not my will, but thine be done." The servant is not above the master, and that is the way to which meditation leads us.

When one comes to the place of meditation, there is a literal leaving behind of our cherished goods: the analytical intellect which wins us a big salary in the marketplace, the articulate way with words which impresses our colleagues and friends, the lively imagination which is such a rich source of fun and creativity. We leave behind that in which we normally take our security, not because they have no value and are not precious—they are!—but because we want to encounter God beyond mind, with the mystical heart. The way to enduring riches is the way of poverty. The way to enlightenment is the way of darkness. If we are to be disciples of Christ, we must be free within from the urgings of the ego for power, possessions, and prestige.

We are consistently caught in the snare of a framework of evaluation in which the reference points are education, human effort, projects, personal goals and accomplishment. Meditation lays the axe to the stubbornly persistent tendency to judge the value of something by performance or production levels. There is no agenda and nothing to accomplish. Just be before the One Who Is. Stop everything for thirty minutes twice a day, and sit or kneel in poverty with only a word-sound before the Mystery present to us. The sacred word is simply a means of turning our attention beyond ourselves, a way of drawing us away from our own self-centered thoughts and concerns to be with God, with Jesus, with the Holy Spirit. Our aim in Christian prayer is to allow God's mysterious and silent presence within us to become *the* reality which gives meaning, shape and purpose to everything we do, to everything we are.

As a friend and fellow meditator remarked, "In meditation I can be momentarily unlimited and undivided, complete. I have an opportunity to be nobody doing nothing, released from the tyranny of time and the confinement of space, no matter how vast. Why is this necessary? Personally, I need to learn, then to be reminded for half an hour twice a day, that I am not my own possession. Knowing this, I have nothing to lose by giving myself, except for what is left of trepidation."

If the life of prayer is to transform our spirit and make us a "new creation" in Christ, then prayer must be accompanied by conversion, that deep change of heart in which we die on a certain level of our being in order to find ourselves alive and free on another, more spiritual level. Here we must frankly admit that there is no way around self-denial and sacrifice. In the spiritual life there are no tricks and no short cuts. Those who imagine that they can employ special techniques and "get there quicker" usually ignore God's will and grace as they try to write their own ticket. They may even appear to succeed to some extent. But one cannot begin to face the real difficulties of the life of prayer and meditation unless one is content to be a beginner and to accept that one knows little or nothing. "Those who think they 'know' from the beginning," says Merton, "will never, in fact, come to know anything . . . . We do not want to be beginners. But let us be convinced of the fact that we will never be anything else but beginners all our life!"[5]

True contemplation is not a psychological trick, but a theological grace. It can come to us only as a gift and not as a result of our persevering use of spiritual techniques. Grace, mercy, faith are not earned commodities, but constantly renewed gifts. The life of the Spirit in our hearts is renewed from moment to moment, directly and personally by God as an expression of God's love for us. The grace of meditation is also a special gift and should never be taken for granted.[6]

John Main called meditation "the first death." What makes death hard is clinging. In meditation, one lets go—of words, images, self-preoccupations, acquisitiveness. It is perhaps hardest of all to let go of the flash of insight that occurs in the middle of our time of prayer, the idea which promises to resolve a problem we've been working on, the feeling or memory that surges up and exercises a strong attraction. Letting go of these, our most prized, interior possessions lets the air out of the balloon of our false selves which would have us believe that in these does our security rest.

The letting go is exacted as well when I am involved in my activities and realize the time at which I normally meditate has arrived. I oftentimes in this situation think of Jesus' parable about a man finding a treasure in a field or a pearl of great price and then going off and selling everything in order to obtain it. In that moment, I have to "sell off" what I am involved in, let go of it in order to retain the pearl of great price: the relationship of intimacy with my Creator, Savior, and Sanctifier who alone can fulfill the yearnings of my heart. This is part of what meditation as poverty, as a work, as a discipline means. This method of prayer is an exercise in letting go of everything.

This doesn't mean that we do not use the good things of this world. It is only the clinging to things that reduces the free flow of God's grace and that hinders our growth in God's love. As the effects of meditating take deeper hold within us, we learn how to let go of things and events that arise outside the time of prayer, including the delightful experience of God's Presence which prayer may give. It brings us to accept and even to embrace those dark places within ourselves in the spirit of Paul's "I boast gladly of my weaknesses so that the power of Christ may dwell in me. Therefore I am content with weaknesses, insults, hardships, persecutions, and calamities for the sake of Christ; for whenever I am weak, then I am strong" (2 Cor. 12:9-10).

The most radical letting go relates to the ego. It is a way of transformation which is gradually effected in us not through time alone nor experience alone, but through the love at the root of our existence. There, the creating and recreating Holy Spirit who has been in secret communion with our spirit all the while is teaching our hearts how to formulate the ultimate Name. The heart's solitude is the home of the true Self.

Our basic core of goodness is our true Self. Its center of gravity is God. Though we are not God, our true Self is in God and one with God. The experience of being loved by God enables us to accept our false self as it is, and then to let go of it and journey to our true Self. The growing awareness of our true Self, along with the deep sense of spiritual peace and joy, balances the psychic pain of the letting go of the false self. This disintegration and dying of our false self is our participation in the passion and death of Jesus. Our inward journey to the true Self is marked by the transforming power of divine love and is our participation in the risen life of Christ. In this journey, freely chosen and entered upon through meditation, the truth of our poverty, of our absolute dependency and our giftedness as "receiver," is revealed.

One day while leading a meditation and yoga retreat at Mount Carmel monastery overlooking Niagara Falls, I stepped out of the monastery at 6:30 a.m. to walk down to the Falls and found myself in a fantasy world of marvelous colors and fantastic shapes. Fifty hot air balloonists, gathered for a summer festival, were using the open field on the monastery grounds to unfurl their balloons and fill them with air. I had literally stepped out of bed and into a field of dreams filled with four-storey dinosaurs, Mickey Mouse and giant running shoes (hot air balloons are no longer just your basic pear shape!).

I walked among them and watched them fill their balloons with air blown into them by large generator-driven fans. As the magnificent shapes filled out and lifted off the ground, a tongue of flame was rhythmically injected into the balloon by releasing gas from cannisters strapped along the sides of the large riding-basket attached to the balloon. This release of hot air into the balloon was accompanied by a sound resembling that of deep breathing.

As I helped a team of balloonists to hold their riding-basket on the ground until they were ready to lift off, I asked one of them: "How do you steer it?" "You don't," he replied. "It's all in the wind. It's ultimately up to God where you go. You just put yourself into the currents that are there and flowing and away you go." "What does it feel like when you're up there?" I asked him. "The surprising thing is that it doesn't feel like you are moving at all," he replied. "But you are. You only become aware of that when you look back. Things that once seemed big now appear small and are fading in the distance. There's this wonderful, peaceful sense of just being up there in your balloon."

I should have had him stay and give my morning meditation talk and let me ride in his balloon, for he had all the theology down pat without knowing it. He had just very effectively described the inner journey of meditation. You open your heart to the breath of the Spirit who fills it up. Then, with a repeated and rhythmical release of energy—your word—you send a tongue of flame firing your faith and your love, and your heart begins to lift heavenward. Without this repeated emission of flame carried on a sound like a deep breath, there's no lift off. Once you're up and going and that enkindling breath of fire comes to a halt, you come back down into the midst of a busy world full of distractions.

Amazingly, when you're up there, you don't feel as if you're moving. You're not aware of progress, of forward motion. You just feel as if you're standing there and not going anywhere. But the wind of the Spirit is carrying you on its currents. And where it takes you *is* up to God!

After a time, when you look back, you become aware that there is movement. Things which once loomed large and seemed really important are now fading in the distance. You see things in better perspective.

It's a gentle journey, one you may have first approached with some fear and hesitation. But once you've experienced the serenity and peace of it, you find an eagerness in yourself to go back to it again and again.

Here we come home to our true selves, without illusion. Here we see that we receive all, our being and everything else besides, from God. And it is here, at the deep core of our being, that praise bursts forth, a song from the true Self. Meditation represents the commitment to return again and again to that sacred place and to be "at home" there.

9

The Kingdom of God Is Among You

We spend most of our lives conjugating three verbs: to want, to have, and to do. We are kept in a state of continuous craving, fussing, clutching on all levels: political, social, emotional, intellectual and even religious. We forget that none of these verbs have any ultimate significance except insofar as they are transcended by and included in the fundamental verb, to be. Being—not wanting, having and doing—is the essence of a spiritual life.[1] The best way "to do" is "to be."

That is what meditation is really about: being. Being before the One Who Is in full, loving attention. God is. I am. In this sense, meditation is the way to reality, to the reality of our own being. It is an utterly simple prayer that simplifies us and teaches us just to be. To be ourselves, to enter into the gift of our own being. When one enters into harmony with the on-going creation that one is, one also enters into harmony with all of creation and its Creator. We no longer live as if we were exhausting a limited supply of life that we received at our birth. The teaching of Jesus is that we tap into eternal life when we become one with the One Who Is, whose very name is I Am.

"Be still and know that I am God" (1 Kgs. 46:10). We simply say our word and allow the gift to be given by God. "Meditation is very simple," Fr. Main was fond of saying. "Don't complicate it." God wants to transform our prayer from an act of thinking to an act of loving. For our part, we must be content with a peaceful, loving attentiveness to God. Since God desires to touch and transfigure every human being, our task is to get rid of our obstructive dispositions and simply be there with personal, passionate presence.

It may seem as though this is very passive, and in a way, it is: we are waiting for God. At the same time we must make a continuous effort to hold ourselves in wakeful attention which requires the constant activity of the will to return to God by returning to the sacred word. It is a process of deepening openness to the Source of all being, the God who is love. The aim and invitation of our lives is nothing less than full union with God. We were made for communion.

The death of someone close to us often makes us take a hard look at the priorities which determine where our time and energy go. Several years ago I was deeply shaken by the unexpected death of a friend and moved to search my life for evidence that God was receiving from me the one thing for which God created me: my personal love. Where in my life was this finding expression? In re-examining my priorities and reviewing my commitments of time and energy, it became very clear to me that meditation responds more fully to my reason for being than anything else I do. I am created to know, love and serve God. There is no other activity wherein twice daily God receives what God most wants from me: my personal love and the recognition that this is the primary relationship in my life. From this deepening bond of love flows the energy and motivation for service. I emerge from each encounter wanting to please this tremendous Lover in everything I do. Service is the natural outflow of knowing and loving.

The spiritual journey is a coming into just such an awareness of who we are and why we are. It is a rolling away of the stone which prevents us from experiencing the union which is at the core of our being. What made Jesus special is that he *lived* in the consciousness of who he was and who others are in relation to God. Everything he did expressed this awareness. He had an experience of his Father which provided him with passion and endless energy in his public ministry.

There is a story which highlights the necessity of each one of us having an experience of the Divine Mystery to keep us going. It seems that a young aspirant to holiness once came to visit the hermitage of an old holy man who was sitting in the doorway of his quarters at sunset. The old man's dog stretched out across the threshold as the young spiritual seeker presented his problem to the holy man. "Why is it, Abba, that some who seek God come to the desert and are zealous in prayer but leave after a year or so, while others, like you, remain faithful to the quest for a lifetime?"

The old man smiled and replied, "Let me tell you a story. One day I was sitting here quietly in the sun with my dog. Suddenly a large white rabbit ran across in front of us. Well, my dog jumped up, barking loudly, and took off after that big rabbit. He chased the rabbit over the hills with a passion. Soon, other dogs followed him, attracted by his barking. What a sight it was, as the pack of dogs ran barking across the creeks, up stony embankments and though thickets and thorns! Gradually, however, one by one, the other dogs dropped out of the pursuit, discouraged by the course and frustrated by the chase. Only my dog continued to hotly pursue the white rabbit."

The young man sat in confused silence. Finally, he said, "Abba, I don't understand. What is the connection between the rabbit chase and the quest for holiness?" "You fail to understand," answered the old hermit, "because you failed to ask the obvious question. Why didn't the other dogs continue the chase? And the answer to that question is that they had not *seen* the rabbit. Unless you see your prey, the chase is just too difficult. You will lack the passion and determination necessary to perform all the hard work required by the discipline of your spiritual exercises."[2]

If we only follow the saints and mystics who have "seen" God, but have no experience of God ourselves, we will drop out of the race.

The Kingdom of God Is an Experience

The full riches of what Christ came to proclaim are available to each of us if we can but enter into his experience. The central thrust of the Gospel is the proclamation of fullness of life, fullness of being: "I came that you might have life, and have it abundantly" (Jn. 10:10). The New Testament witnesses to the transforming impact when people live their lives out in the power of God's love.

"The kingdom of God is among you" (Lk. 21:17), Jesus announced. This kingdom is not so much a place as an experience, and eternal life has to do not so much with the duration of time as with depth, richness, intensity and fullness of living.

A few years ago I spent some months of a study sabbatical in India. I studied Buddhism at the Tibetan Buddhist Tushita Retreat Center at Dharamsala, India, in the Himalayas. Everything in the Buddha's teaching is aimed at breaking the cyclical pattern of death and rebirth through one's own positive efforts. Each one is his or her own personal savior. Each one of us bears a karmic debt and must expunge it by dispelling ignorance and attachments.

Listening to these doctrines being presented day after day, I came to a fuller appreciation of what is distinctive about my Christian faith. It says: we had a karmic debt which separated us from God. And God canceled it through Jesus' life, death and resurrection, sending us the bill torn up in pieces with a note that read: "You are set free! Live now in the freedom of the sons and daughters of God. Live in joy and love, and show your gratitude by helping me establish the reign of freedom, justice and peace in the world." Or in the words of St. Paul:

While we were minors, we were enslaved to the elemental spirits of the world. But when the fullness of time had come, God sent his Son, born of a woman, born under the law, in order to redeem those who were under the law, so that we might receive adoption as children. And because you are children, God has sent the Spirit of his Son into

*our hearts, crying, "Abba! Father!" So you are no longer
a slave but a child, and if a child then also an heir,
through God. For freedom Christ has set us free. Stand
firm, therefore, and do not submit again to the yoke of
slavery (Gal. 4:3-7; 5:1).*

Meditation invites one to come to a personal experience of
what Paul proclaims: our redemption is accomplished. The
power of the Spirit is set free in our hearts. Salvation is the
Hebrew word for deliverance from bondage and slavery into
the glorious liberty of the children of God. The Gospel is that
"Good News" of our deliverance from the imprisonment of our
own egoism and self-seeking, from the limitations which iso-
late us, from the need to redeem ourselves by our own efforts.
Salvation means being taken utterly beyond ourselves into
the limitless love and freedom of the Spirit of God. The call of
the whole Christian life is simply to be open to that glory.
The whole purpose of our lives is a pilgrimage to that experience. The moment of revelation is given in God's time and in
God's way. Our contribution is to dispose ourselves in simplicity and poverty of spirit.

"The kingdom of God is among you," flowing through our
lives and our consciousness, changing our very being from
within, transforming the way we see the world and respond
to people, giving us intuitive glimpses of the Real. And if the
kingdom is expanding within us, then we are doing the work
of the kingdom which is to establish God's reign in the world.
God is not liberating us from the unreal, from our egoism and
false selves in order to display us like so many metaphysical
mannequins in some great spiritual goods bazaar. We're
expected to do something, to bear fruit that gives glory to
God and advances God's project in the world.

In *Conjectures of a Guilty Bystander*, Merton tells how in
contemplation he discovered God, and in God he discovered
people inseparable from God and from one another. The contemplative insight that enabled him to overcome the supposed conflict between contemplation and action came to him
in an experience he had in March 1958 as he was standing in

the middle of a shopping district in Louisville. As he watched the people pouring out of the stores, he was suddenly overwhelmed, as he put it,

with the realization that I loved all those people, that they were mine and I theirs, that we could not be alien to one another, even though we were total strangers. It was like waking from a dream of separateness, of spurious self-isolation in a special world, the world of renunciation and supposed holiness. The whole illusion of a separate holy existence is a dream.[3]

The challenge for contemplatives today is to make the same discovery. It is to this awareness that true contemplation necessarily leads: we cannot separate God from God's creation. So we cannot separate contemplation from concern for and active engagement in the problems of the age in which we live.

The process of establishing God's reign, of putting the kingdom of right relationships into place, expresses itself in many ways, usually as a gentle and gradual change of direction in our lives. One day during that same sojourn in India while I was sitting outside in front of my hut at Shantivanam ashram in South India, I heard a sudden loud "crack" and then a great whooshing sound as a branch from the palm tree right in front of my dwelling landed with a thud six feet away from me. The branches of these full-grown trees are a good twenty feet in length with over one hundred palm leaves like the ones we carry on Palm Sunday growing out of either side. When I moved it I discovered it weighed about fifty pounds. As the tree grows upward and develops new growth in the form of upper branches, the under branches slowly turn brown and die. When one no longer receives from the sun what it needs to survive, it cracks and falls away under its own dead weight.

In looking at the branch, I thought of a woman who had come to me once for counseling. Divorced for a few years, she sought companionship and found herself in a destructive pat-

tern of bar-hopping on weekends, finding someone and frequently taking him back to her apartment to spend the night.
She didn't know how to break out of this cycle. I suggested
learning to meditate might help, and got her started. She came
back a few months later to say she was meditating faithfully
and was finding that she could no longer sleep around.

What she was experiencing was new growth upward. A
behavior which had previously enjoyed a place in the sun at
the top was now in the shadow of new priorities. It had
turned brown through lack of being invested with new energy. She realized one day that the inclination had withered
and fallen away. She had experienced a gradual and gentle
turning, the mark of the kingdom of God becoming manifest.
Her energies are now being channeled into different service-
oriented programs.

Another effect experienced is that instead of approaching
one's life and relationships in an adversarial way, sensitive
to the differences, one approaches life with increasing awareness of our commonality. Prior to the end of the Cold War
period, one fellow I know used to be quite a "hawk" where
war was concerned. Through his entering into the experience
of unity and oneness through meditation, he began saying
things like "the other is me" and became actively involved in
peace efforts.

Meditation also sensitizes our conscience. I used to think I
was too busy to have much time for sinning. Now I see that
my very busyness, my compulsion for doing, is one of my
most constant failings, diminishing the time I give to enter
into the joy of being, inclining me to dignify advancing projects over taking time for people.

Health improves, problems resolve themselves, relationships become richer. We do not meditate primarily to seek
these things, but they come to us because we are drawing
nearer to the Lord who is the source of truth, wholeness, and
love, who came that we might have life and have it to the
full. "Seek first the kingdom of God, and all else will come to
you besides" (Matt. 6:33). From the very first day that one
begins to meditate, the sacred word begins to grow in one's

consciousness like a seed. It germinates and with time grows into a mighty tree, sending its roots deeper and deeper. Through it, the Spirit is at work resolving old conflicts, bringing us to face ourselves with honesty and humor, to accept ourselves and the inevitable gracefully, with joy and even gratitude. It is from this self-acceptance that we most effectively reach out to others, for when we can be with ourselves in tolerance and love, we can be with others in the same way.

I began meditating because I wanted a relationship of intimacy with God. I found it there, and I continue to find it there. Many are the ways that this experience at the center is registered: as a stabilizing influence, providing a steady rudder in all sorts of waters; as a path of gradual surrender which leaves me feeling more given; as a growing freedom from attachment to created things; as an experience of "oneing" that increases my longing for a fuller, direct experience of the joy and delight of God's presence.

Meditation does not take the place of other forms of Christian prayer. Rather, it enhances each one by sharpening our desire for God. The eucharist, image, symbol, psalms, music, chant, prayers—in short, all devotions and rituals— serve to incline us to contemplative prayer. All religious traditions have ways of integrating the senses into higher forms of prayer. The answer is not liturgy alone, or meditation alone, but a full and many-sided life of prayer in which all these things can receive their proper emphasis.

There are many different ways of meditating taught in the religions of the world. But if one wishes to go deep, it is important to choose one's path and be faithful to it. Many Christians have found it necessary until recently to seek lifegiving disciplines for their journey from teachers in other faiths because they did not find them in their life in the church. As I have tried to expose in these pages, Christian faith offers its own deep well of contemplative experience and counsel. We are blessed to live in an age where the full richness of it is being recovered and widely shared.

Part II
Yoga:
Prayer of the Body

10

The Bridging of East and West

The starting point for our reflections on yoga is the interdependent and interconnected world system in which we now live. People of different races and cultures and nations are increasingly aware that they share a single atmosphere and source of water. We are mutually vulnerable and carry a common fear for our future and for the whole of human life. This global awareness has given us a new image for our life together. In the words of the renowned British economist Barbara Ward: "planet earth . . . has acquired the intimacy, the fellowship, and the vulnerability of a spaceship."[1]

Multinational corporations use the forces of technology and commerce to erase the distances between people and countries. Weather scientists and agronomists use global instruments to chart the planting and harvesting of food. Rock concerts, world cup finals and papal visits are beamed around the world by satellite. Medical and military information can be shared instantly. Marshall McLuhan's characterization of our planet as a "global village" has entered into common consciousness and common parlance.

Yet global awareness does not itself automatically produce a new world community; what it does certainly do is make us more aware of our tensions and imbalances. Imbalances in the realm of religious consciousness have been perceptively diagnosed in the writings of Bede Griffiths.[2] His thirty-eight years in India led him to the conviction that we are entering into a new age, and that the age of Western domination is over. The future of the world lies in Asia, Africa and Latin America.

> *This does not mean that we have to reject the Western heritage. The ideas of Western science and democracy have penetrated to every part of the world. The ideal of Western science, of the accurate observation of phenomena, of rational analysis, free from all partiality or emotional bias, of the discovery of the 'laws' of nature . . . these ideals remain of permanent value. So also the principles of democracy, of the value of the individual person, of the 'rights' of each individual to life and growth and health and education; and above all, the right of self-government in whatever political structure it may be expressed . . . the right of woman to equality with man— these are the marks of humanity to greater maturity, to a greater realization of what it means to be human.[3]*

The less felicitous effects of Western industrialism—pollution, unemployment, homelessness, weapons buildup—are due to a fundamental imbalance in Western civilization since the Renaissance: the ascendance of the rational, active, aggressive, dominating power of the mind over the intuitive, passive and receptive power. This balance can only be restored when West meets East, when the two fall in love with one another and marry.

The Reconciliation of Opposites

A central assertion in the work of the Swiss psychoanalyst, Carl Jung, is that the project of every human life is the reconciliation of opposites. Every man has a woman within him, and every woman a man; marriage is the place where they help one another re-own what has been projected onto the other and integrate those "masculine" or "feminine" qualities into their own personalities. This is as true of Western and

Eastern world cultures and approaches to God as it is of individual persons.

The Western world, and other parts of the planet under its influence, have now to rediscover the power of the intuitive mind which has so largely shaped the cultures of Asia and Africa. While this is a challenge for the world as a whole, I wish for the purposes of this chapter to focus upon what this encounter holds for the Christian churches.

The Christian churches have, for example, been shaped by the Western mind, as is demonstrated by our need to express our faith in logical formulas and rational systems. This may be less so of the Eastern churches, but not entirely. Logical, rational thought and scientific system are an inheritance from the Greeks, deriving originally from Socrates and the Greek philosophers. The stamp of their genius not surprisingly finds its way as well into the churches which share Byzantium as a common heritage.

This does not mean that the values of science and reason, of logical and systematic thought are negative or should be abandoned. It simply means that reason has to be married to intuition; it has to learn to surrender itself to the deeper intuitions of the whole person, body, soul, and spirit. In varying degrees then, all the Christian churches are in need, by virtue of their cultural context and philosophical/theological heritage, of giving further development to their intuitive side through an encounter with the religions of the East—Hinduism, Buddhism, Taoism—for whom intuition and receptivity are dominant.

Our Western superiority complex wants to balk at this. We are used to having things on our own terms and to operating from strength. It is useful to consider the cultural limitations of Christianity as the product of a Semitic culture with a narrow horizon. Israel had little if any knowledge of the cultures of India or China and imagined that all those who were outside Israel were without knowledge of God. Its history did not go back beyond 5000 BC and it imagined that it was living in the "last age" of the world.

From this milieu and with these limitations, the Christian

Church came forth into the Greco-Roman world, building itself up with the help of the Greek genius for philosophy and the Roman genius for law. While the intuitive wisdom and imaginative insight of the biblical tradition were never wholly lost, the system of rational thought nonetheless became dominant.

Rational scientific knowledge can improve our lives significantly in certain respects, but it also has its liabilities. When we live in a world where there is more concrete than grass under our feet, more steel and granite than blue sky on our horizon, more plastics than natural materials in our hands, we can easily lose touch with the world of spontaneous feeling and imaginative thought. Science and reason become divorced from, rather than married to, sense and feeling. What we need, and what the encounter of Christianity with Eastern religions represents, is the marriage of reason and intuition.

Christianity and Eastern Religions

Until the last century we had no inkling of the actual age of the world and the human race. With rare and isolated exceptions, no people, ancient or modern, presumed that human history extended back as much as ten millennia. Drawing from Hebrew conceptualizations, Christians envisaged all history before Christ as a period of little more than four thousand years with a relatively small total population. In our time, Australopithecus, the first ancestral man to walk upright whose remains have been found in South and East Africa and Java, takes us back five million years; and in the world we live in today, the total non-Christian population numbers in the billions.

When we look at the peoples of oral cultures who have survived down to recent times, we find an unmistakable sense of the divine and an unrelenting quest for experiential encounter with it. Whether they symbolized this impulse in terms of surrounding spiritual forces, witchcraft, or occult healing, the native Americans, Africans and Australians who retained oral cultures until recently all lived in a very lively spiritual universe. The world over, from Asia to Europe and Africa to South America, native cultures have been far more absorbed with spirituality—questions of meaning, harmony with the divine, ecstatic techniques—than they have with material technology. Genius in adapting to their environments and controlling their social units is much in evidence, but it is this pursuit of meaning and this quest for experiential meetings with ultimate powers that preoccupied them. In the history of humanity's searching for God, we find so many different movements of prayer, so many different struggles to do what is right, that any tradition's provincialism is revealed for those who care to look at the larger picture.[4]

In Asia and Africa, the ordinary person lives much more by the imagination and communicates in the language of the imagination in gestures and rituals often accompanied by music and dance. This is no inferior language, but the medium of poets, artists, dramatists and novelists—in short, those to whom we turn for insight into the human condition. The abstract rational mind creates a world and reflects it in concrete reality, while the imaginative mind recreates the concrete world and reflects it in symbols of rhythmical movements, words and architectural forms. The marginalization of art and imagination in our educational systems (these are "soft" courses for the students who cannot handle the preferred "university track" science curriculum) has contributed to an imbalance in our Western civilization.

From the time of Socrates, reason has gradually eclipsed myth in the Western world, leaving it only as a background to poetry and fantasy. We may be right in thinking that improvements in medical care, education and material technology would enrich native people's cultures, but do we realize our own comparative poverty in contrast to the wealth they carry in their psyches? How can we breathe new life into our own myths, into the master-stories that we have told for nearly two thousand years? Do themes of death and resurrection continue to write the basic plot of our lives, or is this system of meaning a code today's young have little interest in cracking?

Joseph Campbell's television series "The Power of Myth" represents an attempt to resurrect myth in a century where reason's triumph has been almost complete. The basic theme of all mythology is that there is an invisible plane or realm of being behind the visible one which is supportive of it. The function of ritual is to pitch us out toward this invisible Mystery and to facilitate an encounter with it. All religions have rituals the purpose of which is to reveal this transcendent Mystery and to teach the path to union with it.

Christian tradition has always taught that human beings can know God through the things God has made. The basic question is: *what kind* of knowledge can we have of God? Is the only knowledge possible in this life a knowledge *about* God arrived at by natural reasoning or by revelation? Or is it possible to have, even in this life, an intuitive knowledge *of* God?

The word intuition derives from the Latin *intueri* which means "to consider, look at, gaze at." It can have the meaning "to look someone right in the face." This usage introduces us to the traditional meaning of intuition: an instantaneous or immediate knowing of something or someone without going through any conscious process of reasoning. For example, you might come to a decision that you instinctively know to be right, without having gone through, consciously at least, a reasoning process to reach that decision.[5]

Is such an intuitive process operative in coming to know God? Most systematic theology has been reluctant to give an affirmative answer to this question. The flat assertion of such intuitive knowing has not been considered sufficient because it lacks scientific validity. Understandably, theologians, like scientists, find more security in ways of knowing which are verifiable not by intuition but by a scientific checking process.[6]

Mystics are not quite so cautious, however. Some would maintain that an immediate knowing of God in which the subject-object separation disappears is possible in the contemplative experience. Thomas Merton puts it like this: "In the depths of contemplative prayer there seems to be no division between subject and object and there is no reason to make any statement about God or about oneself. God IS and this reality absorbs everything else."[7]

It is not that intuition is a kind of knowing that has no relation to rational knowledge or that dogma is somehow antithetical to intuition. In most instances it would seem that rational knowledge serves as a springboard for intuition. But any attempt by rational knowledge to express fully that which is beyond expression is bound to fail. The catechisms of our churches attempt to put the content of the Christian faith into rational, discursive terms. The aim is illusory inasmuch as the content of the faith ultimately transcends all rational, discursive thought. This is the witness of the apophatic tradition in Christian spirituality: as soon as we have affirmed something of God, we have to turn around and confess that it is inadequate to express the full reality of God. While caught up in a mystical experience of God at the end of his life, Thomas Aquinas, the author of the great *Summa Theologica*, exclaimed that all he had written was so much straw by comparison.

Inasmuch as the Eastern religions have given more place to the intuitive than to the rational ways of knowing in their approach to the Mystery of God, they have lessons to teach. One of their insights is that the way to discover and to experience is not by systematic argument but by self-surrender. Such knowledge and experience cannot be produced or attained by human effort alone. It is more a question of allowing ourselves to be transformed, to become passive with a passivity that is infinitely and actively receptive.

For example, Buddhist *vipassana* meditation seems the antithesis of anything practical, but in the application of its principles one discovers that alert receptivity can be very transformative. The Principle of Clarity urges you to be as alert and precise as possible about your thoughts and feelings. The Principle of Neutrality urges you to become a matter-of-fact observer of yourself and to accept what you become aware of (the opposite of our common tendency to block, to deny, to grasp). In the Buddhist view, such resisting is the source of limitation and all suffering. The Principle of Transformation teaches that precise observation without hin-

drance and distortion brings realization and positive transformation. There is a transformative power in the very fact of
awareness and your non-resistance to it. The mindfulness
itself effects the change.[8]

Because they have these lessons to teach, the renaissance
of Hinduism, Buddhism, and native spiritualities in our time
is of significance for Christianity. To be sure, we have these
lessons of the importance of imagination, intuition and receptive passivity in our heritage as well. But they have fallen
out of equilibrium with the rational and activistic. For me, a
sign of this imbalance is found in the thousands of Western
world people who travel to India and seek out gurus to learn
the secrets of meditation and yoga. They are reflecting an
innate sense that their own religious traditions have not provided them with all the keys to open the doors in their quest
for communion with the ultimate Mystery.

Interfaith encounters provide all parties with a positive
prod to striking a more holistic balance. We stand to benefit
from their gifts, and they from ours. We know that the
Mystery of Christ is always present in the church and is the
secret by which she lives. But until the way we live our
Christian lives defers at least as much to this mystical presence as to laws and doctrinal formulations, we have not yet
learned religion's most essential teaching.

Common Quest for Communion

A full appropriation of the living truth revealed in the New
Testament cannot be realized through the Western approach
alone. In the encounter of the world religions in our pluralistic
society we are being called to recognize the limitations of
every form of religion, as well as the insights born of long
experience that each religion contributes to the common quest
for communion with the ultimate Mystery. Whether Jewish or
Christian or Muslim or Buddhist or Hindu, every religion is
conditioned by time, place, and historical circumstances and

its outward forms will pass away. But in all these outward forms of religion—doctrine, sacraments, devotions, organization—the one eternal Truth is making itself known.

Our encounter with other religions in a pluralistic society is an invitation to open ourselves to the revelation of the divine mystery which has taken place in and through them. Because signs of God which we cannot neglect are found all over the world, we also must pay close attention to the intuitive and imaginative wisdom of aboriginal peoples on every continent. The great myths of the world reveal different aspects of the one Mystery present to us and a way of embodying it in the world. We are all pilgrims in search of truth, of reality, of final fulfillment. Though we may claim to have the truth, we must recognize that this truth will always remain beyond our full appreciation and understanding. Sacramental theology today speaks of Jesus as the "primary sacrament" of God. In other words, Jesus himself belongs to the world of signs, inviting us to go beyond word and thought, life and death, to communion with the transcendent Mystery we call God.

The building of the community of the church as the manifestation in history of the presence of God in and with the human family is, therefore, a work that will go forward best if assisted by people of all communities of faith. Each has something to give and something to receive. No one can claim to have a monopoly on the Truth who is God. What we all are seeking is a way of living that is open to the Mystery present to us, and a way of embodying it in the world.

However, until people of different faiths feel they are fully equal in their humanity and thus all have things to teach and things to learn, the *anthropological* foundations of effective dialogue will still be missing. Until people of different faiths recognize that God has addressed them all in varying degrees and therefore all have religious wisdom to teach and religious wisdom to learn, the *theological* foundations of effective dialogue will still be absent.[9]

The message underlying all our mythologies—understood in Campbell's sense of myth "as a clue to the spiritual potentialities of human life"—is that you, as you know yourself, are not the final term of your own being. You must give yourself, sacrifice yourself, to something beyond yourself, bigger than yourself, that will survive you.

Ever since the meeting of the world's religious leaders in Assisi, Italy, in 1988 to pray for peace, we have held a similar annual event in Montreal on its anniversary. In practice, when people from different faiths come together to be at prayer together, it is not to engage in a formal and communal act, but to listen and to learn as each delegation prays in its own way. It is an act of dialogue in which people of faith bring their forms of prayer, their scriptures and their most valued spiritual traditions together in an act of faithful common witness. It is precisely as the word "interfaith" implies, a meeting between *people of faith*. For the Christian it should be an occasion to discern, and rejoice in, the richness of God's self-revelation. John 3:16 does not say "God so loved the church" but rather that "God so loved the world." This means that Christians will not be the only ones with some light to radiate. We can learn something of value from others.

In the words of Thomas Merton: "The 'universality' and 'catholicity' which are essential to the church necessarily imply an ability and a readiness to enter into dialogue with all that is pure, wise, profound and humane in every kind of culture. In this one sense at least, a dialogue with Oriental wisdom becomes necessary. A Christian culture that is not capable of such a dialogue would show, by that very fact, that it lacked catholicity."[10] Merton himself set out on that quest for "oriental wisdom" on the trip to Bangkok which ended in his accidental death. "The Catholic," he said, "who is the aggressive specimen of a ghetto Catholic culture, limited, rigid, prejudiced, negative, is precisely non-Catholic, at least in the cultural sense. Worse still, he may be anti-Catholic in the cultural sense and perhaps even, in some ways, religiously, without realizing it."[11]

To open oneself to the work of God manifest in other religions and to recognize that many people are saved outside the church is not to say that since all religions mediate salvation, they are therefore all the same. We will give further development to this important question in the final chapter. For our present purposes of introducing Part II of this book, suffice it to say that Christians generally agree that there is one plan of God for the world, leading it to ultimate reconciliation and unity. The scriptural symbol for this unity is the reign of God. All peoples are called to it and are working toward it (Eph. 1:9-10; Col. 1:15-20; 1 Cor. 15:28; Rev. 21:1-5). This unity is not a given, but is something to be achieved in and through an historical process. The Holy Spirit is the active principal in this process (Rom. 8).[12]

This is the global context for the church's identity. Its special vocation is to serve the realization of the reign of God in the world. This realization need not be seen as the whole human family becoming members of the church, but as the unification and reconciliation of all things and peoples, with all their gifts, in Christ and in the Holy Spirit. The reign of God is a cosmic mystery, and other religions have their role to play in its realization. In this perspective, inter-religious dialogue is not an option but a necessity because it is the only way in which the whole extent of the mystery of God active in the world can be discovered, and it is the only way in which the unity willed by God can be achieved progressively through a converging movement.[13]

This is the overarching perspective within which we come as Christians to carefully examine yoga as a spiritual discipline. In the ensuing chapters we shall examine how yogic methods can be applied in the service of Christian spirituality. Yoga was originally developed as a preparation for meditation. As a discipline which engages the body, it invites cerebral Western world people to "get out of their heads." As a method which requires the mind to pay close attention to what is going on in the body, it sharpens our awareness. As a "way into" a contemplative experience of God dwelling within, it admirably unifies body, mind and spirit. In short, yogic disciplines can help people become disposed to receive contemplative graces.

11

The Aim and Origin of Yoga

Quebec City, the capital city of the Province of Quebec, is situated three hours by car north of Montreal. Surrounded by fortress walls, the old city and fort are built above and below the cliffs which line the shore of the mighty St. Lawrence River, which is a mile wide at that point. Here, in 1608, Samuel Champlain founded the first permanent European settlement in America.

Visitors generally regard it as "a little jewel," or "one of the best kept secrets in North America." But up until the mid-1960s, getting there required patience, perseverance and, in winter, even a little fortitude. Those traveling up on the south side of the river to get to Quebec City on the north side were faced with a slow ferry in summer and negotiating the ice floes in winter. Some elected to go across the ice on foot, but others opted for the region's thin version of a rowboat which could be rowed in open water and pulled out of the water and slid over the ice floes like a big ski. Today, the ice boat races during Quebec City's winter carnival are a contemporary throw-back to those times.

The first bridge connecting the south side of the river to the north side was for trains only. Eventually, one of the train tracks was converted into a lane for cars. Still, the crossing took two hours on average because of the traffic line-up at the bridge. It was not until the mid-1960s, with the construction of the modern Pierre Laporte Bridge, that traffic could move for the first time with ease and without delay from one side of the river to the other. Finally, for those journeying to this storied city, there was an easeful and enjoyable way into it.

That is what yoga does for meditation. It is a way into it, an effective, time-tested and enjoyable bridge experience from one state of mind and being to another.

When those seeking to touch the Mystery within through meditation come home frazzled from a day's work, there is generally a grinding of gears as they try to relax their bodies, calm and center their minds in order to meditate. Oftentimes the attempt is unsuccessful and the experience unsatisfying of constantly battling distractions from a mind still racing with the day's traffic. The time for meditation over, they get up and, much like those traversing the ice floes in boats or on foot, mutter: "Is this worth the effort?"

Part II of this book is about taking advantage of the bridge—to get somewhere else, yes, but not only that. The experience of crossing the bridge is itself an enjoyable one, offering views and perspectives one doesn't generally get elsewhere. This is a case in which it is not just arriving that counts, but the journey itself. In other words, while yoga prepares one for meditation, it is in itself meditation-in-motion.

Yoga means to unite, to join, but also to harness, to yoke. The application of these nuances in the meaning of the word is pertinent: to unite, to join, refers to the harmonious integration of the spirit and body. To harness, to yoke, indicates that the one who faithfully practices this spiritual discipline brings the senses and thinking "under the yoke."

Yoga is historically complex. As a universal science for cultivating awareness which evolved over perhaps 5,000 years of self-experimentation by its practitioners, the system was codified by the Indian sage Pantanjali in his *Yoga Sutras*[1] in about the second century before the Common Era (B.C.E.). A *sutra* is a short, clipped phrase or aphorism; it describes the tersely worded phrases of Pantanjali's teaching. The term "yoga" is used in Hindu literature in different senses, but its general sense always remains the same: a unification of two or more diverse elements, a whole which includes or unites several parts. In Pantajali's specific sense, it is the establishment of harmony between the everyday self and its spiritual source.[2]

In classical yoga teaching, yoga leads to meditation or fixation of thought (*dhyana*) which in turn leads to ecstasy or pure consciousness (*samadhi*). These levels deal, respectively, with the body through psychophysiological exercises, with the mind through concentrative meditation, and with the soul through pure consciousness. This holistic union of body, mind, and soul provide the climate, the "space" for a spiritual, intuitive experience of God.

In order for yoga to be authentic, this deliberately sought end must inspire and inform the entire undertaking. The goal of yoga is the spiritual experience of God.[3]

Its techniques aim at facilitating contemplative prayer by bringing into existence the most favorable conditions—quieting of mind and body—for attentiveness to God in an age when much else seems to be making this more difficult. In short, yoga serves to open us up to Mystery, and clues us in to the Mystery which inhabits us and from which our being springs.

Thus, in its original context and conception, yoga is a preparation for meditation. The sages—wisdom seekers of old—point out that the physical exercises simply prepare the body and nervous system for the ensuing meditation. This perspective has been largely lost in the way yoga has been packaged and marketed in the Western world. The objective of this chapter is to refocus the primary intent of yoga as a supplement to the yoga manuals on the bookstore shelves where this emphasis is generally not found. My intention is to address the "why" which lies at the heart of yoga. This *raison d'être*, when placed alongside yoga's proven effectiveness in calming the body and quieting the mind, has much to offer Christians as a complementary discipline to meditation.

When the science of yoga was brought to the West, a discernment was obviously made that the potential market would be greater if the physical health benefits were stressed and the religious and spiritual ends of the practice were allowed to fade into the background. Thus, by making a judi-

cious selection from the postures and methods of training, an
autonomous system of physical culture has been built up to
serve ends which, for many practitioners, have no conscious
relationship to their spiritual life or religious experience. For
most Westerners today, the mention of yoga conjures up a
rather bizarre and contortionist series of exercises with exot-
ic-sounding names. If we know anyone who practices it, the
reasons ascribed would probably fall somewhere among the
following: weight control, well-proportioned figure, firm muscle tone, increased flexibility, coordination, good posture,
restful sleep, and an inner sense of well-being. While these
benefits are real and undeniable, they are also utterly secondary to the aims for which yoga evolved.

The primary aims of yoga are spiritual. In fact, these aims
go far beyond producing psychosomatic equilibrium, and
beyond the harmonizing of vital energies effected by the exercises. Yoga seeks to cultivate a focused awareness of one's
deepest being, one's Self, and in that Self, God. Physical exercises are but the skin of yoga; its sinews and skeleton are
mental exercises that prepare the way for a transformation of
consciousness which is always a gift of God and a work of
grace.

Where Did Yoga Come From?

Yoga has assumed many different forms during the several
thousand years of its practice and thus it is impossible to
trace its development simply and exactly. According to Indian
sources, it stems from an ancient science called *tantra*, a
Sanskrit word derived from two roots, *tan*, meaning extension, expansion (of consciousness), and *tra* meaning liberation
(of energy). The whole practice of tantra revolves around
these two ideas: expansion and liberation. The Tantras are a
body of anonymous elaborations of oral religious traditions
which include both ritual instructions and spiritual teach-

ings. By some accounts, they predate the ancient scriptures of Hinduism, the Vedas and Upanishads.[4]

In any case, yoga and tantra do not belong to India; tantric culture is the common inheritance of all humankind: "yoga was not 'made in India', it was preserved in India. Yoga was made by the great minds of the world."[5] The masters of yoga never stop asserting that their practices are independent of all religions, that they will fit any credo. Contrary to popular belief, the practices are not inseparably tied to the concepts peculiar to Hindu theology. The best practical proof of this is that so many of the yoga teachers in the West provide instruction in the postures and breathing techniques without ever going into concepts of Hindu religious belief.

Tantrism and yoga have been marked by great variety through their history, being practiced with different understandings of the meaning and the end of yoga. There have been yogas which aim at a personal experience of a personal God and yogas which aim only at the vision of consciousness in its proper state. Among these schools, the divinity has been understood in different and seemingly irreconcilable ways, e.g. as the ultimate Person, both transcendent and immanent with regard to finite beings, or as the ultimate value at each state in the evolution of human consciousness. The point is that all practitioners read into their practice the ideas and ideals they received by faith from their own sources of revelation. The Christian who employs yoga as a discipline does the same.[6] Finding one's own particular faith perspective in a practice originating elsewhere has a long precedent among the Eastern religions themselves, to say nothing of the many instances of the same in the development of the Christian rituals around Easter and Christmas. Or as one Christian writer succinctly puts it, "If the God you recognize within is the God you know through Jesus Christ, that experience is transferable into various settings, even into those settings where God is called by other names or by no name at all."[7]

In his *Yoga Sutras*, Patanjali outlined general principles showing step-by-step how a person can find inner peace and knowledge through yoga, but he did not straight-jacket his instructions in any particular religion or philosophy. The methods represent a system that can help enrich one's present philosophy or system through practical experience. It is therefore possible to profit from yoga techniques without conflict with one's own beliefs. The common ancestors of yogis—ascetics and shamans—are the men and women in different lands who used various physical and psychological exercises as vehicles to heightened states of consciousness. The use of such exercises grew into a highly developed and refined art within the context of Indian religious culture.

Before the first invasions of Aryans from the northwest around 2000 B.C.E., an impressive Indian culture already existed for a millennium. The native Indian people were called Dravidians. The cultures of these two peoples, the Dravidians, who pre-existed the Aryans in the Indus Valley, and the Aryans, combined to form the Hindu culture. The religion of the indigeneous Dravidian people ultimately triumphed in the penetration first of yoga, then of Tantrism, into every level of Hindu society and into every school of Hinduism, as well as into Buddhism and Jainism (a religious movement roughly contemporaneous with Buddhism).[8]

Yoga is a systematic approach to attaining the highest level of consciousness of which the human person is capable. This attainment has been a perennial goal of humankind. In order to unravel and dispel the obstacles that stood in the way of becoming centered, rooted, sensitized to the Presence within, the yogic masters were forced over the ages to deal, one by one, with the different aspects of human functioning. The functions of the body were systematically explored through a very precise series of postures or *asanas* which make up much of what is known today as "hatha yoga." Intricacies of respiration and breathing patterns were studied in great detail. The workings of the mind were catalogued and explained. This careful, precise approach to the functions of the mind and body established a series of clearly defined, easily reproducible and beneficial practices which can be studied in modern laboratories and have been since the 1950s.[9]

Within these deceptively simple practices lie the fruits of thousands of years of careful and systematic exploration by a long line of spiritual seekers. These dedicated men and women devoted their lives to the continuing perfection of a system of self-training that would bring the body and mind into harmony in such a way that they could realize their highest human potential as they conceived it.

12

The Heart of Yoga Practice

In its original context, yoga embraces the full range of spiritual paths to union with God that are practiced by people of very different temperaments and personalities. This comprehensive approach to the spiritual quest is called "integral yoga." There are four main pathways, presented here with some corollary examples for our Western context.

Karma yoga is the path of self-realization through action. Suited for people of active temperament, it is the way which leads to God through selfless work. Karma yoga teaches how to work for the sake of the work itself. It invites one to release concern for the fruits of one's efforts, to do one's duty and to leave results to God in a spirit of non-attachment. This approach would be reflected in the lives of people who are on the telephone lists of volunteers for various organizations. They receive a request for assistance and they go to help out. They may work for one or several days. When the immediate need has been met, they are thanked and take their leave. They will not be around to see the results from the mailing for which they stuffed a thousand envelopes, but they are happy to help wherever needed.

Bhakti yoga focuses on the cultivation of intense love for God through devotional practices. It seeks salvation through love and prayer. This pathway would be exemplified by people who spend a lot of time in Bible study or prayer. The daily Mass-goer, the person who prays the rosary nightly or says the Jesus Prayer while walking to and from work, are practitioners of this form of yoga.

Jnana yoga is for people who have a rational and philosophical bent; it aims at spiritual insight through intellectual knowledge. It involves study through which one removes the veil of ignorance and illusion and comes to the realization of beauty, truth and goodness. True knowledge of the inner spirit is sought through reflection and analysis, leading one to a direct realization of unity with the Supreme Being. The person who delights in reading theology and philosophy or who cultivates an appreciation for the arts reflects the approach of Jnana yoga.

Raja yoga is the path that leads to union with God through methods of concentration, control of the mind and senses, ending in meditation. It calls upon the physical and mental discipline of hatha yoga. The monk living in the monastery who dedicates hours to meditation but is also concerned to cultivate the "practice of the presence of God" during manual labor and exercise serves as a contemporary example of one who has embraced raja yoga as a pathway of preference. Also located here are those who try to "do what they are doing" with mindfulness, whether that be housework or office work, and those who preserve time for meditation each day amidst the demands of family life.

Obviously, work, devotion, study, meditation are not exclusive of one another. It is understood that they will exist in various combinations in one's life, depending on one's dominant temperamental disposition. The synthesis of these various paths, integrally practiced, develops the head, heart and hands and leads one to God in a harmoniously balanced life. One begins to see, against this background, how insufficient is the average Westerner's perception of yoga as a series of esoteric exercises to keep one's body flexible.

I wish to underline two points about these four pathways. Firstly, each one has as its aim to take the individual to God. This is explicit and up-front in the treatment of yoga that one finds in Hindu literature. Secondly, many people are already practicing one form of yoga or another as Indians understand it: many people are seeking to "yoke" themselves closer to God through good works, religious devotions, study, or meditation. Each one to the Indian mind is yoga of a different kind.

My remarks in Part II of this book are restricted to examining the orientation of hatha yoga (which is but a particular application of Raja yoga) to meditation. "Ha-tha," from Sanskrit, means "sun and moon." The sun represents the expenditure of energy and the moon its conservation. In various cultural traditions and mythologies, sun and moon represent the various cycles of life (day and night, light and dark, breathing in and breathing out) as well as dualities like male and female, on and off, conscious and unconscious, rational and irrational.

Seekers of conscious union with the divine in various ancient civilizations subjected to careful study the repercussion of various bodily gestures and attitudes on the spiritual in our nature. They discovered, for example, that by keeping the body still you calm the mind; that by concentrating your attention, you settle the body; that by certain methods of breath-control, the mind becomes quiet and focused. This evolved a system of practices: physical postures (asanas), breath-control (pranayama), and mental focusing on what is happening in the body-mind when one enters into and holds the posture. Together, these things make up hatha yoga. During the asanas the mind controls the movements of the body. The aim of self-awareness as one reestablishes contact with one's body is the very foundation of yoga.

Pantajali, the first to offer us a codification of yoga, describes its whole purpose as "stilling the thought waves of the mind" or "the cessation of movements in the consciousness."[1] Yoga shows ways of quieting the movements of the mind, leading one toward a state of silence. The asanas, in fact, are correctly practiced only if they fulfill this central purpose of yoga which is the stilling of the mind.

On the surface, it looks like no more than a collection of stretching exercises and breathing techniques. But "exercises" is not the best word for the series of gentle positions designed to limber the body. "Poses" or "postures" is better, for these stretches are performed slowly and gently, with grace and control, as a type of meditation rather than as a form of calisthenics. Ultimately, their purpose is to bring us to a state of inner quiet, rebalancing the opposing forces within us, symbolized by sun and moon. The result is an experience of equilibrium, peace and inner harmony.

An example of "the opposing forces" within us is the dual functioning of our muscles—contracting and relaxing—which becomes "out of balance" when our muscles are chronically tensed and contracted. During periods of stress, when we experience discomfort in the area of the neck, back, or shoulders, our body is reacting to the chronically tensed muscles. When this happens, the first step toward restoring inner peace and harmony is to quiet down and relax the body. Stretching and lengthening muscles that are chronically contracted helps to rebalance both body and mind. What happens in the body affects the mind, just as the mind affects the body.

Thus there are two aspects to the practice of yoga postures: the external form or the posture that works through the body; and the internal form that works through the mind. Often in popular practice it is the external form, the technique, that is emphasized the most. The internal form—the attitude, the intention, and mental aspect—is overlooked. Actually, the physical postures are to be considered the external vehicle of the more significant "inner posture"—the experience of inner stillness and harmony. This "inner posture" can be maintained even while the external postures are constantly changing. In this way yoga resembles Zen in which archery or a tea ceremony is simply used as a vehicle for entering into a state of meditative consciousness. To the extent that the experience of inner harmony and peace is part of the spiritual quest, one could say that the purpose of the *asanas* is primarily spiritual rather than merely physical. The external form of the posture is seen as secondary to its primary purpose as a vehicle for meditative experience.[2]

It is not at all unusual, therefore, that internal attitudes and perceptions begin to change with the practice of yoga and meditation. One might find oneself having less of a taste for superficial conversation, but a sharper appetite for more in-depth communication around questions of personal and spiritual growth. Doing the *asanas* is a vehicle for inner awareness, a way to practice a different attitude toward everyday life. A letter I received from a friend who had recently gone through some traumatic life changes offers eloquent testimony to this.

There is a new addition in my life: yoga. It now claims my time the way meditation does, as a "tool" which is helping me reach new depths in myself.

It's over a year now since my life "crashed" and I lost everything: job, neighbors, network of friends, financial security, sense of purpose. I was stunned and badly wounded.

A naturopath whom I know said to me one day when he learned I meditated twice a day, "You should do yoga." That's how I wound up at my first yoga class. I remember at the end of my first session saying to James, my instructor, "Is there any point to my being here?" For I inhabited a body that had never been exercised or stretched. Yoga seemed as if it could be just one more contact with failure, and I wasn't sure I needed that. But he only answered, "Come back next time." And I did.

Twice a week since then! Not only do I feel better physically for it, but morally as well. Contact with the people who do yoga and with the teaching at yoga's core has been a really important complement to this new contact with my own body. All of it has been significant for my overall personal spiritual journey.

"Yoga is stretching," James would say, introducing not only the practice of yoga but its teaching. "Allow your body to achieve the maximum stretch without straining." These were words which spoke to me on several levels in terms of what I was living, all the transitions I was navi-

gating. Stretching into new postures means surrendering old ones. My encounter with the inflexibility of my body shed new light on inner inflexible attitudes which, I came to see, contributed to my "crash." "Surrender into the crash," my inner voice whispered. "Don't resist it. Don't judge it. Simply, give yourself to it. Stretch. Achieve the maximum stretch without straining. Let yourself discover how this crash will shape you." The new postures led to silence, and in the silence was peace.

"Yoga is balance," James would say, "and balance comes from stretching. Watch a tightrope walker. When she is about to lose her balance, she stretches further. Her first instinct is always to pull in, to protect herself from a fall, but the secret to balance is to stretch further." So I began to stretch further, in my yoga class, but more importantly, in my life.

"Yoga is openness," James would say. "We achieve openness by letting go. Fear keeps us from letting go, and so we have to listen to our fears and let them go." I would begin by getting in touch with my fear of physically falling and end up facing deeper fears like ridicule and loneliness. Then, as I began to let go of my fear of falling, I also began to let go of other things to which I was holding on tightly: illusions about myself and others. James' invitation to get my head out of the past or future and to "be here, now" helped me to see that we are given what we need in each present moment.

"Listen to your body. Your body is the teacher," James would say. "Listen to the wisdom of the body." As I stretched and listened, not only to my physical self but to the body of people whose love had provided strength and support, my posture, both within and without, began to change. Stretching . . . stretching . . . stretching.

One day, James began the class by saying, "Who am I? That is the essential question we ask ourselves." As I reflected on that question, I realized that I am not at all the same person as a year ago. I'm more aware of my rigidities and my inflexibilities, more conscious that there's stamina at the core of my being. This "crash" cracked the boundaries of what I thought I could bear, and brought me into a whole new appreciation of my capacities. Now I can even say, "This has been a good thing." I'm even grateful for it.

So, as you can see, yoga has become a "way" for me, a path of discovery, a discipline for myself in my encounter with life.

Yoga became a metaphor for life, a place wherein my friend became conscious of internal attitudes, insecurities and fears. By allowing the body, in its own wisdom, to stretch and hold as much as it could without the interference of derogatory mental comments and unrealistic expectations, she began to develop a trust and a faith in her body and in herself.

This is the subtle, internal part of yoga which oftentimes is ignored, perhaps because the external form is easier to see and correct. But the focusing on and dispersal of inner tensions leading to acceptance, integration and peace—this is what plays the vital role and makes yoga truly worth the time and effort. It is, in fact, the heart of the practice. And one doesn't even have to perform the external posture perfectly to receive these benefits.

The postures become a gateway for encountering fears and limitations. When you are intentionally encountering bodily limitations and resistance from stiffness in the joints and muscles, holding the posture becomes a powerful vehicle to show you where you are in that moment. And the way to progress from that point is to accept your condition unconditionally. When you come to the point beyond which your physical resistances will not allow you to go without forcing, you meet some fears that come directly from your self-image—

adopted concepts about your body and what it can or can't do. This moment is a privileged opportunity to learn how to be in your body fully, without struggling or coercing it to fit your mental image of yourself and your flexibility. Reaching and relaxing into the physical toleration point becomes a metaphor for accepting where you are in life.

In challenging life situations, there are two divergent roads. You can say, "Well, I have had enough of this. This is just too uncomfortable or painful." In doing so, you buy into all the limiting beliefs you hold about yourself and take refuge in regret and distracting activity. Or you can say, "I'm going to work with this." By "holding the posture" and relaxing into it as much as you can, you discover that you can actually extend beyond your preconceived limits and fears.[3]

Yoga is much more than physical exercise. Comprehensively understood, it takes into its sweep the major pathways to spiritual growth and development: work, devotions, study, and meditation. In the actual practice of the psychophysiological exercises that make up hatha yoga in particular, the postures become points of encounter not only with our bodies but with our own sense of inner limits and possibilities for living. This "inner posture" is the heart of yoga practice.

13

Yoga and Christian Faith

The doctrine of the Incarnation stands at the center of Christian faith and is the bedrock for our understanding of the major truths of Christianity: the Trinity, the church, the sacraments, grace, and life after death. In broad terms the Incarnation is the doctrine about Jesus of Nazareth as the eternal Word of God become flesh (John 1:14). The second person of the Trinity comes down from heaven and enters fully into the human condition in the life and death of Jesus.

A statement by Pope John Paul II underlined the far-reaching implications of this doctrine:

> *The Incarnation of God the Son signifies the taking up into unity with God not only human nature, but in this human nature, in a sense, of everything that is flesh . . . . The Incarnation, then, also has a cosmic significance, a cosmic dimension: the "first born of creation" unites himself in some way with the entire reality of humanity, with the whole of creation.[1]*

The image of the Word of God coming down from heaven to earth at the time of the Incarnation might mistakenly imply, however, the introduction of a previously absent divine presence into the world. The backdrop to the event of the Incarnation is the general presence of God in the created world and among the people of God in the history of Israel. The human experience of God prior to the Incarnation is reflected in the colorful story of Israel's faith in Yahweh.

The image of the human person in relation to God that emerges from this biblical account is of a being who reaches out beyond the self toward some unifying center of communion. From the Psalms, for example, one derives a picture of a being who experiences an unrestricted desire to know and to love, a being who is restless in virtue of his or her awareness of human incompleteness. The goal of this searching self-transcendence is the elusive Mystery we call God. The Hebrew scriptures bear witness to a tension in our human experience: we have a sense of both belonging to and being separated from this holy Mystery. This story of God's self-communication to the individual and the community in creation and in history, and at the same time the individual and the community's incomplete response to this invitation, sets the stage for the historical process of the Incarnation.[2]

The Incarnation reveals our enspirited bodies, our embodied spirits. "We are the temple of the living God," St. Paul wrote (2 Cor. 6:16); "Glorify God in your body" (1 Cor. 6:20). If ever we wanted to trade in this bodily existence for another kind, in the face of that message we no longer have any grounds to do so. Where we are and what we are is now the intimate habitat of God. If ever we approached life in this world as a second-rate adventure in the service of another world, the Incarnation demands that we revise that assessment in favor of recognizing the inherent value of our embodied earthly life.

It is not so much that the Word entered the world; it is rather that the Word became *flesh*. In the Incarnation, Jesus in his flesh took the world as part of himself. The world quite literally became the body of God. Since God is identified with and discovered within this bodiliness, this fleshiness, this materiality, this sensuality, we have no right to dismiss the world as some second-rate practice field for the real life in heaven. The Incarnation states that there is no practice and nothing is second-rate. Life in this world is the life of God.[3]

We have not been burdened with this world and this flesh in order that we might weasel our way out. Rather, we have been gifted with this world and these bodies because this is where God dwells. All flesh is holy and the ground of all human endeavors is sacred. It is in these bodies that we work out our salvation. This corporeal nature is the place that God chose to call "home."

What we are doing is discovering in yoga a concrete application of our incarnational faith. The use of bodily postures to open us to God is already well-established in our own practice. Going down on our knees, for example, invites our mind and heart to be prayerfully present. At our community worship we stand to express our dignity and shared mission, kneel to express the transcendence of God, and touch one another to recognize our bondedness in the Holy Spirit. Depending on what church one enters on Sunday, one will find a range of other bodily postures expressing openness to God: genuflecting, bowing and kissing icons, sitting quietly in a circle with open hands, prostration and standing with hands raised high toward heaven. Gesture obviously unites mind and body and presents us whole to God. It is deeply embedded in the human psyche as a means to prayerful presence.

The ground for all the spiritual disciplines of the body is the desire to increase our awareness of the deep mystery of the indwelling Trinity. Thus the spiritual disciplines enjoin openness rather than tightness, balance rather than clutchiness, alertness rather than distraction. They inevitably involve our body, mind and spirit as different foci of one unified reality. Our embodied nature is like a hologram of God's cosmic divine embodiment. Within us is a universe of interwoven space, form, and spirit, grown and pervaded by God's Spirit in Christ.[4] Yoga is an example of a discipline which reminds us of this larger perspective and reveals to us what a precious, awesome, divine expression we are in our embodiment.

Yoga is a way to help us fully inhabit our bodies and to begin using them to more fully actualize what God calls us to be. Why do people in good physical condition have a special aptitude for a rich spiritual experience? Because the dancers or the swimmers or the gymnasts know things through, with and in their enfleshed spirits that pass the rest of us by.

Their range of humanity, of awareness, is expanded. The potential God gave them has been actively taken hold of and worked with. How could we not know we were supposed to keep ourselves in good condition? What master craftsman could make such a marvel as the human body and not be disappointed when we allow it to rust?

If yoga helps us blow off angry steam, soothe jangled nerves, eat right, and accept our limits, we should relate to it as a faithful friend and speak more of how it contributes to our spiritual growth. If it helps us to see the created world more sharply and breathe the air more deeply, sensitizes our minds to the ecological pollution and our hearts to the unhappiness of people around us, then we should not hesitate to speak of it as a discipline of the spiritual life.

This truth of Christian faith can never be sufficiently pondered: that God so loved us and our world that the Word of God became flesh. Any regular discipline of exercise that breeds affection for the embodied self, smiling at it gently while urging it on, cultivates a spirit of human solidarity and compassion. When one has gloried in this reality oneself, in however humble a fashion, one can more enthusiastically cheer the ballerina and the ball-carrier, the master of yoga and the mistress of natural childbirth. Fewer things human are foreign, and all things human are more precious.

To carry the life of God in our bodies is both a gift and a responsibility. "The body is not meant for immorality, but for the Lord, and the Lord for the body," St. Paul writes in his First Letter to the Corinthians (6:13). The Holy Spirit's call within us is to use our bodies for responsible living in our work, study, devotions, play and all that we do before God. When our central intent is opening to God's presence through the use of our bodies, whatever we do with them becomes a form of prayer.

We pay a lot of attention to our bodies in Western culture, but rarely is it with the intent to open ourselves to God. Even when we pray for healing of the body, the end prayed for is just to make the body well again, not that our bodily experience might become a means of deepening our life in God. A period of sickness may do that better than health. And in the nautilus rooms and aerobics classes, the hours lavished upon our bodies tend to go more in the direction of looking good and feeling fit with little or no thought given to what place this might have in our relationship with God. Dieting provides another example; it is usually undertaken exclusively for reasons of physical health rather than, as within the context of fasting, to become more available to God.[5]

Some of the Eastern religions have paid much closer attention to the body's spiritual dimensions than we have in the West. Ironically, many Christians today are finding in hatha yoga and other practices the help they have been looking for in order to live more fully an incarnational Christian faith that values the human body as a divine gift. Early cultural and philosophical influences in the Western world led to a separation of body and soul and a relative demeaning of the body. The record is, of course, checkered, as illustrated by the important place given to physical labor (*ora et labora*) as a way to God in the influential rule of St. Benedict. Yet only in recent decades has the church more generally begun to recover a Hebraic view of the body's integral place in our spiritual nature.[6]

New Openness to Contact with Other Religions

Every religion seeks to open people up to the Mystery of God and brings its own symbol system to that Mystery. The goal of them all is communion with the Mystery. In this sense, a Christian understanding of yoga means the perception of the Christian end in all the means employed and experiences had. The Christian must discover the applications of his or her faith in the practice and experience of this or any other spiritual method.

As with meditation, one's practice complements and enriches one's participation in the liturgical prayer of the church and the active exercise of practical love expressed in work for justice and peace or care-giving. The tensions between self-realization and participation in common life, between contemplation and action, are healthy and creative, even if not always comfortable. We simply need to find the balance.

What is at issue where Eastern religious practices are concerned is precisely that question of balance: the harmonious use of the body, mind and spirit as an aid in opening one's whole being to God. Recently, on a retreat, the leader invited us to use a Buddhist meditation technique to "track" the movements of our bodies and to note the thoughts arising in our minds. We soon discovered that to do so we had to slow down. And that was her strategy. Why? Because in moving slowly we are more likely not to miss the grace present to us. That is the main reason we generally go on retreat: to pay careful attention to what God is doing in our hearts and lives. Silence helps us tune in to our own thoughts, and a schedule with lots of open space in it invites us to drop below the surface of our usual preoccupations and become more sensitive to the subtle reality of God's presence. We move more slowly and deliberately, joining our consciousness to the Consciousness that beckons to us. For the same reasons, the movements in yoga are slow and deliberate, and every breath, bodily sensation, and thought is "tracked" with full awareness. The practice of yoga can thus, as a part of day-to-day routine, draw us into contact with the grace that is present to us.[7]

Christianity is not primarily a system of dogmas or conceptualized expressions of faith. It engages one above all in a relationship with the person of Jesus Christ, worshiped with material symbols and gestures in our incarnate nature. Because Jesus revealed God's truth in his whole activity as a human being and embraced all that is truly human, the Christian is "at home" in practices which open us to God's presence in these embodied spirits. I have met some Christians who are wary of yoga because of its origination in other religious contexts. But God seems often pleased to show us the divine handiwork in the lives of those who belong to other religious paths in order that our faith convictions may remain humble and unjudgmental and truly open to the Spirit of God at work everywhere in the world.

The Vatican's "Letter to the bishops of the Catholic Church on some aspects of Christian meditation" was motivated by the increasing contact of Christians with other religions and with their different styles and methods of prayer. It mentioned in particular the Eastern methods of Zen, transcendental meditation and yoga. It responds to the question of what value these forms of prayer or preparation for prayer might have for Christians:

The majority of the great religions which have sought union with God in prayer have also pointed out ways to achieve it. Just as the "Catholic Church rejects nothing of what is true and holy in these religions" (Vatican II's Decree on Non-Christians, *no. 2), neither should these ways be rejected out of hand simply because they are not Christian. On the contrary, one can take from them what is useful so long as the Christian conception of prayer, its logic and requirements are never obscured.*[8]

The document goes on to recognize that Christians are today becoming more conscious of how one's bodily posture can aid prayer and how genuine practices of meditation that come from other living faiths may prove attractive to the person who is divided and distracted. These aids, it says, can "constitute a suitable means of helping the person who prays to come before God with an interior peace, even in the midst of external pressures."[9]

In reflecting on this new openness, Tilden Edwards underscores some important points in his book *Living in the Presence*:

In the wider ecumenism of the Spirit being opened for us today, we need to humbly accept the learnings of particular Eastern religions in relation to the body now available to us. What makes a particular practice Christian is not its source, but its intent. If our intent in assuming a particular bodily practice is to deepen our awareness in Christ, then it is Christian. If this is not our intent, then even the reading of Scripture loses its authenticity.

I say this in the context of the long history of Christian spiritual practice which has included utilization of methods and vocabulary that have originated out of many non-specifically Christian sources. The Bible itself is full of such influences. This is important to remember in the face of those Christians who would try to impoverish our spiritual resources by too narrowly defining them. If we view the human family as one in God's Spirit, then this historical cross-fertilization is not surprising, nor is it the same as a patched-together eclecticism. We realize that God's mysterious Spirit is profligate in the world, creating God-consciousness in endless forms. A faith and understanding of God in Christ gives Christians a distinctive interior center from which to discern and embrace this divine Presence where it is genuinely manifest. In terms of the body, selective attention to Eastern spiritual practices can be of great assistance to a fully embodied Christian life. They also can provide challenge to the secularization of the body dominant in Western science and common life.[10]

Postures for Prayer

In his book *Body, Mind, and Spirit,*[11] Irish Dominican prior and retreat director Louis Hughes, who studied yoga for six years in India, provides an example of a Christian interpreting yoga postures in the light of his biblical faith. In a section entitled "Postures for Prayer," one finds several yoga postures illustrated, accompanied by instructions on how to execute the pose. For each one, there is a brief reflection on how that particular pose expresses corporeally some attitude of faith in Christian life, and a scripture passage to meditate on while doing the posture. Some examples of particular exercises with their corresponding scriptural verse:

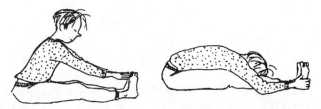

Forward bend — "Bend my heart to obey your law, O God" (Ps. 119:36).

Spinal twist — "Turn to me now and be saved" (Isa. 45:22).

Child's pose — "At the name of Jesus, every knee should bend, in heaven, on earth and under the earth" (Phil.2:10).

Corpse pose — "Into thy hands, O Lord, I commend my spirit."

Once one is shown how Christians do in fact integrate their faith with the practice of yoga, the possibilities for personal application are as limitless as the different combinations of scripture verses, postures, and themes in the spiritual life can inspire. Or, you may wish to create your own prayers, or find that words are not necessary at all. What these examples demonstrate is that, in addition to being a preparation for prayer and for prayerful living, the poses can themselves become prayer.

Carolyn Cronk, a university professor and part-time yoga teacher, offers the following reflection with reference to the corpse pose pictured above:

The symbolism of yoga postures as concrete representa-
tions of inner spiritual dispositions has long fascinated
me. One prime example is the corpse pose, on the surface
a very simple relaxation posture. The letting-go in relax-
ation is in and of itself significant; the entire front of my
body being open and vulnerable is a position of great
trust, calling to mind the trust in God that is the ground
of my faith. Conscious awareness of how I am supported
by the earth beneath my back recalls both my connected-
ness with all of creation and the unfailing support of
God's love. Focusing on nothing but my breath entering
my body reminds me of how there is nothing essential to
life that is not provided through God's love for me.
Finally, my open and upward-facing palms are a gesture
of gratitude and of readiness to receive the gifts of love
and grace.

A variation to this approach is simply to take the posture which conveys the way you are feeling right now before God, whatever it is, from humble and withdrawn to open and joyful, from needy and beseeching to relaxed and accepting. Find your own way of praying with the body in speaking to God, listening to God, and waiting upon God.[12]

One of the gestures I find particularly appropriate for beginning and ending yoga sessions is called the "Trinity movement mantra" by Episcopal priest Nancy Roth in her book *A New Christian Yoga*.[13] Just as a mantra is a repeated word or phrase, this movement is meant to be repeated three times. It can be done standing, sitting or kneeling.

(see figure 5 on p. 154.)

Inhale and raise both arms forwards and upwards, as you look up, reaching and stretching, expressing relationship with God, our Creator.

Then exhale and lower the arms out to the sides at shoulder level, with the palms up, to form a cross. Hold them there and turn your attention to Jesus, our Redeemer.

The third person of the Trinity, the Holy Spirit or Sanctifier, we experience both within us and among us. Inhale, and bring your hands inward towards the heart-center. Then exhale and reach forward, with the palms up in a receptive position.

Finally, return the hands to a folded prayer position at your breast.

Each morning when I arise, I do the following yoga movements called "salute to the sun," slowly and mindfully performing each one to the words of the Our Father. We like to stretch anyway when we get up in the morning. Here is a stretch involving all the muscle groups in the body. As you can see, the movements accord well with the words to form a morning prayer engaging the whole body, mind and spirit simultaneously. I had come to this on my own and have been teaching it to people the last few years. When I discovered it similarly illustrated in Rev. Roth's book, I was surprised and pleased to know others have been working in the same way with yoga postures and Christian prayer.

(see figure 6 on p. 155.)

Figure 5.

Figure 6.

EXHALE

Our Father

INHALE

Who Art In Heaven

EXHALE

Hallowed Be Thy Name

INHALE

Thy Kingdom Come

EXHALE

Thy Will Be Done

RETAIN

On Earth As It Is In
Heaven

INHALE

Give Us This Day
Our Daily Bread

EXHALE

And Forgive Us
Our Trespasses

INHALE

As We Forgive Those Who
Trespass Against Us

EXHALE

And Lead Us Not
Into Temptation

INHALE

(Coming Up) But
Deliver Us From Evil,
For Thine Etc.

EXHALE

Amen

14

Notions Strange to Christian Ears

In every encounter between followers of different religions an exchange takes place. Those who are party to this encounter are introduced to new worldviews, concepts, terminology, and practices. If some aspect is interesting, it is not unusual to find people trying to integrate it into their own system of belief or practice.

When Christians read books on yoga by Hindu authors or attend lectures or take courses given by proponents of Eastern religions, they will probably encounter notions like reincarnation, kundalini energy, chakras and astral bodies, which are strange to their ears. I have been in several sessions when participants of Christian background put questions to the instructor about these notions. In responding, the instructor has tried, with the best of intentions, to find points of correlation with Christian faith but usually ends by misrepresenting it. Such was not the instructor's intention, to be sure, but a result of certain historic misunderstandings which have been perpetuated through the ages and which seem to be enjoying a new resurgence in our time.

In the interest of clarity, I will seek in this chapter to reflect on these questions from the standpoint of Christian faith. Genuine interfaith dialogue is only served by an accurate understanding of our differences as well as our similarities. If we are able to speak clearly to one another, it frees each of us to be who we are and to proceed in our relationship on the solid ground of accurate perception and mutual respect. There does not have to be agreement on everything in order for us to draw real positive benefit from each other's spiritual treasuries. Distinctions can and should be made if the participants in interfaith encounters are to be faithful to their own tradition.

Reincarnation

There is perhaps no better current example of the need for clear communication than the doctrine of reincarnation. Reincarnation refers to the conviction that an imperishable principle (soul) exists in every human being, which soul for some reason comes back on this earth after death, usually in a new human form. In Hinduism and Buddhism one can reincarnate as a plant, an animal or a god in a subsequent life, but in order to attain ultimate purification and liberation, one must be reborn at some time as a human being on this earth. Variations on this general teaching exist, such as in the Self-Realization Fellowship of Paramahansa Yogananda in which a devolutionary reincarnation would not be in an animal form but in a lower state of human consciousness. The notion of having numerous lives on earth, in whatever form, remains key, however. Such terms as *metempsychosis* (Greek for "animate afterward"), rebirth, and transmigration are included in the term reincarnation for the purpose of this discussion.

This doctrine is found in the most varied religions in different forms. It is found among many of the so-called primitive tribes, among the ancient Egyptians, among the Celts as well as in Greek philosophy (Pythagoras, Plato, Plotinus), in the Latin poet Virgil, as well as among the Gnostic Christians, the Manicheans, and even in the Jewish Kabbala. In all these religions and schools of philosophy, however, the theory of reincarnation was only one theory among others. In India (Hinduism and Buddhism), on the other hand, it became a dogma pervading the entire religion and the totality of its thought.[1]

Belief in reincarnation surfaced in modern Europe during the Age of the Enlightenment. In 1780 the German writer G.E. Lessing published a widely-read work called *The Education of Humanity* in which he saw humanity's history as an irresistible climb toward the light of the spirit. In the final paragraphs, he puts forth the hypothesis that this climb might take place during the course of successive lives, each more spiritual than the other. The idea took hold. Goethe and the Romantics adopted it, and Darwin's theory of evolution reinforced in many the conviction of universal progress.[2] In our time, the theory of reincarnation has met with renewed interest through religious movements such as the New Age in which it has an important role.

According to a 1983 Gallup poll, a quarter of Europeans believed in reincarnation, and a similar poll taken in the late 1980s in the United States claimed that 23 percent of the American public believed in some form of reincarnation. There are several reasons today why many find it an acceptable solution to their questions about life:

- One is provided with an explanation for the why of the events which befall a person. Why do the good so often seem to do badly? On account of earlier guilt. Why do the evil so often seem to do well? On account of earlier good deeds. According to karma, the fate of every person in this life and in future lives is determined by the consequences of good or bad actions in the past or present.[3]

- One is provided with a solution to the problem of unrevenged injustice in this life. It is satisfying to believe that those who have committed the most heinous crimes without being punished will receive their just due in a subsequent life.

- In the face of the many things to experience and to learn, it is consoling to think that one can resume one's course in additional lives. Some are convinced that a person should experience everything in life once: being wealthy and being poor, being a man and being a woman. And this is only possible if there are numerous lives.

- Some feel that a single earthly life here and now is too short to be decisive for eternity. The idea of reincarnation seems more compassionate by comparison: one has the opportunity to make restitution for one's mistakes and to progress. Reincarnation is thus seen as a part of God's plan, a process of purification and maturation towards full communion with God. It is God's program in which everyone eventually succeeds.[4]

There are three important observations to make at this point: 1) We are not dealing with a "nonsense" notion; the fact that people all over the globe are acquainted with reincarnation or rebirth means it merits a serious and respectful response. 2) Behind the doctrine of reincarnation lies the search for a meaningful, moral, just world order; the question of where to find just recompense and reparative compensation in a world in which human destinies have been so unequally and unfairly allotted. 3) There is a fundamental difference between the Eastern (Hindu and Buddhist) theories of reincarnation or rebirth and the modern Western ones.

This third point bears further development. In the Eastern religions the cycle of rebirth is a fearful thing, something to flee from and something people want to be liberated from. The wheel of rebirth is tied to notions of guilt and punishment and evokes fright. In traditional Buddhist teaching, for example, the world is on a devolutionary spiral because most people do not "learn their lessons" even in repeated reincarnations. The number of those who do not reach liberation and nirvana far outnumber those who do.

By contrast, in our Western thought, as represented by the examples cited above, reincarnation represents a new and positive opportunity. A recent letter from an acquaintance raised the question in these terms: "I would love to talk to you some day about reincarnation. I find it comforting and logical to know I have been working toward God before this lifetime and will after this lifetime." Not long after, a church member commented in a similar vein: "I see God as love and our lives as a learning experience in which we learn to express that love. If God has loved us enough to call us into the material plane once, why not more than once so we can learn even better?" Here reincarnation is not a burden, but rather a comfort positively associated with new possibilities for self-fulfillment.

In listening to the Christian response to the questions raised, one best begins with the Bible in which Christians locate God's revelation about the way things are.

The Response of the Bible and Early Christianity

Even though today the contrary is often claimed, the Bible makes no mention of reincarnation. There are, however, several biblical passages which speak clearly against what reincarnation teaches without ever mentioning it by name (2 Sam. 12:23; 14:14; Ps. 78:39; Lk. 23:43; Acts 17:31; 2 Cor. 5:1,4,8; 6:2; Phil. 1:23; Heb. 9:27). The most straightforward of these is the verse in Hebrews which summarizes the teaching of scripture on the subject: "Just as it is appointed for mortals to die once, and after that the judgment, so Christ, having been offered once to bear the sins of many, will appear a second time, not to deal with sin, but to save those who are eagerly waiting for him."

While Jesus, too, never mentioned reincarnation as such, some of his teachings bear directly upon notions of karmic retribution or the singularity of our lives. Lk. 13:1-9 provides a good example of this:

At that very time there were some present who told him about the Galileans whose blood Pilate had mingled with their sacrifices. He (Jesus) asked them, "Do you think that because these Galileans suffered in this way they were worse sinners than all other Galileans? No, I tell you; but unless you repent, you will all perish as they did. Or those eighteen who were killed when the tower of Siloam fell on them—do you think that they were worse offenders than all the others living in Jerusalem? No, I tell you; but unless you repent, you will all perish just as they did."

Then he told them this parable: "A man had a fig tree planted in his vineyard; and he came looking for fruit on it and found none. So he said to the gardener, 'See here! For three years I have come looking for fruit on this fig tree, and still I find none. Cut it down! Why should it be wasting the soil?' He replied, 'Sir, let it alone for one more year, until I dig around it and put manure on it. If it bears fruit next year, well and good; but if not, you can cut it down.' "

In the first part of that passage, Jesus refers to two tragedies—the first caused by human malice, the second the result of a freak accident—to correct what he considered were mistaken notions of retributive justice. He focuses squarely on the apparently popular belief that tragedy befell certain people as a deserved punishment for earlier misdeeds. He counsels them not to attribute their death to such, but to take these events as a sober warning to those still alive to repent. Just as the presence of tragedy should not be read as guilt, neither should the absence of tragedy be read as a sign of innocence and approval, but as a gift of God's mercy that allows more time to repent. The light of life is as easily snuffed out for a good person as for an evil one.

In the lesson on the fig tree, Jesus underscores the urgency and importance of repentance. The main point of the parable is that this is the last chance, as it were; the call to reform has to be heeded. If it is not, those who ignore the challenge will find themselves in the same sorry condition as the fig tree. In not giving an indefinite term in which to bear fruit,

the text speaks to all who think the lifetime process of conversion can be begun "tomorrow" or in future lifetimes. Each
human person is given a unique period of time and must
maximize the use of that time for bearing fruit.

Another pertinent example of Jesus' teaching is the parable of the laborers in the vineyard in Matthew 20:1-6. Since
the owner of the vineyard is a good person, even those who
worked only one hour receive complete recompense for a full
day's work, exactly like those who had to endure the heat and
burden of the entire day. When those who have put in a full
day's labor complain that this is not just, the landowner
responds: "I choose to give to the last the same as I give to
you. Am I not allowed to do what I choose with what belongs
to me? Or are you envious because I am generous?" So, Jesus
concludes in a Christian koan that defies the logic of strict
justice, "the last will be first, and the first will be last."

Again, the stress is upon God's mercy rather than upon an
inflexible standard of recompense. The writings of St. Paul
especially make the frequent and insistent affirmation that
we are justified not by our works and deeds, but through
faith in Jesus (Rom. 3:20-28; Gal. 2:16). "For by grace you
have been saved through faith, and this is not your own
doing; it is the gift of God—not the result of works, so that no
one may boast" (Eph. 2:8).

The two names that most frequently surface in attempts to
reconcile the theory of reincarnation with the Bible or
Christian teaching are John the Baptist and Origen. There
was a popular understanding—marginal to the meaning of
the Gospel—spread around among the people in Jesus' time,
that John the Baptist was supposedly Elijah born again
(Matt. 11:14; 17:12). This is not only rejected by the Baptist
himself (Jn. 1:21), but has nothing to do with reincarnation.
The expectation related to the return of Elijah (who had been
carried off to heaven) in his *own* body, not in another body.

Reincarnation literature generally claims that primitive
Christianity knew of and accepted this doctrine. The teachings
of Origen, the greatest third-century theologian, are in particular cited in support of this claim. This lacks any serious histor-

ical foundation. All the Fathers of the church, beginning with Hippolytus and Irenaeus in the second century through and including Origen, criticized the doctrine of reincarnation as advanced by the Pythagoreans and Platonists. Careful study of Origen's texts shows that he explicitly rejects "metempsychosis" (transmigration of souls). What he did teach was the "pre-existence" of souls before their "incorporation," their entering into the body; it is precisely this teaching and not that of reincarnation which the Council of Constantinople attributed to him when it condemned the notion of pre-existence in 543.[5] Even with his teaching on pre-existence, it was essential for Origen that an individual have only one life on this earth. He recognized that the notion of several lives on earth did not accord with Scripture.[6]

In an overall perspective, there are several points where Christian faith clearly diverges from the theories of reincarnation and rebirth:

1) *A different view of time and history*—Many other religions see time and history through the image of an eternal cyclical return and view every event as a cyclical repetition of a primordial event. This view is symbolized by such rhythmic patterns as star movements, seasons, day and night. For Christian thinking about history, the idea that time is irrevocable plays an essential role. The Bible places full stress upon the singularity and irrepeatability of God's action in history. History is therefore not cyclical but linear, having a distinct beginning and end. God is the Creator and sovereign over time. God is not caught up in the cycles of time or being, but is "the Alpha and the Omega," the one who began time and the one who will bring it to an end. Genesis tells of the beginning of time—the creation—and the book of Revelation tells of the end of time—the second coming of Christ and the last judgment. After that, the brief day of time will yield to eternity.[7]

Hindu and Buddhist understanding proceed on the assumption that the world will end, but only to begin a new cycle. Jewish-Christian-Islamic tradition, by contrast, assumes there will be not simply an end to human life and history but also a consummation, the completion of something radically new: "a new heaven and a new earth." Consequently history is a meaningful, coherent, continuous, goal-directed process brought to eternal fulfillment by God. This worldview posits the individual's inalienable responsibility and the meaning of what each one does while keeping the final consummation in sight.[8]

2) *Unity of body and soul*—Christian hope in the after-life does not concern merely the soul's immortality but the entire person who is called to be with God as an embodied spirit. The body is not the soul's prison; it, too, is created by God. Furthermore, it is destined for eternal life, thanks to the resurrection of the body, an idea completely alien to the Hellenistic world. So while Christian faith sees the body as inseparable from the soul and cannot imagine our salvation outside the totality of our embodied nature, reincarnation offers no salvation to the body. It is, in fact, expressive of an extreme dualism, seeing the soul manifesting itself in different bodily forms.

The assumption of an independent existence for the soul either before or after the body, of the existence of a separate soul-substance independent of its bodily substrate, corresponds neither to our experience nor to the findings of modern medicine, physiology, and psychology which in general work from the supposition that human beings are a psychosomatic unit.

3) The centrality of grace as opposed to human effort—the central message of the Gospel is that our fulfillment is not our doing or the result of our own efforts, but rather a gift of God's grace. Communion with God and life with God cannot ever be properly a work of the human being but only a free gift of God. Therefore, neither one nor many lives can be adequate for reaching perfection. The

bottom line is that all is grace. It matters little if a life is long or short. What is decisive for our eternal salvation is welcoming the saving love of God who wants nothing but to save all those who desire to be saved, even if they have led a bad life and are taking their last breath. Thus Jesus' exchange with the thief who said to him from the cross to his right: "Jesus, remember me when you come into your kingdom." He replied: "Truly I tell you, this day you will be with me in paradise" (Lk. 23:42-43).

Hindus are familar with the notion that God can intervene and blot out human guilt, that God can "extinguish" karma. Some Christian theologians however, still perceive a difference of emphasis in the Christian understanding that God, manifested in Jesus of Nazareth, "forgives" guilt.[9]

4) *Joyful life with a personal God in eternity versus blissful absorption into a cosmic All*—Christians believe that the individual human person is not to be absorbed into a cosmic All because an encounter of love requires persons. God is also personal. While it is Christian faith that all things will be reconciled and made one in Christ and presented to the Father that "God may be all in all" (1 Cor. 15:28), Christians do not believe that individuality is lost.

5) *Different perceptions of suffering*—Christian theology does not claim to have solved this problem and speaks about it as a "mystery." Essentially, however, the Christian view of suffering is not to see it as a punishment for past failures or sins but as a test case for basic trust in God, who is challenging human beings to make decisions. Christian theology draws an image of hope from the Bible in the attitude of Job: an unconditional, unshaken, and yet not unreasonable trust in an incomprehensible God despite all the suffering that racks this world. Christian faith lives on the tried and tested hope that a hand is stretched to us across the abyss of pain

and evil. This trust in a God of compassion, concern and
solidarity is based on the experience of Jesus' death, resurrection, and elevation to eternal life.

From the Christian standpoint, the experience of suffering has nothing to do with resignation or passivity.
Rather, the Christian seeks to transform it through acts
of hope and trust in God's transforming power. The
irrevocable responsibility of the individual before God
therefore requires that one fight a battle for justice,
freedom, and peace against the forces of evil, injustice,
misery and death. While the present unfolding of things
may seem inexplicable, belief in a God who creates and
completes means that individuals and the cosmos have
their first and last security and permanent home in
God, their Creator and finisher.[10]

6) *The Resurrection of Jesus*—Although ancient religions
had many legends of gods and goddesses who would die
and rise, none of them incorporated the Christian elements of a glorified risen body and the power to share
this new risen life with others. Even the Jewish hopes
that the righteous dead would return to earth with their
bodies were hopes for a physical resuscitation like
Lazarus' (see Isa. 26:19; Ezek. 37:10; Dan. 12:2). Other
philosophies and religions have held such beliefs as the
immortality of the soul, total annihilation at death, survival as ghosts or disembodied spirits, or reincarnation.
But the Christian belief in the resurrection is unique.

Christian faith understands the death and resurrection of
Jesus, which happened "once and for all," as being valid also
in an analogous way for the redeemed. In the Apostles' Creed
we profess belief in "the resurrection of the body" as the final
destiny of all people. St. Irenaeus of Lyons, in the second century, spoke of our own bodily resurrection being inseparable
from faith in Jesus Christ dead and risen: "It is clear that the
very same thing will happen to his disciples since it was for
them that the Lord did all that. Their souls, therefore, will go

to the invisible place assigned to them by God and they will sojourn there awaiting that resurrection. Afterward they will be reunited with their bodies and will rise intact, that is, bodily, in the same way in which the Lord is risen, and they will enter this way into God's presence."[11] What will this risen body be like? No one knows exactly. Similar in some way to our earthly bodies, but transformed and glorified. "Beloved, we are God's children now; what we will be has not yet been revealed. What we do know is this: when he is revealed, we will be like him . . . " (1 Jn. 3:2).

There are some points of convergence between theories of rebirth and Christian faith. One is the notion of purification after death. Purgatory is a reference more familiar to Catholics than to other Christians, but the notion of cleansing suffering endured after death by those not yet fit to enjoy the full light of God's presence figures in the thinking of Christians generally in one way or another. It basically relates to an experience of transition beyond space and time in which the unfinished person, still immature in love, encounters the holy, infinite, loving God. It is not difficult to understand why there might be some humiliating, painful, and purifying aspects to the encounter. The Council of Trent (1545-1563) maintained the doctrine of purgatory, but said nothing about its nature and duration.[12]

A second point where all concerned could benefit from further dialogue and sharing of experience is the whole notion of enlightenment as a goal of our spiritual development whether conceived of through one or many lifetimes. Awareness of and reflection on the experience of enlightenment is quite new to Christians. Enlightenment could be described as an experience of the unity of things, an almost overwhelming sense of the oneness of things and of our interior bond with them through a common "isness." It is the culmination of a natural process of development in which we experience our true natures as sharers in the mystery of existence. Further sharing on this subject could only enrich Christianity and allow it to enter into deeper dialogue with those religions of Asia that hold this experience so much to heart.[13]

A final thing which can be said equally of reincarnation and bodily resurrection in a singular and unique existence is that both are unprovable convictions rooted in faith. Despite the many reports of reincarnation or transmigration of souls, there are no scientifically undisputed, generally recognized data to back them up; neither could such be said to exist for the resurrection of Jesus. In discussions of "previous lives," even when the facts of what someone "remembers" prove to be precise, the distinction is often forgotten between the facts of experience and their interpretation.[14] Two cars collide in an intersection. None of the occupants of either car dispute the *fact*, but they may have very different *interpretations* of how it happened.

When we move from facts of experience to interpretation we move into a different realm. When we interpret events that touch upon the afterlife, we do so with reference to a philosophical or religious understanding of human nature and of our origin and destiny. Those who accept the concept of reincarnation will interpret certain experiences as "proof" of their beliefs. Those who do not accept it will give other explanations in the conviction that telepathy, clairvoyance, or the unconscious, as Freud showed, can be explained without going beyond the present life. It is not likely that there will ever be scientific proofs or refutations of either reincarnation or the bodily resurrection of Christian faith.

However, Christians who accept reincarnation and try to integrate it into their beliefs cannot help but modify thereby certain key tenets of Christian faith, most notably the atoning role of Jesus' work and the key role of grace and forgiveness. Many people in the Christian tradition who more or less accept the notion of reincarnation have probably never thought through its implications for other aspects of their faith and are unaware of the theological connections and correlations of one belief to another. Their belief in reincarnation very likely stands on its own, is interesting and helpful, but does not exist in a well-considered system of faith.

From the six points of divergence traced out above, it should be clear that modern theories of reincarnation contradict not only single scriptural passages or individual doctrinal teachings, but go against basic concepts of Christian faith and are in contrast to the coherency of Christian faith taken as a whole. As such, they are irreconcilable with the nature of Christian hope in eternal life.

Kundalini Energy, Chakras and Astral Bodies

In yoga centers everywhere, references are commonly made to the chakras and kundalini energy, leaving Christians who have no familiarity with them quite adrift. Imprecise understandings abound, and foggy thinking rolls in on the waves of New Age journals and books which are eclectic in the composition of their perspectives. Clear, balanced thinking in these matters that respects the inner coherency of Christian faith is hard to come by.

The best place to start with an exposition of kundalini is with reference to enlightenment. As we have already noted above, Christians are neophytes to this dialogue. If enlightenment is understood as a direct, non-conceptual awareness or experience of the unity of things, then kundalini appears to be a particular kind of enlightenment. Enlightenment allows us to experience the wondrous mystery of existence that embraces all things. It could be seen as the flowering of the instinct to return to God that is deep within all things, as an expression of the drive within us to become fully what it is in our nature to be. When, in the case of the human soul, this instinct blossoms into an intense spiritual experience with psycho-physiological impact, it is described in yogic literature in terms of the "awakening" or the "rising of kundalini energy."[15]

This experience, called the kundalini process and involving references to chakras and perhaps one's astral body, is poorly documented among Christian contemplatives and saints. They were certainly not working with the same categories of interpretation that grew out of the Hindu culture and spiritual experience, and their own categories may not have been as serviceable. Let us look at some of these categories of thought as represented in the following definitions: [16]

1. *Astral Body*—This is the psycho-spiritual body in Hindu literature. It mediates between the material body and what is known as the causal body, which is pure spirit. It has its own energetic physiology, which roughly parallels the systems of the material body. It might be conceived as an aura or field of energy surrounding the physical body.

2. *Chakras* (Sanskrit for "circle")—These are the energy centers in the astral body, roughly corresponding to the spinal plexi. Spinal plexi are relay terminals along the spine at which the central nervous system (brain, spinal cord, and their nerves) communicates with the autonomic nervous system which modulates the activities of the glands, organs, and other involuntary processes. Most texts speak of seven chakras, five of which are located along the spine. The sixth is located in the center of the forehead, and the seventh atop the head.

3. *Kundalini*—The term means "the curl of the hair of the beloved." It is described as a very powerful form of psycho-spiritual energy that is curled or coiled at the base of the spine in the first chakra. According to yogic literature, when awakened through the disciplines of yoga this energy uncoils and moves up through the spinal canal, piercing the chakras and eventually entering the brain. Great energy, power, insight and bliss are said to accompany the experience of kundalini in the brain. Though some yogis are reported to have the ability to keep the kundalini current flowing up to the seventh chakra, for many it is a short-lived experience after which the kundalini slowly begins falling, eventually coiling again in the first chakra.

Scientific studies which attest to the reality of these things are now available. Dr. Lee Sannella's conclusion is that the kundalini process is basically desirable, signaling a transformation to another state of consciousness that may lie on the frontier of our evolutionary future.[17] But how are we to appraise them from the perspective of Christian faith?

The first thing that must be said is that what we do not know about these topics outweighs what we do know. The first book in which a Christian reflects on these processes out of his own personally documented experience of them was recently provided by Philip St. Romain under the title of *Kundalini Energy and Christian Spirituality*.[18] Until I came across this book, I looked in vain for some reliable Christian literature to help me make sense of these foreign notions. St. Romain concurs, and says with regard to his graphically described experience of the kundalini process: "To be quite frank, I learned nothing from the Christian literature to help me understand and cope with my condition. I learned even less from Buddhist and Zen literature! Christianity, Buddhism and Zen provide a wealth of literature concerning the psychological, philosophical, metaphysical, theological and sociological implications of the spiritual life. Only Hinduism, however, with its abundant literature concerning the teachings of the yogis, offers comprehensive teaching concerning the role of physiology in the process of transformation."[19]

Professionally trained as a biologist prior to his becoming a spiritual director and psychotherapist of a diocesan pastoral life center, St. Romain understands both physiological processes as well as the workings of divine grace. His work is an offering to spiritual directors, pastoral counselors, contemplatives, New Age readers, and those interested in Christian-Eastern dialogue. As knowledgeable Christian evaluative data is extremely limited, I will seek to present a concise summary of his research and reflections, quoting him directly where what he says already represents an effective synthesis for our purposes. There are at least nine points which seem particularly pertinent from the perspective of Christian faith.

1. These experiences are real.

Chakras: on the level of physiology, the spinal plexus centers are very real. When used in the context of spirituality, however, St. Romain finds it more plausible to think of them as "places" in consciousness rather than actual physiological centers *of* consciousness. "I sincerely doubt that these centers of consciousness are actually situated in the chakras, as most New Age writers insist. Rather it seems that this is merely a way of structuring a spirituality along organic lines."[20]

Astral body: "I am quite aware that the life of the physical body is one thing and the life of the energy body is another. The energy body is patterned on the physical and was given birth by it, but it now lives on an energy Source that transcends the physical . . . . I wonder if this energy body is not a glimpse of the resurrected state. Sometimes it seems to me that this physical body is merely a seed, from which, if all goes well, the energy body will sprout . . . . Later, perhaps, in the fully resurrected state, another physical body will be given, but this time to serve the purposes of the energy or spiritual body. I am sure that many readers will think this is all very far-out, and I quite agree! Nevertheless, it is also very real . . . . Human nature is most mysterious, if we can drop our attachment to the familiar."[21]

Kundalini energy: In Christian theology, the soul is the life principle of the body, with which it is one as an embodied soul. It is a creation endowed by God with its own unique qualities and energies. Kundalini, for St. Romain, is an energy from that "place" or ground where the energies of body and soul are one: "Kundalini is, then, a kind of primal human energy, simultaneously impacting the physiological, psychological, and spiritual levels of human existence. It is a Soul energy, for it is the Soul that gives life to the body in all its dimensions. The awakening of kundalini signals the awakening of the powers of the Soul in the body. Whether this is for good or evil is another question altogether."[22]

Every religion includes accounts of the awakening of kundalini. If, then, psycho-physiological energies in the body are real and their "uncoiling" cannot be denied, what "triggers" this process? The theory St. Romain finds most plausible is that the "push" to uncoil these energies comes from an intensification of the currents in the sensory cortex of the brain which increases the amount of electrical energy in those parts of the body stimulated by the cortex. In other words, kundalini is an experience of our natural, human psycho-physiological powers.

2. *One can be taught how to awaken this energy.*

The best explanation we have for how this primal energy is awakened or uncoiled is that it is related to an intensification of the currents in the sensory cortex. The abdominal breathing advocated in yoga and Zen can provide the spark. The *asanas* taught in hatha yoga also facilitate the uncoiling of repressed psycho-physiological energy in the joints and the nerve plexus areas. "The most effective method is a combination of meditation and yogic postures such as those taught in hatha yoga."[23] So the state of consciousness which results from the awakening of kundalini can be taught and can be attained through one's own efforts.

The soul is a creation that may realize itself as one with the body and with God. "This is, I believe, the enlightenment experience, a natural (perhaps original) state of human consciousness available to all who will undertake the right kinds of disciplines."[24]

3. *The possibility of self-accomplishment is sufficient to distinguish kundalini awakening from contemplative prayer, which cannot be attained on one's own.*

The essence of contemplation is the sense of being grasped by God. It is just being-here-now-in-love. One becomes aware that there is nothing to do to effect this union except to avoid sin and to gently turn the attention toward God. God does the rest. One can experience kundalini phenomena without contemplation; one can experience contemplation with kundalini; one can experience contemplation without kundalini phenomena, as, it would appear, is the case with most contemplatives.

4. *The higher states of consciousness are not tantamount to holiness.*

The chakra system seems more concerned with *states of consciousness*, while the three classic stages of spiritual growth in Christian literature are concerned with the degree of the experience of *union with God*:

Purgative. A time of struggle in which counterfeit values are rejected, but they are also still attractive. One experiences an intense civil war, but begins progressing in virtue.

Illuminative. One finds it less difficult to resist temptation. One's true center is God, and one works at progressing in virtue and understanding.

Unitive. The person is united with God in his or her center. Virtue comes easily, although the possibility of sin remains.[25]

God, the Evangelist John tells us, is love, and *love is not just a state of consciousness*. Rather, it is an *orientation of consciousness* that wishes the happiness of another and is willing to become involved in the struggle to that end. The Holy Spirit is more interested in the *orientation* of consciousness than in its psychic powers, in the primacy of love over psychic gifts. Kundalini does not in and of itself bring forth the fruits of the Spirit that Paul lists in Galatians 5:22: love, joy, peace, patient endurance, kindness, generosity, faith, mildness, and chastity.

5. *The awakening experience can help one to bring greater energies into the service of love.*

There is significant positive potential in a kundalini awakening. St. Romain acknowledges that there is a great overlap among the three Christian stages of growth and the seven stages of chakra consciousness. He notes how one finds in reading the lives of Christian mystics that their growth in union with God was accompanied by growth into the higher states of consciousness. As they progressed in union, they "ascended the chakras" as well, manifesting greater psychic gifts, creativity and inner freedom. In the context of spirituality, these could clearly help one to bring greater energies into the service of love.

6. *The continued operation of free will means that one cannot know in advance whether an awakening experience will count for good or for evil.*

Just as before an awakening experience so in its aftermath free will continues, and with it the possibility of misusing the considerable powers released. Awareness of this no doubt accounts for the secrecy traditionally surrounding kundalini yoga teachings. Kundalini is an enormous energy for good, but like all human potentials, it could also be used for selfish motives and thus become a source of serious harm. Thus the kundalini awakening may or may not bring about a deeper union with God, *for union with God is effected through love and surrender and not through consciousness awareness.* Love is a life stance, a decision that one must reaffirm until death settles the question forever.

7. *The view of the soul and its relation to the body and to God in Christian metaphysics is not held in the East.*

In Hinduism, for example, it is held that Brahman (the transcendent God) equals Atman (the immanent God). Catholics would agree that God's presence can be experi-

enced within the Soul, but would staunchly deny that the Soul is God. This distinction is important, for it helps to clarify the significance of kundalini in the spiritual life. It is one thing to say that kundalini is an energy of the Ground, or body-Soul union, and quite another to say that it is the Holy Spirit. Because Hindus do not recognize the existence of a Soul that is both one with God and a creation of God (not-God), they naturally conclude . . . that kundalini is really the same thing as the Christian experience of the Holy Spirit.[26]

8. *What we think about the nature of God's relation to the soul also affects our understanding of sin.*

It is the view of Hindu yogis that there is no sin for enlightened individuals. Given the Christian understanding of soul, awakening of kundalini does not in any way signal the end of our potential for sin.

9. *The Christian theological perspective is significantly different from that which informs Hindu literature.*

These religions (Judaism, Christianity, Islam) take a very different approach to salvation. Where Eastern religions begin with the human being reaching out to the divine, Western religions begin with the divine reaching out to humans. Eastern religions emphasize practices that transform the human to a divine being; Western religions emphasize divine grace as the transforming energy . . . . The East offers sophisticated spiritual "technologies," specifically designed to divinize the person; the West offers very little in the way of "how-to" spirituality, emphasizing instead faith and love. The East regards the Ego as an obstacle to the experience of God; the West sees grace working in and through the Ego to bring about transformation. The East holds that absolute non-duality is the highest level of consciousness; the West seldom drifts far from duality in its descriptions of relationship with the divine. Given these and many other differences between Eastern and Western religions, it is obvious that the metaphysics and spiritualities of these two great traditions should also differ.

There is nothing in Christian teaching comparable to the Hindu notions of chakras, astral body, and kundalini energy. Neither will one find in Christianity anything like the spiritualities associated with the yoga system, which are designed to lead one up through the various centers to the experience of union. Nevertheless, the chakras, the astral body, and the awakening of kundalini are experiences that can be identified in the experiences of many, many Christian mystics. In contrast to the East, however, these experiences were not sought as means to union; they were experienced as a consequence of prayer.[27]

Conclusion

St. Romain's last statement—that these experiences came as a consequence of prayer—serves as an appropriate introduction to our next chapter. His willingness to describe the kundalini process as experienced by a Christian is sure to be appreciated by spiritual directors, since this energy can arise through the practice of ordinary Christian prayer forms.

Some knowledge of these terms and the experiences behind them also provides an insight into the origins of yoga. The *asanas* are said to have originated as spontaneous postures often accompanying the awakening of kundalini. The origin of the various *asanas* practiced in hatha yoga are thought to be derived from observation of these spontaneous *asanas* produced during the early phases of kundalini awakening. Practitioners sought to reduce the pockets of resistance to be encountered in the much-hoped-for event of a kundalini awakening by consciously and deliberately practicing these poses. One sought, in this way, to lovingly prepare the body to receive its new and precious energies.[28]

One cannot fail to be impressed in all of this exploration and discernment with the holistic nature of the process of spiritual transformation. It is only logical that the experience of growing intimacy with God, who is a real Being emanating real energies, is going to impact us physiologically, psychologically, and spiritually. "For the contemplative, kundalini is the psycho-physiological consequence of a spiritual union with God," writes St. Romain. "In a spiritual context, the purpose of kundalini can be viewed in terms of opening the person to a deeper experience of union with God."[29]

The nature of yoga as a bridge experience, a unitive exercise, is clearer than ever. It seeks to effect an alignment of the forces residing in body and soul. Asceticism, that process of "artful shaping" in the spiritual life, means extinguishing neither the appetites of the flesh nor the desires of the mind. It means restoring the balance between the different dimensions of our being. To set in order is not to destroy; it is to discipline, to govern our various appetites, to foster our holistic well-being. In all this there is no magic, but simply a setting into action of the means placed in us by the wisdom of the Creator. By becoming more balanced in body, mind and spirit, one becomes more receptive to God as well as more able to shoulder one's responsibilities in Christian life. Grace (the Holy Spirit) brings nature to fulfillment, turning the harmony thus established to marvelous account.

15

How Yoga Can Help a Christian Pray

The test of any individual and any culture is how deeply and well it attunes itself to the highest influence it knows. Nothing less than such attunement will draw out of us that which lies dormant within awaiting fulfillment. Until we are tuned in to a larger reality, we are like a television set sitting in a corner of the room with a blank screen. If it is to produce pictures, it has to be tuned in to power and light. By itself it doesn't make pictures, sound, or anything else; neither do we unless we are plugged in to our power source. When we are attuned, then we can act as transformers of the energy that comes through us.

Or, to vary the image slightly, attunement to God is like looking for the FM classical music station on your radio. There are often pop rock or country and western stations that come in easily and drown out the others; finding the signal you want and getting a strong, clear sound may require some fine tuning and the closing of windows to reduce other external, competing noises. The signals are in the air. It's essentially a question of attunement. The spiritual life is similar: to align with the Holy Spirit within requires a fine tuning dial and a readiness to make our inner dwelling quiet, especially if we're just beginning to cultivate a taste for this kind of music.[1]

Attunement doesn't involve competing for God's attention,

as though God were a great switchboard operator in the sky who is very busy attending to many people and who can only plug us in periodically for the briefest of communications. The Divine One whom we seek is within us and around us. It is not even strorg enough to say that God lives in the very depths of our being. God *is* the depth of our being, our true Self. That is the great mystery at the heart of our existence. The more we tune in to this profound reality, the more we realize the truth that we are unique and special persons with a particular contribution to make in establishing the reign of God in the world. Our hearts begin to open up as we cooperate in the process of letting a larger power of love do its work in us. As we begin to experience our communion with God, we become aware as well of an increase of joy and serenity in our lives. All of us have this capacity, this "mystical heart," enabling us to live with a sustained awareness of the Divine Presence present to us. We were made for communion.

How do we become attuned? We have a vital role to play. We don't wait passively for God to do all the work. We send some signals that show we want to be attuned. We dispose ourselves. We demonstrate our willingness. That is what the disciplines of the spiritual life are all about. When you get down to them in practice, they work through our makeup as enfleshed spirits, attuning both our material and spiritual elements to the signals emanating from the indwelling Holy Spirit. Like the Incarnation, they are scandalously concrete. They seek to empty us of all we cling to that is not God, to make us open and receptive to the Spirit's transforming touch.

Of course, none of our efforts is essential to God's graced presence. That presence exists apart from our efforts. However, these methods help us to notice rather than miss the grace at hand and to allow that grace to work in us in our ongoing way of life. University professor and yoga teacher Carolyn Cronk witnesses to what yoga has meant for her:

From the very beginning of my yoga practice, it has been a means for quieting and centering my being, for letting go, at least for the time of my practice, of that which is not of the essence. It is in that focused state of being, leaving aside the rush of doing that is otherwise so much a part of my life, that I find myself most in contact with the divine. Over time, and with repeated practice to remind me of what that space feels like, yoga has helped me learn to move more naturally into setting aside all else, however briefly, to experience the presence of God. The Protestant church tradition in which I grew up has so few models of meditation or a contemplative path. Yoga's concept of focused quietness, as a source of energy for world-changing action was quite a revelation to me.

The yogic accent on having a certain quality of being as the source of action has much to show the Christian about the appropriate attitude toward grace. So much more of the kingdom of God can be actualized in our lives by being open to the flow of grace than by straining after specific results. In the physical movements of yoga, the flow from one position to another is just as important as the final posture itself. There is much emphasis on letting the movement be carried by the breath, in contrast to effortful striving. To see the breath of life as an expression of the action of the Holy Spirit sets even the most ordinary of movements in a whole new light, emphasizing the power of grace when our lives resonate in harmony with it.

The aim is to bring our whole selves into harmony with God's designs for us so that we can increasingly experience a vision and power beyond ourselves. The author of *The Practice of the Presence of God* complained often of our blindness, constantly crying out that we are to be pitied for our willingness to be satisfied with so little. "God," he says, "has infinite treasures to give us and still we are satisfied with a brief passing moment of piety . . . . By our blindness we restrain the hand of God and so stop the flow of the abundance of His graces. But when He finds a soul imbued with a living faith, He pours into it His graces in abundance."[2] The gift of our calling is, in the words of Maximus the Confessor, "to be by grace everything that Christ is by nature."

The Function of the Postures

How can yoga make a contribution to what we are able to do by our human efforts for attunement? How can yoga help a Christian open to the Mystery?

The goal of yoga is to center us, to ground us, to sensitize us, to make us present, to make us all here, now. It quiets the body as the environment of the mind, and then empties the mind and makes of it a blank page. In this state of focused awareness, one is not aiming at a deeper understanding of a truth, but at a direct, intuitive experience of the Presence at the center of our being. Thus techniques, which bring the body and mind to a quietude where we can tune in to this Presence, have an appreciable place. They bring us to a point of openness and surrender to God so that God can do the work of healing and "oneing" in us.

What I am really doing is recollecting myself in the true sense of the word: gathering myself together, possessing myself, bringing myself under control so as to hand myself over to God. One creates an atmosphere of calm, peace, and silence without and within, establishing a harmony between body and spirit so that nothing hinders the working of grace, the Holy Spirit. The aim is to bring tranquillity to one's whole being; to render the body a faithful servant; to free the mind from anxieties and problems; and to render it available to the Spirit.[3] Given the seamless unity of the human person and God's incarnational embrace of our totality, one's spiritual life cannot help but be affected by exercises in which body and soul are in possession of each other and work together. As the various complex elements in us become more harmonious, we unfold and expand like the petals of a flower under ideal conditions of moisture and sunshine.

Pat O'Rourke is a patient representative at a large urban

hospital. Her job is highly stressful; she talks about yoga's contribution to her prayer life.

For me, yoga and prayer are inextricably linked. When I perform the various asanas (postures), I am praying with my body. These series of physical exercises help me to achieve a sense of stillness and peace in which prayer becomes easier and the nagging worries of the day seem less urgent. Yoga has helped me to feel centered and grounded, not only when I do the exercises, but, increasingly, in all of my life. It helps to quiet my over-active mind and has led me to be more receptive to other people and to God. After a stressful day at work, I have often arrived at a yoga session feeling unraveled. The postures of yoga help me to knit body and spirit together. At the end of many yoga classes I have been overcome with a profound sense of awe, gratitude and adoration. The transcendent God seems somehow closer.

Yoga is unlike any other kind of physical exercise and is no more like gymnastics than Holy Communion is like eating breakfast. For that reason, a yoga class in a noisy YMCA would be, for me, a blasphemy. Yoga is, in a sense, part of my sacramental life because it gives physical expression to my deep sense of connectedness to God. When I do yoga I feel, as the psalmist says, like a child resting in its mother's arms.

It is precisely because yoga is a spiritual practice that I have always taken seriously those Christian leaders who warn of its dangers. Yoga is a technique that can help prayer, but Christian prayer is never merely a technique to achieve a state of transcendence. However, I am grateful that something as ordinary as a set of exercises can leave me feeling so peaceful and joyous. Although grace is a gift that no method can manufacture, I feel that yoga disposes me to pray more tranquilly and to be open to whatever gifts God may wish to give me.

The surprise is always that "something as ordinary as a set of exercises" has such an amazing ability to alleviate stress and dispel our scatteredness. All the masters of prayer dwell much on the importance of preventing the mind from moving away from God once it has been focused there, preventing it from engaging with the distractions which present themselves. But insufficient attention is given to how one arrives at such a state of self-possessed calm and control. The basic postures of yoga and simple breath control exercises offer themselves as an answer—not the only answer, but one that certain people will find very helpful. When one teaches them, one almost expects to hear "Is that all there is to it?" They are, like the Incarnation, scandalously "ordinary." People should not simply take my or anyone's word for it, but try them over a period of time and judge for themselves.

Yoga helps us to pray by getting at the major difficulty in prayer: the wandering mind, which shows up in the restless body. By focusing the mind, the body becomes calm and quiet.

How Is Yoga Different from Other Forms of Exercise?

The *asanas*—sometimes referred to as exercises because in order to attain them a certain amount of effort and motion are necessary—are those postures which directly engage and benefit our bodily self. Referring to the stretching exercises as poses or postures emphasizes that these movements are done very slowly. That is one of the salient differences between the poses and our idea of physical exercise. Aerobic exercise is not one of the benefits that yoga provides, so you may want to alternate your yoga practice with other activities like swimming, biking, and jogging, bringing to them the same awareness of the body-spirit connection that marks your yoga sessions.

Approach your yoga period as an oasis in which you will relax and enjoy each movement, taking your time without any sense of hurry. There is a minimum of motion involved, and everything is done at a slow tempo. There is no forcing or bouncing; the movements are carried out gently, with the grace and control of a dancer. The poses don't have to be hard to do in order to be of benefit. Many are simple enough for anyone to assimilate comfortably; others, while difficult at first, soon respond to patient application. Andre Van Lysebeth was a pioneer among yoga experts in the West. This, to his mind, is the best definition of an *asana* that he had yet found: "an *asana* represents a position in which one can keep still for a long time without effort."[4]

One pays attention to the areas being stretched, holding the posture to one's point of natural toleration. If it hurts, ease off. One is usually much looser toward the end of the day than at the beginning. The point is to pay attention to this and to stretch accordingly, not according to some idea of what you should be able to do. The key words are "slow" and "steady." The emphasis is upon pressure applied to certain organs, glands and muscles rather than on movement. When movement is necessary, it is gentle and graceful. Therefore, people of any age can do it.

The secret of suppleness is quite simple: relaxed muscles lengthen as the result of slow and progressive traction. To stretch muscles after relaxing them is one of the key points regarding the *asanas*. That is why this form of exercise produces flexibility in the body more thoroughly and quickly than other forms which are designed to develop the muscular structure of the body through repeated contractions of the voluntary muscles. Muscle is easily stretched and can be extended within normal limits of elasticity. When these limits are reached, the muscle may still be further lengthened, but only slowly. A sharp pull on a muscle which is not relaxed may injure it, but slow, continuous and progressive stretching of a relaxed muscle is completely safe. The effect is beneficial: blood is squeezed out, and as soon as the activity ceases, the muscle returns to its normal size and takes in fresh blood which serves to bathe, cleanse and nourish it.[5] Relaxed muscles are the most amenable to stretching.

It is not necessary to be regularly learning new, more advanced positions. Centuries of experimentation evolved a catalog of eighty-four postures, but most manuals indicate that only about a dozen of these are especially useful. Therefore, it is enough just to hold longer the basic ones which cover the different muscle groups and massage the various internal organs and glands. This is not an aerobic workout in the sense of getting one's heartbeat to accelerate and holding it there for fifteen or twenty minutes. *The time relaxing between the poses is as important as the stretches themselves. The goal is restoration of equilibrium in the forces of contraction / relaxation.* They are like the back and forth swing of a pendulum: both have an integral part to play.

The application to meditation is readily apparent. For example, if one comes to meditate but the body and mind are not prepared and the energies are not balanced, there is inner conflict. The mind resists because it is unable to concentrate, or the body suffers because it is not accustomed to holding one position for an extended period of time. The image of yoga as a bridge is once again pertinent: it unites the two shores (body and mind) in one embrace, allowing an easy flow of energy or traffic from one side to the other and back again. If one has been practicing certain recommended postures and using a simple technique to regulate breathing, there will be fewer mental distractions and difficulties coming from the body. The postures stimulate the glands and increase the flow of blood to all organs. They also loosen the muscles and joints, releasing tension from and giving greater flexibility to the body.

This synergistic interplay between the body and mind evokes a second way in which yoga is different from a physical workout: yoga combines the mental with the physical. Its exercises produce a mental freedom from preoccupying thoughts, and induce relaxation. In effect, body control leads to mind control. The main purpose of the postures is to gain bodily poise and mental tranquillity so that the mind can enter into contemplation.[6]

In its original inspiration and practice, yoga is thoroughly integrative. If you practice only yoga postures, you have but a form of physical exercise. If you devote yourself only to controlled breathing, you are engaging in a simple but effective form of stress management and concentration. If you repeat your sacred word or mantra at various intervals throughout the day, you will be recalling the presence of God. The distinctive contribution of yoga is that it puts all three together in order to facilitate an experience of God. When body, mind and spirit are harmonized, the Mystery residing in our deep being comes through more clearly.[7]

How the Postures Work

Most forms of physical exercise are characterized by intensive, prolonged movements of the muscles, e.g. running, rowing, swimming, cycling, aerobics. These prolonged muscle movements produce large quantities of lactic acid in the muscle fibers, thus causing fatigue. The effect of this acid and the fatigue it causes is neutralized by the alkali in the muscle fibers, as well as by the inhaling of oxygen. Fatigue is the result of the muscle's inability to get enough oxygen to oxidize a sufficient amount of the lactic acid formed. When too much lactic acid accumulates, the muscles become temporarily unable to contract. Most athletes have experienced the resulting cramping and soreness.

During prolonged, strenuous exercise, we are unable to breathe in sufficient oxygen to meet muscular demands. An oxygen debt is created. This debt is the difference between the amount actually needed by the active muscles and what is actually received. Thus, even after stopping, we continue to breathe more deeply and faster than we ordinarily do; the lungs are working to pay off the debt. There is a limit to the size of the oxygen debt that an individual can incur. This is where yoga emphasizes moderate, slow-motion exercise.[8] In moderate exercise the oxygen supply can keep pace with the oxygen used and no oxygen debt results. Deep breathing during the poses allows for more oxygen absorption. Less lactic acid is produced and, as this is easily neutralized by the alkali and dispersed with the gentle and steady stretching, no muscle fatigue results.

Owing to twisting and other movements of various joints, blood vessels are pulled and stretched and blood is equally distributed to every part of the body. The stretched muscles and ligaments are immediately relaxed, carrying more energy to the muscle fibers. As water flows through an open tap, so energy flows into the relaxed muscles. All the exercises of yoga are based on the formula of stretching, relaxation, deep breathing, concentration, and increasing blood circulation.[9]

When the bloodstream in the arteries is not circulating effectively, the vitality of every cell in the body is diminished. Each cell in the body is ready to serve us to its utmost, but it relies for its supply of oxygen on that magic liquid, the blood. Proper circulation, indispensable for carrying oxygen to cells and food particles from digestive organs to tissues, is a matter of correct breathing and strong muscles, since the heart itself is basically a giant muscle constantly at work. Deep, slow breathing is a powerful driving force in circulation. The heart is the pump propelling the blood into the arterial network, while the lungs act as a suction pump on the venous circulation. Circulation depends upon the interaction of these two driving forces. Unimpeded circulation is the finest tonic of all for the heart.[10]

All the postures which have an effect on the diaphragm help massage the heart at the same time as they massage the abdominal organs. They achieve this by subjecting the heart to alternate pressures. Improved circulation and digestion directly affect the health of the nerves, from which we begin to see that this effect is more than a purely physical one.[11] A better supply of blood to the brain inevitably results in overall alertness—a key ingredient for making a period of prayer prayerful—and a revitalization of one's mental faculties. A person's whole outlook is therefore affected by what in the beginning looks like no more than a series of physical exercises. There is nothing mysterious, mystical or mythological about the claim that the yoga exercises have a direct bearing on the human mind and spirit.

Breath as a Bridge Between Body and Mind

Because the relationship between breath and life itself is so intimate, our way of breathing has a profound effect on the quality of our lives. Yet, how many of us are aware of our manner of breathing at any given moment, or of how it is affecting our body, mind and emotions? The act of breathing, for most of us, is an automatic process which we take completely for granted.

Consider these facts of human existence:

Changes in your body affect your breathing. When you exercise, your oxygen requirements increase, and you breathe faster and more deeply.

Changes in your mind affect your breathing. When you are in a crisis situation and feeling anxious, your breathing is rapid and shallow. When you are asleep or relaxed, you breathe more slowly and deeply.

Changes in your breathing affect your body. When basketball players are at the free throw line, they first take a deep breath before shooting. Their muscles know what to do from thousands of free throws in practice; a deep breath helps them to relax and let the muscle memory take over and perform. Singers practice deep diaphragm breathing to improve the strength and quality of their voices.

Changes in your breathing affect your mind. When you are driving late at night and feeling drowsy, several deep breaths can make you more alert at the wheel. When you are feeling worried, a few deep breaths help to calm you down.[12]

Our breathing pattern is like a weather ball that sits outdoors and changes color with the temperature. It reflects changes going on in our bodies and minds. But the simile stops there, for if someone intervenes and intentionally changes the color of the ball, it won't affect the weather, whereas deliberately changing our breathing patterns will affect our bodies and our minds.

There is a system of nerves which provides a direct connection between the brain and the heart. These nerves, called the sympathetic nervous system, stimulate receptors in the heart that make it beat faster or slower. Breathing techniques decrease sympathetic nervous system stimulation and thus produce a calming effect on the mind and the body.[13] In the tradition of yoga, the subtle effects of the breath on the mind and body have been the object of study for thousands of years.

Basic to all yoga is *prana* (pronounced "prah-na"), the life force. Essential to life, it is found in every living thing from the most elementary form of plant life to the most complex form of animal life. It is in matter, but it is not matter. It is in the air, but it is not air. It is inhaled along with oxygen, but it is not oxygen. Too subtle to be graphically pinpointed, *prana* has an abstract quality comparable to what is termed "the soul." Perhaps the closest we can come to the conception of *prana* is vital energy or vitality. In our daily language we make frequent reference to "our energy level." Some days it is high, and other days low. Though we can't measure this energy level with our scientific equipment, we know the reality of it in our experience. This vital force is what yoga texts refer to as *prana* which, in Sanskrit, similar to the Hebrew *ruach*, Greek *pneuma*, and Latin *spiritus*, means both breath and spirit. Breath is the vehicle for *prana*.

Prana is distributed through the body by *pranayama* (literally, "control of *prana*") or yoga breathing exercises. Its particular contribution is to provide more vital energy to the body, revitalize the nervous system, and oxygenate the brain.

When sufficient prana is distributed throughout the body, the mind moves more easily toward one-pointed concentration.

In a single day we breathe about 23,000 times. The average volume of air taken in with a single breath is about twenty cubic inches, allowing for some variations due to a person's size, posture, the nature of the surrounding environment and one's physical and emotional state. However, with proper attention given to breathing, this volume may be increased to 100 cubic inches per breath. In other words, learning good breathing habits can provide you with five times the amount of oxygen, and rid you of five times the amount of carbon dioxide which which you habitually function. If you take the time to watch your manner of breathing and train yourself to breathe more slowly and deeply, the new rhythm will become automatic. From about fifteen breaths a minute you may reduce your tempo by possibly three breaths a minute, which is twenty percent, or 4,320 per day. Such a slowing down means less work for the heart, lower blood pressure, a relaxation of body tensions, and quieter nerves.[14]

The foresight of the yogis who, thousands of years ago, established the rules and methods of ideal breathing is remarkable. They advised us to breathe as though at our birth we had been allotted a certain number of respirations, and as though our lives would last until this capital number of respirations came to an end. Today we can only confirm their insight that to breathe deeply and slowly is to live longer and enjoy better health.

Before we go to some brief exercises which will allow you to see for yourself the different levels of your breathing capacity, it may be helpful to review a little physiology. The trunk is divided into two portions, the thoracic cavity and the abdominal cavity. The thoracic cavity is occupied mainly by the lungs and the heart and is bounded by the spinal column, the ribs, the breast bone, and at the bottom of the lungs by the diaphragm. The diaphragm is the muscular partition that separates the thoracic cavity from the abdominal cavity. The science of *pranayama* starts with the proper control of the diaphragm and respiratory muscles which will bring about the maximum degree of lung expansion in order to absorb the greatest amount of life-giving energy from the air.[15]

Now, perform the following experiments with your respiratory system.

Experiment No. 1: Sit erect by keeping your spine, neck, and head in a straight line. You are going to count the number of seconds while you inhale. Now take a long, deep breath from your diaphragm area without raising your chest or shoulders. Breathe in this manner several times, counting the number of seconds it takes you to fill your lungs each time.

Experiment No. 2: This time, keep your diaphragm still and do not allow your abdomen to expand. Now expand the chest and take a long deep breath, counting the seconds it takes to breathe in. Here the breathing is done through the actions of the respiratory (intercostal) muscles of the ribs which partially expand the lungs. If you want to differentiate more clearly between these two manners of breathing, repeat the experiments alternately, letting yourself experience which way brings more air into the lungs.

Experiment No. 3: Sitting erect as for the previous two experiments, contract your abdomen and draw it toward your thoracic cavity. Now take a deep breath by raising the shoulders and collar bones while the abdomen is contracted. Count the seconds. Repeat it several times and then compare it with your first two experiment results.

The No. 1 breathing is known as deep breathing; No. 2 as chest breathing; and No. 3 as high breathing. These simple experiments demonstrate that No. 1 brings more air than No. 2 and No. 3—and with less effort. No. 2 is inferior to No. 1 but better than No. 3. Many people regularly breathe from their chest and some even rely upon "high breathing." Chest breathing is usually rapid, shallow, and irregular. When the diaphragm is used in deep breathing, it presses upon the abdominal organs and forces out the abdomen. The lungs are given a freer play in this type of breathing and the lower lobes, which receive the greatest amount of blood flow, are more effectively oxygenated.

Here is a simple way to determine whether you breathe from your chest or your diaphragm. Once again, sit erect. Place your right hand on your chest and your left hand on your abdomen. Inhale. If your right hand rises more than your left hand, you are breathing from your chest. If your left hand rises more than your right hand, you are breathing from your diaphragm.

Abdominable breathing is the best of the three methods. Yet any one of these breathing methods fills only a portion of the lungs—deep breathing fills the lower and middle parts, chest breathing the middle and a portion of the upper regions, and high breathing the upper portions of the lungs. In yoga, the first lesson is to use all three methods of breathing simultaneously, starting with low breathing and continuing to chest breathing and finally finishing with high breathing.[16] In this type of inhalation process, the whole respiratory system comes into play and no portion of the lungs is left unfilled with fresh air.

The wonderful thing about deep breathing is that you can do it anywhere, anytime: at work, while walking, relaxing. Breathe consciously and easily, without straining. Remember that the ideal respiration is deep, slow, silent, easy. It becomes more effective and natural with practice. It is one of the most beneficial stress management techniques there is. Even when you can't control the situation, you can always control your breathing and thus help to change your reaction to the circumstances which are upsetting you. Once you can maintain a relaxed breathing pattern when you are angry or tense, you are breaking a chain reaction. When you feel tired, depressed or discouraged, do a few breathing exercises to help restore your mental balance and to help you turn to the tasks at hand with renewed will.

Take advantage of those odd or idle moments in your day while you are waiting for a red light to turn green behind the wheel or standing at an intersection; while waiting for an appointment or a meeting to begin; or in the interval that naturally takes place as one goes from one task to another. Harness your mind to your breathing and let your breath bring you back to the present moment. As you are able to catch those moments and live them fully, you will begin to notice a qualitative difference in your day. Instead of losing those moments fidgeting or getting impatient or anxious, those moments become connectors that tie your life together. They are like little oases, quality rest stops.

The simplest way to still the waters of an agitated mind and body is to pay attention to your breathing. Allow the breath to slow down. Rapid, shallow breathing usually reflects and reinforces tension. It generates rapid, panicky thinking to match the breathing. The mind is by nature unsteady and is at every moment being affected by sight, sound, and other external objects which it perceives through the agency of the senses. How can the deeper Spirit get through all this surface disturbance?

Attention to breath is a vital part of yoga practice. Inhalation and exhalation not only keep us in life, but symbolize the pattern of Christian living—of giving and receiving, of emptying and filling, of death and resurrection. Relaxation is a matter of breathing into the stretch and breathing out our tension. Meditation begins with attention to breathing, which becomes ever more gentle and quiet as we relax into God's presence.[17]

Beneath the surface world of flux with its constantly changing sensations, thoughts and feelings lies a deeper and different form of consciousness. Here the permanent Self resides with its own rhythms and perspectives. Awareness of the breath gives access to this Self. The medieval mystic Tauler calls the place "the ground of the soul"; Meister Eckhart calls it "the little castle"; for Teresa of Avila it is "the inner castle," for John of the Cross it is "the interior home of the heart."

It is the place where the human spirit touches the presence of God.[18]

Our breathing is the physical manifestation of our spirit, that place in our being that touches the Divine Spirit. Thus, our physical breath is an appropriate symbol for our spirit and God's Spirit. It enlivens, purifies and pacifies us. Breath is a symbol of life in Scripture from Genesis (God breathes life into Adam: Gen. 2:7) to Revelation ("the breath of life from God entered them and they stood on their feet," Rev. 11:11). It even becomes a symbol of God's life. When Jesus appears to his disciples on the evening of the day of his resurrection, "he breathed on them, and said to them, 'Receive the Holy Spirit' (Jn. 20:22).

John of the Cross wrote in his *Spiritual Canticle*:

The breathing of the air is properly of the Holy Spirit, for which the soul here prays, so that she may love God perfectly. She calls it the breathing of the air, because it is in a most delicate touch and feeling of love which habitually in this state is caused in the soul by the communion of the Holy Spirit. Breathing with His Divine Breath, He raises the soul most sublimely, and informs her that she may breathe in God the same breath of love that the Father breathes in the Son, and the Son in the Father, which is the same Holy Spirit that they breathe into her in the said transformation. And this is for the soul so high a glory, and so profound and sublime a delight, that it cannot be described by mortal tongue, nor can human understanding, as such, attain to any conception of it.[19]

Yoga and Meditation Working Together

One final experiment will serve to show why yoga prescribes various breathing exercises to get control over the mind. If you have a clock in your house that ticks, go and sit about fifteen feet from it. (If you have no ticking clock, then open your faucet just enough so that it begins to drip regularly.) Now concentrate on the ticks or drips, keeping all other thoughts from your mind. Stay at it until you are able to keep the mind free from distraction, for at least twenty seconds or so.

Most people will have nearly suspended their breath while concentrating on the ticking or dripping. Nearly everyone will have had very slow breathing.

The point is that where there is concentration of the mind, the breathing becomes very slow. This kind of focused, one-pointed concentration is called for in meditation. Learning to slow down your breathing makes it easier to concentrate and therefore to pray. One's breathing in meditation is slow and deep. Furthermore, the suspension of conscious mental activity increases in proportion to the slowness of breath. This suspension of thinking is also called for in meditation.

The breath is a bridge between your body and your mind. Mind, body and breath are interdependent, each unable to act independently of one another. The focused concentration of meditation helps take your breathing to a deep, slow, rhythmical plane. And breathing exercises also serve to prepare you for meditation by slowing down your breathing and engaging deep breathing.

The most common of these *pranayama* exercises are described in detail in Appendix I as a preamble to the illustrations of certain basic postures. This chapter primarily serves to heighten appreciation for the positive contribution that the postures and proper breathing can make to the experience of meditation. The point is simply this: while each of these yoga methods is powerful by itself, combining all of them in their original context has an effect even greater than the sum of their parts. That's because these techniques were designed for something much greater: to be tools for transformation.

When the breath is under control, the nervous system coordinated, the glands stimulated and functioning properly, the mind focused and the body comfortably positioned, one is primed for meditation. The automatic bodily functions have come to a low ebb: the heart rate and breathing rate fall and the digestive process slows.

At the same time, the brain is stimulated beyond normal, resulting in a heightened awareness. The body is relaxed, the mind calm, quiet, and alert. This is yoga's contribution to prayer: to effect coherence among the forms of vital energy by making them the foundation, the "climate" for our coming to know and experience our true nature and calling.

As often as I am able during the week, I come home early enough to do a half hour of yoga before my evening meditation. My mind, revved up by the day's activity, is bouncing ideas and thoughts around like balls in a squash court. In order to slow down the activity of the mind, I use my breath as an anchor for my awareness even to the point of mentally "noting" each inhalation with the note "in" and each exhalation with the note "out." When I become aware that I am thinking or remembering, I note "thinking" or "remembering" and let go of it, returning my attention to my breathing.

While continuing to use my breath as a stable "anchor" for awareness, I begin to allow my awareness to go out and "track" the sensations arising in my body as I enter into a stretch. I focus my attention on what is going on in my body in that posture, watching it for a few moments, and then bringing my attention back to my anchor, the breath. While holding the pose, I focus on my breathing and relax into the stretch. Awareness, which was scattered and fragmented minutes earlier, is being taken firmly in hand and directed like a laser beam, first to the breath, then to sensations arising in the body, then back to the breath, and so on.

It is not difficult to see how, after thirty minutes of this one-pointed directing of awareness, one's whole being is primed for relaxed, alert attentiveness in meditation. The constant letting go of thoughts, memories, and feelings clears out the mental debris and establishes an inner environment of emptiness, receptivity, and poverty of spirit. It is less a concentration of mental faculties than a turning of one's whole being toward Another.

There is no comparing the quality of inner silence, stillness, and openness that I experience in meditation on "yoga days" with those other days when I come home and go right to meditation without the benefit of some breathing exercises and some postures. On the days when meditation is preceded by yoga, there is a greater feeling of being truly re-collected, gathered together, and presenting myself to the Lord, saying, "Here I am, Lord. Do your work."

16

Holistic Benefits

To this point we have dealt with yoga at the level of its original and highest goal, clearly expressed by a leader of the modern yogic renaissance, Swami Satyananda Saraswati: "It is true that *asanas* are practiced for the cultivation of better health, physical beauty, body flexibility and so on, but *asanas* and *pranayama* were originally developed with the intention of providing a perfect means of preparing the body and mind for meditation."[1]

That being said, let these other benefits be given their just due. Researchers began discovering in the mid-1970s how effective stress management techniques and a low-fat vegetarian diet could be. Studies in Boston, New York, California, England, and in other parts of the world were proving, for example, that meditation can lower blood pressure, decrease the frequency of irregular heart rhythms, reduce cholesterol levels, and so on.

In his book *Program for Reversing Heart Disease*, an internationally acclaimed scientific study, funded in part by the U.S. National Institutes of Health and based on thirteen years of research, Dr. Dean Ornish observes that "almost all of these techniques ultimately derive from yoga. It's a testimony to the power of these techniques that entire careers have been built around different aspects of yoga, sometimes even renamed after the person who rediscovered that practice."[2]

He gives several examples: Dr. Edmund Jacobson, a

Harvard physiologist, rediscovered the benefits of deep relaxation and renamed it "Jacobson Progressive Relaxation." Dr. Herbert Benson, a well-known cardiologist at the Harvard Medical School, has spent the past two decades conducting pioneering research on the beneficial effects of meditation. He found that regular elicitation of the relaxation response can lower blood pressure, inhibit gastric acid secretion, and produce other positive benefits. John Kabat-Zinn, Ph.D., director of the Stress Reduction Clinic at the University of Masachusetts Medical School, has found similar results in using yoga techniques with his patients. Carl Simonton, M.D., a radiation oncologist, and Stephanie Matthews Simonton studied and popularized the importance of visualization and imagery as adjunct therapies in treating cancer. Millions of women have used Lamaze breathing techniques as powerful aids in childbirth. Athletes have found that slow, gentle stretching reduces the risk of injuries, and many are finding that use of visualization, imagery, and meditation improve athletic performance. All these techniques originate from yoga.[3]

Bill Moyers brought meditation and yoga to the attention of mainstream America in 1992 with his public broadcasting series on "The Body-Mind Connection," in which long segments were devoted to the beneficial effects of both practices.

Even airline journals are promulgating the good news. An article in one flight magazine,[4] aimed at the harried traveler trying to cover too many bases, worked off a foundational principle of meditation: one-pointed attention. The writer ascribed a fancy name—polyphasic activity—to the modern penchant for trying to do two or more things at the same time. The difficulty with polyphasic activity is that it becomes habit-forming. Once you accustom yourself to trying to respond to two or more sources of stimulation at once, you feel uncomfortable doing just one thing at a time and are no longer able to become absorbed in and enjoy just one activity. You are distracted by problems and irrelevant issues due to the ingrained habit of constantly splitting your attention. Busy men and women are caught in the fundamental clash between healthy living and the technology—modular phones, portable TVs, fax machines—that is invading our lives and leaving us with little or no tranquil time and private space.

The author offered several antidotes; he may have had meditation or yoga in mind:

1. Find a pleasant activity that you truly enjoy, and practice it when you are least likely to be interrupted by the telephone, the children, or a beeper. Be careful not to do more than one thing so that you can relearn how to relax.

2. Redress your work-produced mental and emotional fatigue at the end of the day by doing something physical. Using energy in a pleasant, physical activity generates even more energy.

3. Opt for a slower pace. Spend time in leisure activities that have no demands, no goals, and no need to get anything done.

4. Choose simpler and more basic experiences. Simpler activities are more fulfilling and they keep you in touch with deeper parts of yourself.

5. Disconnect on a regular basis. Pull the plug on the telephone, television, beeper, home computer, and turn the modular telephone to "off." Then relax and enjoy the silence.

The clincher: "Living well lies not in new and better technology, but in the selective use of it so that life can be enjoyed in a simpler and more emotionally fulfilling way. Learn to balance your lifestyle between technological marvels and the satisfaction of inner peace and contentment."[5]

All of the above describe in some way what those who meditate and practice yoga regularly do. The benefits for body, mind, and spirit are very real. Hatha yoga is more than just a collection of stretching and breathing techniques. It is a whole system of physical culture which seeks to begin rebalancing the opposing forces within ourselves so that we might experience the equilibrium, peace and deep unity that underlie these dualities. People begin praticing yoga for many different reasons, but what they report of their experience usually contains elements of the physical, mental, and spiritual. The testimony of Chris Witt, a university campus chaplain, is a good example:

When I first started practicing yoga over four years ago, I was looking for an alternative form of exercise. I had been addicted to running since my college days, some fifteen years earlier. Although I relished the runner's high a good long run often gave me, the ache in my joints— first in my ankles, then in my knees—became more and more debilitating. I hoped yoga would allow me to exercise without harming a body creeping reluctantly toward middle age.

My first yoga class, on a sweltering, humid evening in a church auditorium in Washington, D.C., was something of a revelation. Although I was so stiff that I couldn't approximate most of the asanas, *I instinctively knew I was on to something. What I was on to, I couldn't say until a couple of years later when I talked to one of my teachers about his first experience with yoga. He said it felt as if he had come home, and I knew what he was talking about.*

I now take classes three times a week, and I practice on my own once or twice more. I'm now able to sit in meditation without my back or my knees staging a mutiny. I'm more limber than I've been since I was a baby. My stress has become manageable, and I have an enviable resting heart rate. But as much as I appreciate all the benefits, they're not why I practice.

I practice yoga because while I practice yoga that's all I do. Normally it's hard for me simply to do what I'm doing while I'm doing it. I've learned to be efficient, to prize speed, and to work on several projects at one time. While I accomplish a lot, I also find it hard to slow my mind down, to be still, silent, and attentive. While I'm doing yoga—breathing exercises, asanas, *chanting, sitting—that's all I do, at least for brief moments. I'm present to the moment. I don't think pious thoughts. I don't work through pressing problems. I haven't seen or heard from God. I don't use yoga as a prelude to meditation.*

Yoga is a discipline for me, a discipline of presence. It is teaching me not to use one thing to accomplish another, not to be in one place in the hope of getting somewhere else, to be where I am when I am, to be still and know that God is God.

A holistic spirituality recognizes that, generally speaking, if some practice or other is good for my body, it is also good for my soul, and vice versa. There is only one "I" to which all benefits redound. Mental health and physical vitality, proper sleep and digestion all contribute to the fullness of life here and now to which Christ invites us: "I came that they may have life and have it abundantly" (Jn. 10:10). These, and many other other benefits, are part of the picture where yoga is concerned and warrant a very honorable mention even in such a brief and uncomprehensive treatment as this.

Mental Health. In yoga there is no boundary line between mental health and physical health. The body and the mind are intertwined. We are constantly being reminded of the relationship between the mind and the body when our emotions manifest themselves physically. Anger and excitement raise the blood pressure. Fear tenses the muscles and nervousness dries the mouth. Conversely, a person with a throbbing toothache will find it difficult to concentrate while reading. Within the human person, thoughts and emotions always produce a muscular reaction. The experience of yoga is that the mind can be stilled through muscular relaxation. Mental tension corresponds to muscular tension. Thought, movement, and feeling occur simultaneously. Yoga teaches one not only how to face tension but how to set it to work for one's benefit. Through the contractions and holding of postures, the body is tensed, then consciously relaxed, unblocking tensions. As tension is chased away, relaxation takes over.

Once one has learned the techniques, one can apply them anytime they're needed, whenever one is beset by a crisis or anxiety. One of yoga's greatest contributions to mental and physical health is preventive. Western techniques, such as drugs and surgery, can be very helpful in a crisis, but they are limited. Yoga represents a stress management technique that addresses the more fundamental issues that predispose us to illness. People break down or develop cancers as a result of stress. The tragedy that causes one person to jump off a bridge merely causes another to make adjustments in life. Two doctors at the Ohio State University College of Medicine recently found that medical students who practiced relaxation techniques during exams increased their levels of helper cells that defend against infectious diseases. Those who did the relaxation techniques (which were derived from yoga) the most regularly had the strongest immune effects.[6]

Yoga can assist a person to make adaptations to life rather than being overcome by its trials and tribulations. It helps quiet down the mind and body, thus enabling us to experience an inner sense of peace and joy. This is the state of being desired for us by God, but we disturb it. At the end of a half-hour of stretching, I am struck by the realization that the feeling of tranquillity didn't come from anywhere outside me, but from within. I did my part by acting to dissolve some of the physical and emotional stress that blocks awareness of the Source of peace within, and the rest is God's gift of graceful being.

Physical Flexibility. If you watch a dog or a cat when it awakens, you will see that it often stretches and contracts its spine. Flexibility of the spine is lost as the body grows. As we age, the backbone stiffens because the ligaments become tighter. The whole skeleton, which provides a framework of attachment for muscles, tendons, and ligaments, becomes less flexible. The flexibility of the spine lessens at thirty and continues to decline at forty, until at sixty and over, any bending may be difficult and painful. Yoga exercises are designed to keep the proper curvature of the spine and to increase its flexibility by stretching the anterior and posterior longitudinal ligaments. Ligamentous stiffening can be kept at a minimum through these exercises, and the body's pliability retained even at an advanced age.[7]

Most of us neglect flexibility of muscles, ligaments and tendons. Not stretching our muscles leads to a loss of mobility and injuries which could have been prevented. One of the key disabilities in the work force is low back pain. In many cases this is related directly to reduced flexibility of the hip and back, with reduced elasticity of the hamstrings and weak abdominal muscles. Everyone can learn to stretch. You don't need to be in top physical condition or even have athletic skill. The methods are gentle and easy (see Appendix III). Stretching can be done any time you feel like it: in the morning before the start of the day; at work to release nervous tension; after sitting or standing for a long time; when watching TV, listening to music, or even sitting and talking. It feels good!

Posture. Your muscles and ligaments move and hold your body, adjusting it in accordance with the laws of gravity without your even being aware of it. When you sit still, your spine, the central support of your body, has to hold the weights of the chest, arms, and head in line with the pelvis. If your posture is less than perfectly balanced, in a relatively short time the muscles will be reporting a strain from some quarter. Muscles are designed for movement; they should not have to take on the role of holding weights which are wrongly aligned with the force of gravity. Learning how to sit correctly, for example, is of utmost importance for meditation if you are not to be constantly distracted by aching back muscles.

The yoga exercises will improve posture in general by making you more sensitive to skeletal equilibrium.

Vitality. More than any other form of exercise, yoga releases energy without strain to the individual. Energy is the power that enables one to function at a high capacity without undue fatigue. Everyone has potential energy stored within the body which does not simply release itself but requires an expenditure of energy to make it available. Yoga stretching, postures, and breathing release this untapped energy, thereby increasing one's endurance and vigor.

It may seem incongruous that slow, gentle movements increase vitality; we've been brought up to think that any exercise that doesn't exhaust us isn't doing us any good. However, yoga is interested in efficiently using and conserving energy. One of the reasons why marathon runners develop muscle cramps is that the body has been given no period of respite in which to dissolve and absorb the acid buildup. In yoga exercises, one enters into total relaxation at regular intervals to allow this physiological process to take place and to enable the body to continue to perform at optimum level. Yoga exercises are designed to enable the body to produce more energy while retaining the supply it already has.

Ordinary exercise seldom has any direct bearing on the proper functioning of the endocrine and thyroid glands. Through the subtle effect of certain postures and movements, though, the normal healthy functioning of these glands is stimulated. As is the case with the kidneys, large intestine and colon, often the beneficial effect is obtained by some slight pressure, stretch or twist of the body which sets otherwise seldom-used tendons and sinews into play.

Most of us are aware of how tension drains our energy. Stretching and breathing away your tension releases the energy that has been pent up and immobilized by stress. With less tension we're better able to handle the annoyances and frustrations that beset all of us in our work and relationships with others. Using less energy to cope with these situations, we're conserving more energy for constructive action.

Improved Sleep. No one can be bursting with vitality without adequate sleep. And all too often it's hardest to get a good night's sleep when you need it most. There are times when the quality of a person's sleep is so poor that even after sleeping for hours, one wakes up feeling as tired as when one went to bed. The body and mind need a chance to unwind. When one is having difficulty finding the "off" switch to the mind at the end of a full day, some yoga postures and breathing exercises provide the necessary unwinding and send one back to bed relaxed and able to sleep. And when the quality of our sleep improves, we actually require less sleep.

Digestion. Many people are never at peace with their digestive system. While not exactly ill, they are continually plagued by chronic discomforts like constipation, flatulence, and heartburn which they sheepishly attribute to "something I ate." They falsely seek relief in symptom-masking pills. While diet plays the major role, exercise to stimulate and relax the digestive system is also helpful. Yoga exercises, especially the abdominal exercises, massage the inner organs and promote their healthy functioning without medications or laxatives.

The digestive organs—stomach, small intestine, pancreas and liver—depend for health in part at least on the proper functioning of the abdominal muscles, especially the diaphragm. For as the diaphragm rises and falls with breathing, the organs in the upper abdominal cavity receive a regular massage; but if breathing is shallow, the beneficial massage effect is minimal. Stomach acid is then secreted improperly and digestion suffers, resulting in minor disturbances such as gas or "acid stomach."[8]

While in India, I occasionally encountered spices or "tummy bugs" which resulted in a condition of gastritis. One morning in particular the intestinal discomfort was so bad I could hardly stand up straight when I got out of bed. I had plenty of antacid tablets with me, but I looked at them on the table and said, "No, tablets and pills will take hours before having any noticeable effect. I want immediate relief." I got down on the floor and proceeded to do a series of yoga exercises which effectively dispelled the painful buildup of gases and left me feeling quite normal again. Afterward, the thought came to me: suppose I didn't know anything about yoga. And suppose a friend had come by, found me in discomfort in bed and said, "Let me show you a few exercises that will help you feel much better in no time." After having experienced their immediate and positive effects, I would certainly want to know more about them!

Relaxation. Our minds and bodies function most efficiently when we are relaxed. For most of us, the duality of our muscles—contracting and relaxing—is out of balance, for our muscles are chronically tensed and contracted. The first step toward experiencing inner peace is to quiet down and relax the body. This is precisely the immediate aim of the yoga methods: to help calm your mind and quiet down your body, thus enabling you to experience an inner sense of relaxation, peace and inner harmony.

Through its related series of exercises for both body and mind, hatha yoga techniques are intended to rejuvenate and bring into proper balance all aspects of the body: endocrine system, vascular system, nervous system and musculature. With regular practice, the benefits will not be difficult to recognize: increased relaxation, normalized blood pressure, relief of minor back problems, and a steadied metabolism. When combined with deep breathing exercises and meditation, these practices also bring a sense of emotional calmness and mental peace.

Am I Too Old To Learn?

Yoga can be started at any age without strain. The slow gradual movements build up energy without depleting the existing supply of it. Never forcing, never straining, the body builds its endurance by stretching to its capacity, holding the stretch, and progressing to increased capacity. The breathing exercises, performed by themselves and in conjunction with the postures, increase the supply of oxygen to the blood, naturally stimulating the heart. Doctors have recommended yoga to combat the tension and stress at the root of so many heart disorders. The part that it plays in controlling weight and discouraging smoking and the consumption of alcohol adds to its benefits in keeping the heart healthy. Patricia, a health care professional in her mid-forties, shares how her yoga practice is helping her live more healthily:

> I went to my first yoga class almost three years ago. At that time, I felt tense, scattered and frequently very anxious. After several months I observed that, without any conscious intention on my part, I had begun to practice moderation in all aspects of my life. Never a very moderate person, I found that I forgot to drink coffee all afternoon. A heavy smoker, I reduced my consumption by half (yoga did not perform the miracle of making me quit altogether, but that will come). I found myself less anxious, more optimistic, less driven in my work and more efficient and effective. I found that I trusted God more and worried less.

One instructor with students in her classes in their sixties and seventies said that as a group they suffer less from the ailments that are so common among the elderly—discomforts like constipation, muscular stiffness, and low resistance to respiratory infections.[9]

My very first experience at leading a week-long meditation and yoga retreat quickly opened my eyes to age being no barrier. I expected to be greeted by a group largely made up of people in their thirties and forties. You can imagine my surprise when the retreat house director handed me the list of participants and I learned that fully half the group were in their mid-to upper fifties, 15 percent were in their sixties, another 15 percent in their seventies, and there were two people in their eighties! We had a wonderful week, with the two in their eighties providing daily inspiration for everyone else. At the end of the retreat, again to my surprise, it was the older members in the group who repeatedly expressed their appreciation for the holistic approach and the opportunity to engage their bodies as well as their minds.

On the lower end of the age scale, yoga attacks the problems that beset most teenagers too, by helping to control weight, stimulating proper circulation, improving coordination and poise. In addition, the relaxation and breathing techniques help the adolescent to better handle his or her emotions, as well as improving the power of concentration.

For the active adult, yoga exercises every area of the body, stretching muscles and ligaments in all directions. The qualities it develops—coordination, balance, breath control, flexibility, endurance and a sense of physical confidence—can be carried into any sport or fitness activity.

In courses taught at health centers, in continuing education or wellness programs, look for a teacher who teaches yoga for the individual and not yoga for the sake of yoga. Yoga is a personalized type of exercise. You go along at your own speed to the best of your ability. For you to get the most out of a class, you must have a teacher who can focus on the individual, giving encouragement and help when it is needed. You will probably not find a teacher who is tuned into precisely your wave length, but you can learn from him or her just the same and use what you learn for your own ends.

If by chance your explorations in the yellow pages and with local health centers don't turn up anything, take the initiative and organize a class. Ys, fitness centers, even churches would probably be glad to sponsor a class and help in finding a competent instructor if made aware of the interest in yoga and its benefits.

The point I wish to make with regard to these benefits is that while these phenomena make their appearance in the bodily self, they affect the soul and spirit as well. Improvement in the circulation of the blood, the relief of congestion in certain organs, the stimulation or relaxation of nerves and muscles, the calming of the mind, the tonic effect on the brain, the clearing of the respiratory tracts, the cleansing of the lungs, the stimulation of the internal secreting glands—these are factors of the physiological life, but they are also factors in our emotional, rational and spiritual life by virtue of the body, mind, and spirit's manner of working in unity with each other, for each other and in each other.[10]

The meaning of yoga—union—says it all. This union, or harmonious integration of spirit and body, is not about uniting separate things. Rather, the practice of yoga fosters realization of the union which is already present. Union with parts of ourselves, with others, with all of creation, and with God. For a Christian, any method which positively contributes to our awareness of this union deserves consideration as a discipline leading to a more abundant life.

17

Theological Reflections from the Christian East

The catalyst for this book was a series of encounters with Western Christians who were turning to Eastern religions in an attempt to rediscover mysticism and direct experience of God. In responding to their critiques of Christianity, I found myself frequently referring to my heritage in the Christian East with its rich mystical tradition. It combines in an admirable synthesis the prophetic quality found in the Hebraic Bible of Judaism with the immediate, immanent experience of the indwelling Trinity that Jesus preached and made available to his followers through the Holy Spirit. Among the religions, Christianity added a revolutionary element of the divine indwelling. Jesus taught, "Those who love me will keep my word, and my Father will love them, and we will come to them and make our home with them" (Jn. 14:23).

We have already offered in Chapter 4 some reflections on the applications of Christian faith to be found in yoga. In this chapter we will consider some additional reference points in Christian theology and spirituality which speak encouragingly to those who may be inclined to use yoga as an adjunct to meditation or for its grounding, centering, and focusing capacities.

Theological developments in the West resulted in an opposition between "nature" and "grace," whereas the Christian East never felt the need to develop a separate doctrine of grace.

Greek patristic anthropology is "theocentric," according to which we are not fully human unless we are in communion with God. We are by nature "open outwards" toward God and destined to share in God's communal life. The Christian East thus speaks of "being deified," being "in Christ," and being penetrated with divine life or "energies" as a participant in his body. Deification or communion between divinity and humanity does not imply a confusion of essences or natures. It remains nevertheless real communion between the Uncreated and the creature, and real indwelling of the divine—not by essence, but by energy. The humanity of Christ is penetrated with divine energy and Christ's body becomes the source of divine light and deification for all who are "in him." The distinction between "essence" and "energy" is nothing but a way of saying that the transcendent God remains transcendent at the same time as God's life is communicated to us.[1]

In the Incarnation of Christ, God enters into immediate communion with humanity. The New Testament church, founded on sacramental communion and "life in Christ," offers participation in the very reality of the divine life. Granted to all the baptized, this participation is personal and conscious: it happens in the "hearts" of the saints. This real communion, this intimate familiarity with the One who is, is possible because "the Word became flesh and lived among us" (Jn. 1:14).

Throughout the centuries, Christian spirituality has often been influenced by Platonic terminology and ideas which tended to describe the fallen state of humanity in terms of an opposition between spirit and flesh or matter. For example for Origen, the principal theologian of the early Greek church (184-254) and Evagrius (fourth century), the ultimate goal of prayer and contemplation is for the mind to become free from all matter. Later theologians, like St. Symeon the New Theologian (eleventh century) and the hesychast Nicephorus (thirteenth century), aimed at reestablishing the unity of spirit and body as a single organism in the act of prayer. As one can see from the following excerpt from Nicephorus, they employed breathing disciplines and instructions regarding posture as an aid to prayer:

You know that we breathe our breath in and out, only because of our heart . . . so, as I have said, sit down, recollect your mind, draw it—I am speaking of your mind— in your nostrils; that is the path the breath takes to reach the heart. Drive it, force it to go down to your heart with the air you are breathing in. When it is there, you will see the joy that follows: you will have nothing to regret . . . . Have no other occupation or meditation than the cry of: "Lord Jesus Christ, Son of God, have mercy on me!" This practice protects your spirit from wandering and makes it impregnable and inaccessible to the suggestions of the enemy and lifts it up every day in love and desire for God.[2]

Nicephorus' language is, of course, figurative. When he speaks of "drawing the mind in through the nostrils," he means, in effect, focus your attention on your breathing at the point of the nostrils. The "heart" here refers more to the deepest psychological ground of one's personality, than to the actual organ of the heart. It is in this ground of our being, this inner sanctuary that we encounter, in the prayer of the heart, the One who is more intimate to us than we are to ourselves. The theme of "placing the mind in the heart" is a recurring figure of speech in Eastern Christian treatises on prayer.

As we described in Part I on Meditation, there is in each of us a contemplative faculty, a yearning to be with God in the temple of our hearts. This is why we can say that mystics are not special kinds of persons, but every person is a special kind of mystic—or at least, is called to be. In other words, our faith ought to give us a new vision, a different consciousness of ourselves, of the world, of other persons, and of God. Believing in God's revelation in Jesus Christ, we see things in a different light, because faith penetrates to the deepest levels of consciousness, transforming not only our external behavior but also our motives, thought patterns, and emotional reflexes. This transformation of consciousness by faith is the essence of Christian life. However, many Christians are content to live "unconsciously," deflecting the personal experience of God and stifling the Spirit. If we become ever more conscious of the world *around* us as we advance in years, should we not also become more aware of the grace *within us*?

The Fathers and Mothers of the Eastern Church, no less than Western theologians, recognized God's freedom and initiative in the work of human salvation and sanctification. But they also affirmed as a dogma of faith our own freedom and responsibility in this work. Symeon the New Theologian taught that from our side two factors are essential: expectation and effort. From God's side the indescribable is given: our total nature having been assumed, once for all, by the second person of the Trinity, our nature itself is now graced. We who share the humanity taken up by the Son of God have only to recognize and appropriate the grace which, in Christ, blesses our nature.

The Christian East attributed great importance to what it called praxis. Praxis is the active life of the Christian, not in the sense of the apostolate or the corporal and spiritual works of mercy (although these are included), but in the sense of the "struggle for virtue." It includes all that we do, under the influence of grace, in order to reintegrate our being—body, mind and spirit—in the quest for God. Symeon teaches that the gift of contemplation, of living with a recurring sense of joy, awe and wonder at the Mystery always and everywhere present to us, will not be given unless it is sought. The disciplines of the Christian life like regular participation in the eucharist, scripture reading, fasting, meditation, yoga, time with friends, time alone, exercise, living with a sabbath rhythm, service—these are the ways we seek the gift, seek to be made aware of what is, and to live with that awareness as our constant companion.

This heightened consciousness is not in itself an altered or extraordinary state. It was for this that we were made. This is our proper state. Eastern Christian theology has always emphasized the unity of the natural order and that of grace, so that our participation in God is seen as both a gift and a task. We are by nature open, evolving beings, and grace is offered to us as a challenge, an invitation to grow; by it we are given the power to participate actively in effecting this growth. This is not just a project for the mind. *The body shares the goal, and so it must also share in the way that leads to the goal.* This is the basis for approaching yoga and a physical fitness program as important and integral components in our spiritual lives. This is the reason why there is a place for the practice of breath control in order to focus our awareness and open ourselves to the divine Presence which dwells in the depths of our being.

Our striving does not contradict the gratuity of divine grace. God is totally free, and God's greatest gift to us is a share in that very liberty. In using the oft-repeated patristic phrase, "God became human so that humans might become God," the implicit addition at the end is "by adoption and grace." God takes our mind, our thinking, and shapes the way they perceive other people, other things, and God's own self. God acts upon us in order to assimilate us to God's likeness which is our true Self. The other polarity, always in tension with God's freedom to act upon us, is our freedom, our receptivity to God's action. One of Symeon's favorite Gospel verses was: "Blessed are the pure in heart, for they will see God" (Matt. 5:8). He understands the two clauses of this beatitude in close and reciprocal connection: the purification and integration of our whole nature—body, mind, and spirit—are both the *condition* and the *effect* of our vision of and union with Christ.[3] This process of purification and integration is not something that God does from God's side unilaterally. We must be willing. We must dispose ourselves. We must employ real and concrete ways of making ourselves open and receptive. Thus the notion of synergy has an important place: the action of two or more energies to achieve an effect that neither could do alone.

Christianity insists on the body's role in the spiritual quest. The starting point is human nature as it is, so corporal asceticism is a practical necessity. There is an inherent tension in the union of spirit and matter in our nature; we are engaged in a gradual process of transformation of the material component and the attainment of a more perfect union of these two poles. We unambiguously declare our faith in the resurrection of the body, and it is in this dynamism of resurrection and transformation into spirit that the body is seen to have a key role. We speak about "the spiritual life" but we know our embodied nature is an important part of the project.

In fact, most of the core doctrines of Christian faith involve the body: the incarnation; the passion, death and resurrection; the (bodily) ascension into heaven. Add to this the church's faith in the presence of Christ in the liturgy and sacraments through the material mediums of bread and wine, water and oil, a hand laid upon the head of a sick person or a penitent sinner, the gift of one's whole self to a partner in marriage. Physical bodies, substances drawn from the material world, become instruments and media of spiritual action. The Holy Spirit makes use of them all to work a wonder within us.

It should come as no surprise then that the mystery of God's redemption becoming real and effective in us is also linked to physical exercises, postures, attitudes and breath control. The repercussions of certain bodily states on the soul and the influence of various rhythms of living on the depths of the inner life testify to our nature as enfleshed spirits. Anyone who has ever knelt or prostrated oneself in prayer knows that certain ways of holding the body promote a sought-after attitude in the soul. This is an illustration of synergy, or the dialectic of grace and human activity, which relates to the mysterious interpenetration and cooperation of the two freedoms, human and divine.

And yet, all is grace. We need a grace even to accept a grace. In the various practices treated in this book and its companion volume, *Disciplines for Christian Living*, I have tried to keep in clear focus the distinction between God's freely bestowed grace, and our free cooperation in using various techniques to dispose ourselves to receive God's invitation to communion of life. A few summary points may be useful at this stage.

First, the conviction upon which all these reflections have been based is that God wishes to share life with us through our immediate experience and that we, through the faculty of our "mystical heart," can know God directly. This communication is made to a human person, an embodied spirit. Therefore we have need of concrete methods of bringing our whole being to a point of receptivity to receive from God the gifts God wants to give.

Second, the disciplines we employ are preparatory acts seeking to establish within us a prerequisite condition of openness and readiness for a state of union with God through grace. On our own, our best efforts leave us absolutely impotent to reach such a communion of life by dint of our own striving. Union with God is a free and gratuitous gift of God. Its bestowal cannot ultimately be dictated by a human will, nor can it be assumed that, how, and when it will be given.

Third, synergy (the mysterious interpenetration of God's freedom with our freedom) means that all our efforts, entered into in faith, hope, and love, are given an efficacy by the Holy Spirit to move us to a plane of experience which would, normally speaking, be impossible for us to reach. This is the difference between "making" things happen and "allowing" them to happen. The physiological "high" is what we get when we force things to happen, but there's nothing spiritual about it.

Finally, if our uses of the disciplines or psychosomatic techniques are truly to help transform us into channels of God's love and action, they will be in harmony with what God has revealed in the Gospel and in church teaching. In other words, it will become clear by our actions whether our experience is the result of a purely physiological high brought on by intense effort and intellectual concentration or whether we are being moved by the Spirit of God. This will be seen in the type of life we live according to God's revealed word in scripture and in the church's doctrine.

Without these norms by which to judge, too much emphasis may be placed on human methods and efforts and not enough upon God's allness, God's indwelling, Trinitarian life; not enough emphasis upon our need for the sacraments and the teaching church to guide us and strengthen us; not enough emphasis upon our own need for inner healing through God's forgiveness and mercy. Techniques must never be divorced from the teaching of scripture and the church's tradition of liturgy and sacraments. We are seeking the glory of God and surrender to God's will and work in our lives, not a self-satisfying psychic experience. Without this as our constant reference point, techniques tend to become ends in themselves and the heightened state of consciousness a goal in itself. Poverty of spirit and humility should be the true test of growth in prayer and Christian living, not how "high" one gets.[4]

The following statement by Vasileios Gondikakis effectively recapitulates these perspectives. He is the Father Abbot of a monastery on Mount Athos in Greece and he wrote it for monks. As what he says applies to all Christians, I will insert the broader reference into his text.

> *The Lord did not come into the world merely to make an improvement in our present conditions of life. Neither did He come to put forward an economic or political system, or to teach a method of arriving at psychosomatic equilibrium. He came to conquer death and to bring us eternal life . . . . (The Christian) is not one who by employing certain forms of abstinence or certain techniques has arrived at a high degree of self-control or at various ascetic exploits. All these things are only achievements belonging to his (or her) present world, unimportant in themselves, incapable of overcoming death . . . . The true (Christian) is one raised up, sharing in the resurrection. (His or her) mission is not to effect something by thoughts, or to organize something by personal capacities, but by his or her life to go give witness to the conquest of death.[5]*

18

Jesus Christ at the Encounter of World Religions

The disciplines of meditation and yoga have become a frequent meeting place for members of different religions. Yoga institutes, *vipassana* insight meditation centers, Zen meditation retreats all have residential programs where people from different faith backgrounds meet one another and share. This is a natural and rich instance of interfaith dialogue. Further information is provided for participants through books, pamphlets, and publications of the particular organization. And because of their deep and mutual interest in the contemplative dimension of living, these participants often discover deeper bonds of mutuality across religious lines than they experience with many people of their own respective groups whose interest in deepening the spiritual life is not as pronounced.

The communality of our quest for union with the divine is amply illustrated by the monastic vocation, which is not primarily a Christian but a human phenomenon. This makes monasteries the ecumenical centers of the future for interfaith dialogue and encounter. These "monasteries," I would suggest, are finding their expression wherever people—almost always now from different faith traditions—gather to seek deeper communion with the divine.

It is meditation, the life of prayer, which equips us for encounter with both Christians of other churches and people of other living faiths. From a Christian perspective, an ecumenical spirituality is characterized by mutual appreciation, a cosmic sense of the presence and work of Christ and the Holy Spirit, and a reverent regard for the uniqueness of each person in God's love and providence.[1]

My discussions with Christians in these places of encounter generally surface fundamental questions of how to relate their Christian faith to what they are hearing or reading or practicing which, not uncommonly, is drawn from the context of another religion. The distinction and the unity between world religions and Christianity eludes a perfect analysis. We are only now engaging in direct and frequent dialogue and encounter with one another. In past centuries, each religion has stayed largely within its own cultural borders and framework of reference. The shifting populations and patterns of immigration are creating a new cosmopolitan society in which followers of several different religions now inhabit the same cities in significant numbers.

It took Christian theology nearly five centuries (Council of Chalcedon, 451) to evolve a statement that most Christians could agree upon regarding who and what Jesus Christ was and is. It will take us a long while yet to work out a theology of the history and meaning of other religions. We are only now developing the language and categories of thought. We will surely make some mistakes and discover ourselves in some *culs de sac* in the process. Among the many theological voices, one which seems to me to be both faithful to the New Testament witness and open to God's work in other religions is that of Jacques Dupuis. Some of the perspectives presented here from his book *Jesus Christ at the Encounter of World Religions*[2] provide contemporary Christians with an orientation to the important question of where and how to situate Jesus in the context of this new dialogue.

The message we announce has always been problematic: that universal salvation has been effected in a determinate time and place, by the death on a cross of a human being, Jesus of Nazareth, who was the anointed one of God. To suggest that one particular culture could have received the legacy of a solitary salvation event occurring in a particular religious tradition—this seems to constitute a belittling of other religious traditions and cultures such as those of Asia which are actually older and possess remarkable treasures of their own. When confronted with what Christianity claims for Jesus of Nazareth, thoughtful Hindus and Buddhists understandably find it sectarian if not scandalous, parochial if not inequitable.

But as Christians, we can only seek the meaning of the phenomena of the history of religions from within the standpoint of Christian faith. It is for Buddhists or Hindus or others to do a theology of religions from their perspective. A Christian theology of religions is necessarily a Christology of religions. The mystery of Jesus Christ, the center of Christian faith, is our principle of understanding, the yardstick by which the data of other religious traditions can be measured. Our task is to show that a Christian theology of religions can and should be truly universal and adopt a global perspective. It is not closed or narrow, stingy or mean, but cosmic in its dimensions. As Christian theology shares certain basic intuitions with other religions, it can itself be enriched by contact with them and their theological traditions. Our task is to demonstrate that a theology of the history of religions based on Christian faith establishes, on a cosmic scale, a wonderful convergence in the mystery of Christ of all that God in the divine Spirit has realized and continues to accomplish in the history of humanity.

The Holy Spirit at Work Throughout the History of Humanity

If we broaden our perspective and consider the economy of salvation throughout the history of humanity, we may distinguish four successive periods in the history of salvation, each one corresponding to a divine covenant. First, the covenant with humanity in Adam and Eve. Second, the covenant with Noah, who symbolizes the religious traditions of the nations. Third, the Abrahamic and Mosaic covenant with Israel. And finally, the covenant established by God in Jesus Christ with the new people of God. The whole economy of salvation is dynamically ordered by the providence of God toward its full manifestation in Jesus. At each stage of this development, God's commitment to humanity is renewed.[3]

The covenant with humanity's religious traditions represented in Noah remains in effect even during the time of the church, wherever the Gospel of Jesus Christ has not been effectively preached. Put another way, followers of other religions who have not been personally summoned by the Gospel in their conscience continue to lead their lives under the cosmic covenant to which other religions belong. For these members, these religious traditions serve as a means of salvation, a role which they perform in relation to the mystery of Christ and under the influence of his power. The coming in time of "special" salvation history (i.e. the post-Incarnation period) does not abolish the validity of "general" salvation history.[4]

We must acknowledge that many men and women in these traditions have encountered God in an authentic religious experience. For example, one does not pray to an impersonal God; prayer entails a personal relationship between an "I" and an infinite "Thou." Authentic prayer is a reliable sign that God has undertaken the initiative of a personal approach to human beings and has been welcomed in faith. However incomplete and imperfect their conception of God might be, those who entrust themselves to God in charity and faith are saved. Salvation, after all, depends on the response made by sinful human beings in faith to a personal communication initiated by God.[5]

Sometimes we try to make sense of the destiny of those not Christian by allowing them the possibility of salvation on the basis of their *personal* sincerity, thereby denying any salvific value to their religion as such. But the religious traditions of humanity take their origin from the religious experience of the persons or groups that have founded them. Their sacred books contain the memory and record of concrete encounters with the Divine. Their practices result from the codification of these experiences. Thus it makes no sense to assert that their religion plays no role in their salvation.[6]

The Bible does not see all truth confined first to Israel and then to Christ or the church. Melchizedech, a non-Jewish priest, is seen by Abraham as a priest of God. The letter to the Hebrews says Christ's priesthood is like Melchizedech's. Proverbs has chapters taken from an Egyptian wisdom book. Stoic truisms appear in Paul. Many other scriptural verses acknowledge truth elsewhere. We can infer from them that we will find truth in other religions.[7]

In short, this theology of world religions posits that, before uttering the ultimate divine word in Jesus Christ, even before speaking through the prophets of the Old Testament, God has already uttered an initial word to human beings through the prophets of the nations. The echoes and traces of this word can be found in the holy scriptures of the world's religious traditions. The Old Testament itself in its Genesis stories of Adam and Eve, Cain and Abel and Noah, bears witness that God spoke to the nations before ever addressing Israel. Thus the holy scriptures of the nations, along with the Hebrew scriptures and the New Testament, reflect the various modes in which God's divine self-revelation continually found expression throughout human history.

In the first stage, God grants to the hearts of seers and sages a secret word, at least traces of which are contained in the sacred scriptures of the world's religions. In the second stage, God speaks officially to Israel by the mouth of its prophets, and the entire Hebrew Bible is the record of this word. Both of these words find their full revelation in the third and last stage wherein God utters the decisive word in the divine Son. It is to this incarnate Word that the whole New Testament bears formal witness. In this overarching perspective, the history of salvation and revelation is one, revealing the influence of the Holy Spirit in all its stages: cosmic, Israelite, and Christian. Throughout this long and complex history, God has been personally guiding humanity toward the goal divinely set.[8]

From the viewpoint of Christian faith, Christ is universal. He belongs to all religions. More precisely, they all belong to him, since he is present and active in them all, just as in all human beings. In order to see this, we need to recall that the divine Word is the universal agent of all God's historical self-manifestation—even before God's incarnation in Jesus of Nazareth. Thus a Christian theology of religions finds its advantage everywhere. It is able to enrich itself with the intuitions of other religious traditions since they contain an authentic manifestation of God through the mediation of the divine Word. It will also be able to recognize in the holy scriptures of other traditions not only a word addressed by God to their members, but a word through which God speaks to Christians themselves, even though in Jesus Christ God has spoken the decisive divine Word to the world.

May we think that God speaks to us Christians through the prophets and sages whose religious experience is the source of the sacred books of these traditions? The fullness of revelation contained in Jesus Christ and transmitted by the church does not gainsay this possibility. Nor is it opposed to the use in Christian prayer, even in the Liturgy of the Word, of the words of God contained in the sacred books of other traditions. Indeed, this ought to be done, with prudence and with respect for the different stages of revelation history. Also required will be the discernment necessary to avoid any ambiguities by a responsible selection of texts, in harmony with the mystery of Jesus Christ in which the Liturgy of the Word culminates. Under these conditions, we shall discover, with joy and surprise, astonishing convergences between the words of God and the divine word in Jesus Christ. Certain aspects of the divine mystery may actually be given more emphasis in other sacred scriptures than in the New Testament. We need only think of the deep sense of the divine majesty and the holiness of the divine decrees on every page of the Qur'an, or the sense of the immanent presence of God and the interiority in which religious experience is steeped in the sacred books of Hinduism. Paradoxical as it may appear, a prolonged contact with the non-biblical scriptures—practiced within their own faith—can help

Christians to a more in-depth discovery of certain aspects of the divine mystery that they behold fully revealed in Jesus Christ.[9]

Two Fundamental Axioms of Christian Faith

In its interface with other world religions, Christian theology is experiencing a renewal today as it did in ages past through contact with Greek philosophy. Just as the dialogue with the rediscovered Aristotle enabled Thomas Aquinas to deepen his theological understanding and to recast Christian theology in the medieval situation, so is the dialogue with Hindus, Buddhists, Muslims, Jews and others in different parts of the world enabling us to deepen our theological understanding and to recast some of our theological ideas in the modern situation.[10]

That said, one should be aware that Thomas Aquinas did not accept everything that Aristotle had to say. In order for us to have similar powers of discernment concerning what to appropriate and what not, we need to maintain a firm grasp of our own faith convictions. There are two fundamental axioms of Christian faith that find application here: the will of God to save all, and the central place of the mystery of Christ in the concrete realization of the divine salvific plan.[11]

These axioms may seem at first contradictory, but when properly understood they find their linkage in what theology calls "the Christic mystery." One explicit New Testament text which utters both axioms in quick succession is found in 1 Timothy 2:4-6: "God wants *everyone* to be saved and to reach full knowledge of the truth. For there is only one God, and there is only one mediator between God and humankind, himself a man, Christ Jesus, who gave himself as a ransom for *all*" (emphasis mine).

The second axiom, relating to the central place of Christ in God's plan to save all, places Christ in the role of universal Savior. He is at the center of the mystery of salvation, as obligatory mediator and the way leading to God, because God and no one else—not human beings or Christianity—has put him there. This is the message of the New Testament in its entirety, the assertion underlying every part of it, the deep faith without which none of the books that comprise it would have been written.[12]

These two axioms—that God's salvific will is truly universal, and that salvation comes through God in Christ alone—are the touchstones of orthodoxy in any Christian theology of religions. By holding these two axioms in fruitful tension, a Christian theology of world religions can be characterized by an openness and a commitment to explore the many and various ways in which God has spoken to all people. This exploration has the potential to transform, enrich and fulfill Christianity, giving the church a future shape quite different from the one we know today.[13]

"To say that Christ is at the center of the divine plan for humanity," writes Dupuis, "is not to consider Him as the goal and end toward which the religious life of human beings and the religious traditions of humanity tend. God (the Father) remains the goal and end. Jesus never replaces God. Jesus Christ is at the center of the mystery as obligatory mediator, constituted by God and no one else, as the way leading to God."[14]

The historical Jesus, constituted Christ and Lord in his resurrection, is God turning to human beings in self-revelation and self-giving. He is God in a personal relationship with men and women, God turned toward human beings in self-bestowal. Christians are those who come to an *explicit* discovery of God personally present to them in Jesus. This Christic mystery remains *implicit* for those who do not recognize the mystery of salvation actively and universally present to them in Christ.

The place Jesus Christ occupies in Christianity is central. No other religion attributes such a unique place to its founder. For Islam, Muhammad is the depository of the divine message, the prophet through whom God speaks. For Buddhism, Gautama is the great teacher, the Enlightened One showing the way. For Christianity, however, Jesus claims equality with God. He never refuses the title Messiah. He corrects holy writ. He insists that prophecy is fulfilled in him and that the Kingdom appears through his acts.[15]

It is the mystery of Jesus Christ himself, and not just his message, that is at the very heart of faith. The message and the Messenger blend into one. Christianity is not, then, a "religion of the book," as Islam is sometimes described. It is the religion of a person, the Christ.[16]

The uniqueness of Jesus Christ and the universal meaning of the Christ event represent more than a central belief for Christian tradition. These truths are seen as the very foundation of faith. They have always been, and still are, a stumbling block for those who do not share our faith. Uniqueness and universal are understood here in the strict sense: by and in Jesus, God effected a self-manifestation in a manner that is decisive for all and can be neither surpassed nor repeated. In the last analysis, of course, the sole valid theological foundation of the uniqueness of Jesus Christ and the universal import of his life, death and resurrection is his personal identity as Son of God. To confess him as such is to make an act of faith. As St. Paul says: "No one can say 'Jesus is Lord' but under the impulse of the Holy Spirit" (1 Cor. 12:3). But our dialogue with other faiths will need to include the particularity of claims for Jesus as having been in the form of God and having taken on the form of a servant—a claim that the church has early and often made (Phil. 2:6-11).

Christianity advances no claims concerning Christians themselves. Its claims regard Jesus. He is the one who is unique, not us. While we have received a commission to be worthy witnesses to our faith, history provides ample testimony that we often fail. Fortunately, God's fidelity does not depend on ours, just as Jesus' mystery and uniqueness does not depend on the quality of our witness.[17]

Given the central place of Jesus in Christian faith, it comes as no surprise that Christian spirituality is deeply personal, locking onto the person of Christ, studying him in the gospels with a steady gaze and purity of heart, wanting only to know him personally and what he wants of us. Gradually, this becomes "the one thing necessary": to do what our heart

tells us that he would have us do. Other things begin to matter less and less. It is this affair of the heart, this deepening
sense of intimacy and trust, this relationship of love that
becomes the center of our lives.

If Christians adapt Eastern methods of meditation and
yoga, they will center them on the person of Jesus. In their
use of various methods they will seek to enter into his experience of intimate relationship with God, into his very consciousness which makes us cry out, "Abba, Father." This is
only possible in faith. It is faith and not techniques which
must be at the center of any meditation or yoga that styles
itself as Christian. In his own pattern of discipleship, Jesus is
the model for Christian living and the goal of the journey. He
is the one, true yogi. His life, his mysteries, his person are
the Christian's yoga or path to union with God.[18]

Interfaith dialogue assumes that we have in some fashion
wrestled with the fundamental questions of Christian faith
and that we are committed to Christ. This does not mean that
we never suffer doubts about the assertions of Christianity,
but it does mean that, day by day, we find enough sense and
beauty in the venture of loving Christ to sustain us without
great trouble. Thus we are in a position to serenely and joyfully cross the bridge of dialogue with Eastern religions.

The hidden presence of the mystery of Christ in other religions has profound implications for us. Since all God's communications with humanity have been through the eternal Word
(become flesh in Jesus of Nazareth), salvation is both present
and effective in the religious traditions of the world both
before and after Jesus Christ. Thus we may approach in a
spirit of alert openness and discerning receptivity. Since others have an experience of God through the Christic mystery,
their religious traditions have something to offer Christians.

In *Jesus Christ at the Encounter of World Religions* Jacques
Dupuis writes:

> *They (other religious traditions) can help them
> (Christians) to discover new facets of the mystery of
> Christ. Certain aspects of the mystery of Christ may be*

felt more profoundly by others than by many Christians.
A sharing in the religious experience of others in the
interreligious dialogue can help Christians deepen their
own perception of the Christian mystery, even though
they have already received its authentic revelation. After
all, Truth is not an object to be possessed, but a person
by whom to allow oneself to be possessed. The others are
possessed by the same Truth. Thus, while it may seem
somewhat paradoxical, it is theologically correct to say
that they can teach us something of the mystery of Christ
. . . . Christ can be just as personally present—or even
more so—to some of their deeply committed members
than to less committed Christians.[19]

In the early part of this century the slogan of the mission-
aries was "the world for Christ in this century!" At the end of
this century, we are in front of the permanence of world religious pluralism not greatly affected by the Christian mission
of conversion. Does this mean that such pluralism is part of
God's grace?

What does this mean for the situation of interreligious dialogue? It would seem appropriate to cast it as mutual evange-
lization in the sense that, through dialogue, the partners
evangelize each other under the impulse and movement of the
Spirit of God. This is because the partners in dialogue live—
consciously on the one side, unconsciously on the other—the
same mystery of Christ, active in them through the work of
the Holy Spirit. The encounter and exchange have value in
themselves, are an end in themselves. Such encounters pre-
sume from the very beginning openness to the other and to
God; and along the way they effect a greater openness to God
in each through the other. The dynamic is one of conversion,
yes—of each to God through the Christic mystery at work in
them. The same God speaks in the hearts of both partners;
the same Holy Spirit is at work in all. Thus they become for
each other a sign leading to God.[20]

Therefore, concludes Dupuis, "The proper end of the inter-
religious dialogue is, in the last analysis, the common conver-

sion of Christians and the members of other religious traditions to the same God—the God of Jesus Christ—who calls
them together by challenging the ones through the others."[21]

Thus there is both fruit and challenge in this encounter for
Christians. The fruit: we will gain an enrichment for our own
faith through an experience in greater depth of certain aspects
of the divine mystery communicated less clearly by Christian
tradition. The challenge: we will be forced to revise certain
gratuitous assumptions, to uproot certain deeply embedded
prejudices, or to overturn certain narrow outlooks—in short,
to purify our faith.[22]

At the heart of our faith is the grateful and joyful assertion
that, in this human being, Jesus of Nazareth, a member of our
race, God has personally come to meet us on our own level.
Jesus places God within our reach and offers to us the gift of
divine life. He is God in a human way, and a human in a divine
way. Apart from Christianity, God encounters human beings,
but the human face of God remains unknown. In Christianity,
God encounters us in the human face of Jesus who reflects for
us the very image of God. While every religion contains an
approach to the human person on the part of God, in
Christianity God's advance toward us becomes fully human.[23]

So it is that we can find God at work in everything that is
human, in every decent, noble, intelligent thing that people
do or say, as well as find God grieving over and sharing in
every suffering. For a Christian spirituality rooted in scripture such as John's gospel, all things came to be in the Word
that became incarnate, and the Word's taking flesh is a profound expression of God's solidarity with the world and everyone in it. There is a light at the heart of everyone which no
darkness can overcome. In that comprehensive, uncompre-
hended light, Christian spirituality finds all things holding
together in the grace and truth of the cosmic Christ celebrat-
ed in Colossians: "He is the image of the invisible God, the
firstborn of all creation; for in him all things in heaven and
on earth were created, things visible and invisible, whether
thrones or dominions or rulers or powers—all things have

been created through him and for him. He himself is before all things, and in him all things hold together" (1:15-17).

Christians in the exchange of interfaith encounter may have the opportunity to humbly and simply share that the eternal Word of God, become flesh in Jesus of Nazareth, is the source and center of their salvation history. For me personally, his Holy Spirit has shaped and guided the decisions of my life. Other people may report a similar experience and attribute it to other sources. But my own actual history has been formed by the love of Christ. I want to be faithful to that, to him. It is a joy to speak of him to others, a delight to share his good news that we are set free from sin and death, and a privilege to serve him in love with a grateful heart.

Part III
Praying with Heart and Body

Appendix I

Recommendations

There are certain conditions regarding time, space, clothing, and attitude which will enhance your practice.

Time. Do your yoga exercises at whatever time of the day suits you, but try to do them at a regular time. Your exercises should never be practiced just after eating. Many people find that morning practice puts them in top form for the rest of the day. The long time spent lying still during the night means that you are less supple in the morning, so some exercises may be more difficult then. Make allowances for this and avoid forcing your body to do something it may not yet be ready to do. If you prefer later in the day, as a general rule allow three to four hours after a main meal and two hours after a light meal. Set a quartz timer (quiet) for the amount of time you have and then release your preoccupation with time and enter fully into focusing on your breathing and your stretches.

Place. Choose a place where you can be uninterrupted. Demarcate your space by spreading out a yoga mat or a blanket folded in half. When climate permits, outdoors in the fresh air is ideal. When indoors, choose a well-ventilated room. Open the window a crack even in winter to give yourself the benefit of some fresh air. This is particularly helpful for the breathing exercises. At the end of the session, cover yourself with a blanket during the relaxation pose and wrap it around you when you sit up for meditation. The body cools down considerably once you stop moving.

What To Wear. Light, loose clothing that allows for complete freedom of movement with no restriction anywhere. Keep some socks handy to put on during the relaxation period, but take them off during the session itself so your toes and feet can feel the grass or the mat.

Attitude. Come to your practice as to a bubble bath or a jacuzzi. Luxuriate in it. There is no pressure on you to perform or to compete. Focus your attention on what your body is feeling; clue in to where it wants to stretch. Once you learn the postures, you can employ them in different arrangements, depending on how you feel that day. Omit poses that don't feel comfortable. Enter into them with your eyes closed, conscious of your breathing, to foster a sense of interiority and concentration.

Showers, Vigorous Exercise, and Eating. Wait a half hour before taking a very hot bath or shower after your session. Your body is circulating a large amount of blood that has been accumulated in the deep-lying organs; a hot or cold shower or bath draws the blood away to the peripheral regions of the body and neutralizes the effect. A lukewarm shower, however, approximating blood heat, will not influence your circulation significantly and may be taken immediately afterward if you desire.[1] It is recommended as well to wait about a half hour before undertaking vigorous exercise. Allow yourself to revel in the feelings of calm and relaxation. They will pass soon enough! There is nothing to prevent you from eating a meal directly after your practice. The ideal, however, is to sit in meditation afterward. Transforming the environment of the bodymind and priming it for meditation is the primary reason for the development of the yoga postures and breathing exercises.

Appendix II

Yoga Breathing Exercises

When you come to meditate, one of the most useful rules of thumb for focusing your awareness is simply to pay attention to your breathing. Yoga breathing exercises can be used at any time, but are particularly effective before or after yoga practice and just prior to meditation.

First, some physiological notes about breathing. Your nose is lined with erectile tissue that expands and contracts during the day, causing your nasal mucosa to swell and shrink. Although you probably are not aware of it, the flow of air through your nose shifts from one nostril to the other during the day as the lining of each nostril expands and contracts in a biological rhythm.

You can check this out for yourself by placing your palm near your nostrils. One of the nostrils is partially blocked, and the flow of air in and out of the lungs will be mainly through only one of the nostrils.

For most people, the breath will flow predominantly through one nostril for about two hours, and then the predominance will begin to shift to the other nostril. Although Western physiology does not have much to say about this phenomenon, yoga texts state that this rhythm and alternating pattern is important in maintaining physiological and psychological equilibrium. Research has not yet been done to confirm or refute these concepts. But we do know that the two hemispheres of the brain function somewhat differently. It may be that this is reflected in one's breathing.

In any case, the techniques of alternate nostril breathing were developed to "rebalance" the equilibrium of breathing. Whatever the way it works, alternate nostril breathing is an exceptionally powerful technique for calming and relaxing the mind and body.[1]

Yogic breathing gives great attention to the process of exhalation.

The ratio between inhalation and exhalation is 1:2. If the inhalation is four seconds, the exhalation will be eight seconds. There are two reasons for this: the exhalation is the more relaxing phase of breathing; and a longer exhalation serves to squeeze the stale air out of the air sacs. As long as the air sacs are filled with old air, no amount of inhalation can effectively bring fresh air to them from the atmosphere. In ordinary breathing we squeeze very little air out of the base of the lungs.

Therefore, the first lesson in yogic breathing is simply inhalation and exhalation according to the 1:2 ratio. When you awake in the morning and are still lying in bed, take some deep, slow breaths. If you walk to and from work, breathe in for six steps as you walk (or whatever seems right for you), and exhale to the count of twelve steps (or whatever doubles your inhalation). As a general rule, exhalation should last twice as long as inhalation.

When a proper inhalation and exhalation pattern is established, the next step is to retain the breath proportionately. Retention has the effect of slowing down the breathing process and bringing it under control. According to yogic breathing, the ratio between inhalation and retention is 1:4. Retention is four times inhalation, and exhalation is always twice inhalation. Therefore the ratio between inhalation, retention, and exhalation is 1:4:2. The minimum schedule to start with is three seconds of inhalation, twelve seconds of retention, and six seconds of exhalation. Once one can do that comfortably, the ratio can be increased over time to four, sixteen, and eight, then five, twenty, and ten.

Almost all the yoga books and teachers warn that any breathing techniques more involved than those outlined here should be avoided by the beginner or, at the very least, performed only under close supervision with an experienced teacher. It is always advisable to do all the breathing exercises under the guidance of a yoga teacher. For the purpose of the following exercises, if at any time you feel that you are not getting enough air, simply resume normal breathing.

If at all possible, always breathe through your nose, which filters and warms the air.

Breathing Exercise No. 1
The Complete Breath

To practice the three-part or complete breathing, sit comfortably with your back straight or lying down on your back. Place your right hand on your chest and your left hand on your abdomen. Then begin by filling your abdominal area with air. Your left hand should begin to rise but your right hand will not.

After filling your abdomen with air, keep inhaling as you allow more air to rise, filling your lower chest. This should cause your right hand to rise. Feel your rib cage expand as you inhale.

Keep inhaling and feel the air rising even higher in your chest. As the air reaches the top of your lungs, you will feel your collarbone begin to rise.

To exhale, repeat the process in reverse, from top to bottom, feeling your collarbone descend, and the upper and lower parts of your chest contract. Finally, contract the abdominal muscles at the end of the exhalation to squeeze out all the residual air. Exhaling is the most relaxing phase of breathing, so take twice as long to exhale as to inhale. Practice the complete breath for five minutes, focusing on the sensation of breathing. If at any time you feel short of breath, light-headed or dizzy, just resume normal breathing. You might want to schedule a few minutes each day just to practice deep breathing, and to do it especially when you're feeling stressed.

Benefits: Relaxes the body. Calms the mind. Revitalizes the entire system. Strengthens the abdominal muscles, diaphragm, heart, and lungs. Improves digestion and elimination. Very soothing during menstruation. Can be practiced during postures, relaxation, meditation, and anytime, anywhere.

Contraindications: Recent surgery to abdomen or chest. All breathing exercises are best done on an empty stomach.

Breathing Exercise No. 2
The Sounding Breath or the Ocean Breath

1. Sitting with your spine straight or lying down on your back, take a few deep breaths and relax.

2. With a slow and steady breath through the nostrils, gently contract the back of your throat (the glottis) creating a soft but audible sound like ocean surf. To learn how to create this sound, practice whispering "Ahhhhh" with your mouth closed on both the exhalation and the inhalation.

3. Lengthen the breath as much as possible and focus on the sound. Repeat for five minutes.

Benefits: Same as for the Complete Breath, but more pronounced. The mind becomes absorbed in the sound which has a tranquilizing effect.

Contraindications: Same as for the Complete Breath.

Breath Exercise No. 3
Single Nostril Breath

1. Sit in a comfortable position with the spine, neck and head in a straight line.

2. Close the right nostril with your thumb. Inhale slowly through the left nostril, counting "one second, two seconds, three seconds, four seconds."

3. Exhale through the same nostril, counting to eight seconds in the same manner. Exhalation time is always twice inhalation time. Repeat this exercise fifteen to twenty times through the left nostril.

4. Now close the left nostril with your right ring finger and little finger, closing down the index and middle fingers, and inhale through the right nostril, counting four seconds for inhalation, eight for exhalation.

That completes one round. Repeat for fifteen to twenty rounds.

Do not make any sound during inhalation. Apply the basic rules for the Complete Breath, inhaling into the three chambers of your lungs: low, mid, and high. In exhalation try to expel as much of the stagnant air as possible from the lungs.

In Exercise No. 3 there is no retention.

Stay with this simple daily exercise for two weeks to a month, increasing the proportion from 4:8 to 5:10 and 6:12 if you are able to do so comfortably. Do not try the higher proportion until you are able to do the lower one easily and without strain. That is the main rule in every breathing and other yogic exercise: *keep within your capacity and never overdo it.*

The purpose of inhaling and exhaling through one nostril is to develop the capacity to do low, mid and high breathing automatically through either nostril. If one patiently practices the basic lessons in breathing and lays down a good foundation, the more advanced exercises can easily be taken up.

Approximate practice time each day: ten minutes.

Breathing Exercise No. 4
Alternate Nostril Breathing

After two weeks to a month of daily practice of Exercise No. 3, advance to the alternate breathing exercise.

Traditional yoga texts recommend arranging the fingers in the following manner for this exercise: make a gentle, relaxed fist with your right hand. Then open only the thumb and the last two fingers. The side of the thumb is used to close off the right nostril, and the side of the ring finger, with the little finger pressing against it, is used to close off the left nostril. Do whatever is most comfortable for you. Some prefer to place their first two fingers between their eyebrows rather than having them curled back into the palm of their hand. Experiment with these or other methods and use what works best for you.

1. Close the right nostril with your right thumb and inhale slowly through the left nostril.

2. Now close the left nostril immediately with your right ring finger and little finger. Remove your thumb from the right nostril and exhale through that nostril. This is half a round.

3. Now, without pausing, inhale through the right nostril.

4. Close the right nostril with your right thumb and exhale through the left. This completes one full round.

Use the inhalation-exhalation proportion to which you had comfortably arrived in your practice of Exercise No. 1. If five seconds inhalation, then ten seconds exhalation. If six seconds inhalation, then twelve seconds exhalation. The same general rules apply to Exercise No. 4 as for No. 3. The ratio of inhalation to exhalation is 1:2. There is no retention of breath in Exercise No. 4.

Fifteen to twenty rounds will take ten to fifteen minutes.

Breathing Exercise No. 5
Alternate Nostril Breathing
with Retention of Breath

The only difference between the fourth and fifth exercises is the retention or holding of the breath. The correct ratio between inhalation and retention is 1:4. However, in the first month or two of practicing this exercise, it is advised to follow a 1:2 ratio before taking up the 1:4 ratio.

The minimum starting proportion is three seconds inhalation, six seconds retention, and six seconds exhalation. If you have been comfortably inhaling for a duration of four, five or six seconds, the count in this exercise would be 4:8:8, 5:10:10 or 6:12:12.

1. Close off the right nostril with your thumb and slowly inhale through your left nostril, counting off five (or your preferred number of) seconds.

2. Keeping your thumb on your right nostril, close off your left nostril with your ring and little fingers and retain your breath for ten seconds.

3. Release your thumb from your right nostril and exhale through that nostril for ten seconds.

4. Inhale through the right nostril for five seconds, closing it off with your thumb, and retaining the breath for ten seconds.

5. Release your ring finger from your left nostril and exhale for ten seconds.

This is one round. Fifteen rounds will take twelve to fifteen minutes.

When you are able to do 8:16:16 comfortably, change the ratio to 1:4:2. Start with four seconds inhalation, sixteen seconds retention, and eight seconds exhalation.

You're not in competition with anyone and you don't need to perform for anybody. So there's no need to push yourself beyond your comfort level. These exercises are for your own benefit.

When we come to meditate, our minds are usually racing and full of preoccupations. Devoting five minutes to one of these breathing exercises prior to meditation is a wonderful aid to slowing down the mind through slowing down our breathing, and focusing awareness through attentive counting of the breaths. These exercises can be used to good benefit on any occasion in which we want to achieve calm, one-pointed concentration.

Contraindications for Alternate Nostril Breathing with Retention: holding the breath should be minimized or omitted for those with unmedicated high blood pressure, abdominal inflammation, lung conditions, or hernia.

Appendix III

What You Should Know About Stretching

All the yoga postures involve stretching, so before getting into the poses themselves, it is worthwhile to present some basic considerations to keep in mind while stretching.

The development of good breathing habits gained through practice of the breathing exercises will serve one particularly well when it comes to stretching. The reason is that proper breathing enables the stretch.

Everyone can learn to stretch, regardless of age or flexibility. The methods are gentle and easy, taking individual differences into consideration. So if you are basically healthy, without any specific physical problems, you can learn how to stretch safely and enjoyably. The benefits are many: reduction in muscle tension and increase in feeling of relaxation; promotion of blood circulation; improvement in coordination; increase in range of motion; and prevention of muscle strain injuries. The stiffer you are, the more you stand to benefit from stretching. Your half-inch stretch may represent more than the foot-long stretch of a supple person.

While stretching is easy to learn, there is a right way and a wrong way to stretch.

Right way: stretch slowly and gently in a relaxed manner, breathing into the stretch as you exhale. Sustain it while you inhale. Focus your attention in particular on the muscles being stretched and in general on any associated sensations taking place in your body as you stretch. As you exhale slowly, you will find that you are able to extend the stretch by millimeters. This is what is meant by "proper breathing enables the stretch."

Wrong way: stretch hurriedly, pushing yourself to the point of pain, bouncing up and down on the muscles to make them loosen up faster.

The authoritative book on the subject is Bob Anderson's *Stretching.*[1] In it he distinguishes between the The Easy Stretch and The Developmental Stretch. In The Easy Stretch, you go to the point where you feel a *mild tension* and relax as you hold the stretch for 10-30 seconds. The feeling of tension should subside as you hold the position. If it does not, ease off slightly and find a degree of tension that is comfortable. The Easy Stretch diminishes muscular tightness and prepares the tissues for The Developmental Stretch.

In The Developmental Stretch, as in the Easy Stretch, there is never any bouncing. It is just a matter of taking your stretch a fraction of an inch further until you again feel a mild tension. Hold the stretch once more for 10-30 seconds. The tension should decrease once again; if it does not, ease off slightly. You are in control. Silently counting the seconds will ensure that you hold the proper tension for a long enough time. After a while, you will learn to stretch by the way it feels, and be able to dispense with the distraction of counting.

While doing these stretches, your breathing should be slow, rhythmical and under control. If, for example, you are going to execute a stretch that requires bending forward, inhale deeply and then exhale as you bend forward. *Breathe slowly and deeply as you hold the stretch; do not hold your breath while stretching.*

The muscles have a built-in nerve reflex to prevent injury. Holding a stretch when it is causing pain, or bouncing up and down, strains the muscles and activates the nerve reflex. Ignoring the nerve reflex signals can result in microscopic tearing of muscle fibers, which leads to the formation of scar tissue in the muscles and a gradual loss of elasticity. This is one of the reasons why it is important to pay close attention to what is going on in your body during a stretch. Pain is an indication that something is *wrong*. There is an unmistakable difference between the tension you feel in properly stretching a tight muscle and the pain that results when you have gone too far.

Stretching, when done correctly, is not painful. It actually feels very good. By regularly stretching, your flexibility will increase and you will come to anticipate more and more the good feeling that comes from being loose and supple.

Stretching is entirely individual. In aerobics or yoga classes sometimes too much emphasis is placed on maximum flexibility. There should be no comparisons made between what you are able to do and what others are able to do. Everyone is different. Simply concentrate on the feeling of the stretch and not on how far you can or cannot go in relation to someone else. This is not a contest. Each person has a certain potential. All you are asked to do is to stretch toward *your* potential. So be sensitive to where you feel your own limits are. If you stay close to what feels good to you, you will improve naturally and enjoy your stretching.

Keep the following considerations in mind:

- You are different every day. Some days you are more tight or loose than other days.
- You have control over what you feel by what you do.
- Regularity and relaxation are the most important factors in stretching. If you start stretching regularly you will naturally become more active and fit.
- Don't compare yourself with others. Even if you are tight or inflexible, don't let this stop you from stretching and improving yourself.
- Do not try to be flexible. Just learn to stretch properly and flexibility will come with time. Flexibility is only one of the many by-products of stretching.

- Proper stretching means stretching within your own limits, in a relaxed manner, and without comparisons.
- Stretching keeps your body ready for movement.

Stretch whenever you feel like it. It will always make you feel good.[2]

Appendix IV

Yoga Warm-Ups

From a standing position

1. Neck Stretches

Press your chin toward your chest. Bring your head back to center and then lift your chin, lengthening the back of your neck as you tilt your head back. Bring your head back to center again. Repeat this movement a few times. Next, lower your right ear toward your right shoulder but do not raise your shoulder. Return to center and repeat to opposite side. Finally, turn your head to face the right, bringing your chin toward your right shoulder. Repeat on opposite side.

2. Shoulder Openers

a) *Shoulders to ears:* inhaling, squeeze your shoulders to your ears and hold for a few moments. Allow the tension to build and then exhale with a sigh as you drop the shoulders back down. Repeat a few times.

b) *Shoulder rotations:* slowly rotate the right shoulder in a
   clockwise direction by squeezing it up to the ear, then
   back and down, forward and up. Repeat several times
   and reverse the direction of the circles. Repeat on the
   opposite side. Then rotate both shoulders at the same
   time.

c) *Shoulder blade squeeze:* interlace your fingers behind
   your back and press your hands away from your shoulders, lengthening your arms. Allow your chest to open as
   the shoulder blades squeeze together. Tighten the buttocks and breathe deeply as you hold.

d) *Elbow press:* extend the right arm overhead and bend
   your elbow, placing your palm on your back as if to pat
   yourself on the back. Hold your right elbow with your
   left hand and gently begin to pull the elbow to the left.
   Repeat on the opposite side.

3. The Standing Swinging Twist

Stand with your feet shoulder-width apart and your arms relaxed by your sides. Begin to turn your hips from right to left, allowing your arms to swing side to side, flapping them against your body like empty coat sleeves. Lift the heel of the opposite foot in the direction you are twisting to give hips more range of motion.

4. Hip Circles

Stand with your feet hip-width apart and place your hands on your hips. Rotate your hips in a clockwise direction, pressing the hips forward, to the right, back, and to the left. Keep your torso as straight as possible, letting the rotation come from the hip. Repeat several times in both directions.

5. *The Rag Doll*

Stand with your feet shoulder-width apart, knees slightly bent, and arms relaxed at your side. Exhale deeply as you begin to bend forward, pressing your chin into your chest and rounding the spine down. Allow your head, neck and arms to hang freely as your torso hangs from the hips. Gently allow the torso to bob up and down. Then sway slowly from side to side, making figure eight motions with your hands and arms. Inhaling, curl the spine up slowly, consciously stacking one vertebra on top of another, bringing the head up last. Slowly lift your arms overhead, take in a deep breath, and exhaling, let your arms come back down to your sides.

6. *The Squat*

With your feet shoulder-width apart, bend your knees and bring your hips toward the ground, keeping your spine relatively straight, your head lifted, and allowing your heels to naturally lift off the ground. Place your hands on the ground in front of you between your knees. (For stiff or sore knees, lower the hips partially and place your hands on your thighs.)

7. Leg Extensions

From the squatting position, extend your right leg out to the side. For an extra stretch, slowly extend your torso over your right leg, bringing your chin toward your knee. Repeat on the opposite side.

From a kneeling position

8. Movements of the Spine

a) *The dog stretch:* down on all fours with your back level like a table top and your arms and upper legs like the four legs of a table (table position), inhale as you lift the tailbone, looking upward. Allow your lower back to arch downward as your chest opens.

b) *The cat stretch:* from the dog stretch position, on the exhalation tuck the tailbone under and round the spine upward, lowering the head. Move slowly and smoothly several times from the dog stretch into the cat stretch, coordinating breath and movement. Originate each movement from the pelvis.

c) *The puppy stretch:* from the table position, move your hands forward about two to three feet in front of you, pressing your chest down toward the ground while lifting your tailbone. Hold for several breaths. Make micromovements with your shoulders, hips and torso.

dog   cat   puppy

d) The leg pump: from the table position exhale, bringing
your right knee and forehead together. Inhale as you
extend your right leg behind you, pressing out through
the heel as you lift your head and look upward. Repeat
several times, then reverse sides.

From a sitting position

9. The Butterfly

Bring the soles of the feet together, heels in toward the
groin, and hold your feet either at the ankles or the toes.
Gently move your knees up and down like the wings of a
butterfly, but without bouncing. Then, apply gradual pressure downward to the inside of the legs with the forearms
and elbows. Avoid rounding the spine and hunching the

shoulders by keeping the head up and fixing your gaze on the
floor a few feet in front of you.

10. Knees Side to Side

Bend your knees, bring your feet flat on the ground about
six inches outside your hip width. Place your palms behind
you for support and lean back slightly. Slowly move your
knees from side to side.

11. Spinal Rocking

Bend your knees in toward your chest and hold underneath your knees. Begin to rock slowly forward and backward on the spine, with a thick rug or padded mat
underneath you. Inhale rocking backward, exhale rocking
forward.

12. Sacral Massage

Lie on your back with your knees in toward your chest and your hands on your knees. Rotate your knees in a clockwise direction, pressing down through the tip of the tailbone, then the right hip, lower back and left hip. Repeat several times and then reverse direction, rotating in a counter-clockwise direction.

13. The Crunch

Place your fingers lightly on the sides of your ears and bend your knees with your feet flat on the floor. Exhale as you lift your head and shoulders and bring your elbows toward your knees. Inhale as you release and go back down. As a variation, bring your right elbow toward your left knee as you come up one time, and the next time reverse it with your left elbow toward your right knee. Repeat several times.

Another variation: interlace your fingers behind your head and bend your knees, bringing the feet a few inches off the ground. Exhale as you lift your head and shoulders, bringing your elbows toward your knees and your knees toward your elbows. Inhaling, release and repeat.

14. The Knee Down Twist

Lie on your back with your arms out to the side in a "T"
position. Bring the sole of your right foot on top of the left
knee. As you exhale, gently twist to the left, lowering your
right knee to the left side. Roll your head to the right,
bringing the right ear toward the ground. Keep both shoulders in contact with the ground. For a little extra stretch,
place your left hand on top of the right knee, bringing it
more toward the ground. Hold for several breaths before
repeating on opposite side.

Appendix V

The Yoga Postures: An Orientation

Much like different Christian denominations, there are various schools of yoga, each with its own emphasis on what is most important. For example, the Bikram school encourages performance of the postures in a hot room in order to work more effectively with the connective tissue in the muscles. The Ayengar school emphasizes knowledge of the physiology involved in the postures and works on particular details in each pose. The Sivananda school ascribes a special place to the sun salutation medley. The Kripalu school of yoga, in which I have taken my training, seeks to draw one into the inner experience of yoga by integrating hatha yoga (*asanas* and *pranayama*) with raja yoga (meditation) in what it calls "posture flow" or "meditation-in-motion."[1]

Kripalu yoga practice is approached in three stages. **In the first stage, you must learn how to do the postures precisely and correctly while maintaining deep, relaxed breathing.** Perfection is not required. Some people have tight hamstrings and lower backs and will never be able to touch their head to their knees without bending the knee. What is important is to understand which muscles and ligaments the posture is intended to stretch and to make a conscious effort, adapting the pose as necessary for your body, but respecting the integrity of the posture by maintaining its basic structural dynamic.

Avoid labeling your performance ("bad" or "not good

enough"). Avoid comparing your physical ability with others' or holding an unrealistic ideal in your mind. Whenever you have a negative, self-critical reaction to what you see in yourself, it creates physical, mental and emotional tensions that undermine your ability to improve. Avoid exaggerated and generalized self-judgments ("I'm terrible at yoga!"). Just describe to yourself what is happening with non-judgmental awareness without bringing in any ideals or comparisons.

The second stage consists of learning how to tune in to the feelings and sensations that are arising in your body as you slowly move into and hold the posture at full extension for 20-60 seconds. The mind is thus anchored into the body and what is happening there, reestablishing a friendship between body and mind. This is, in itself, a significant benefit.

This focusing technique increases body-mind harmony, reduces the restless wandering of the mind, and takes you inward. Your powers of concentration improve and the mind becomes sharp and focused. All your movements, slow and gracefully made, are "tracked" by the mind, as well as the sensations arising from these movements. The body is closest to nature and more attuned than the mind to the natural laws of health and harmony. By keeping your attention on the instinctual urges and feelings, you become more attentive to the messages of the body, thereby promoting a harmonious and cooperative working of body and mind.

Body-mind conflict creates blocks and tensions. In all the experiences you've lived, your body hasn't just been a detached bystander. It was more involved than you may have realized. And if the mind encountered some things it didn't like and didn't want to face, they got stored somewhere in the body and are embedded there. Stages one and two help access and release deep-seated physical, mental and emotional blocks that sap your vitality and keep you from living as peacefully and joyfully as you would like. Stages one and two are predominantly hatha yoga (*asanas* and *pranayama*): correct execution of the postures with deep breathing and conscious awareness of body sensations. Stage three incorporates elements of raja yoga (meditation) into hatha yoga.

After you have learned 1) the correct technical performance of the postures, 2) to coordinate your body movements with continuous deep breathing, and 3) to focus your attention upon the feelings and sensations arising in your body, you are ready for stage three.

During stage three, all rules and restrictions that you have carefully learned and assiduously practiced can be put aside. Methods in the spiritual life are never akin to the points in an instruction manual. A proper method is more like a language. Discipline and attention is required in learning the grammar and usage of a language. But for true communication, one must eventually go beyond rules and logic and grammar. We go along with them until our conscious use of them becomes instinctive; then we go beyond the methods and techniques into spontaneous exercise. In the beginning, one needs the discipline of a method to create an environment in which the inner spirit can move. However, a true method has the dialectics of self-transcendence in it and eventually leads one beyond the method and allows for freedom of spirit.

Most traditional yoga stays within technique and is controlled performance. In Kripalu yoga, postures are a tool for transcendence. **In stage three there is no routine, no sequence of postures to follow. After sufficient warmups, you give free reign to however your body wants to stretch.** You choose freely from the "menu" of postures you have learned and employ any pose or series of poses that respond to your inner urgings. The one "book" from which you read is the book of your body.

Some of the ways you move may not even be traditional postures or may not be like anything you have ever seen in a yoga book. In stage three, however, you let go of your preconceived ideas of yoga postures. When your body choreographs and orchestrates its own movements, they are precisely and finely tuned to your inner needs. This harmonious, rhythmic, and balanced flow of postures becomes a form of meditation-in-motion, a prayer without words. It is possible to have some deeply prayerful experiences in this process of "posture flow." Your movements might progress, for example, from the yearning expressed in the mountain, to the surrender of the forward bend, to the imploring attitude of the yoga mudra, to the open receptivity of the triangle and the fish, to the worshipful child's pose, and end with the sun salutation, accompanied by the words of the Our Father. The more postures one learns, the more "vocabulary" one has for this form of prayerful communication with God that fully engages body, mind and spirit.

Stages one and two—correct execution of the postures with deep breathing and awareness of bodily sensations—represent a more "willful" practice. There are days when this is what you will prefer to do: focus your attention on performing the postures with exactness and in a definite, planned sequence, maintaining a balance between consciously induced muscle tension in the postures and intermittent relaxation poses. In willful practice, your energy is directed; you "make" things happen. Concentration is your base of operation, and your yoga period is akin to a "body-mind workout" with stretching exercises and focusing techniques. In the willful or learned practice, great attention is given to respecting, honoring and trusting your body's needs, capacities and limitations.

On other days, you may feel more inclined to a "surrendered" practice, and move immediately to stage three where the application of precise form or technique is an inhibition and limitation. That which is a core value in the willful practice—directing your energy—becomes a liability in the surrendered practice where you "let go" and follow the urge to move according to an intelligence originating from somewhere deep within you. "Meditation-in-motion" is the by-word here.

Being able to enter into either "willful" or "surrendered" practice keeps yoga a refreshing experience and a constant source of joy. If one were always to stay in willful practice, it could become mechanical and dry, if not boring. If you move methodically through the same sequence of postures every-time you come to your mat, you may after a while begin to lose interest. In "surrendered" practice, however, you let go of routine and just move the way your body wants.

In effect, this generally means you employ your own instincts or the postures you have learned in an order and for a length of time that feels right and good to you. You may spend your whole time just entering into a few postures and holding each one for a longer time, surrendering into it, and allowing your body to express to God what is in your heart.

When stage three (raja yoga) is integrated with stages one and two (hatha yoga), body, mind and spirit work harmoniously together. Yoga postures and breathing methods are simply used to dispose one for the contemplative grace of a prayerful, meditative experience. In this way yoga and meditation serve as positive means for spiritual growth.

Both "willful" and "surrendered" practice are ideally followed by a period of sitting meditation as described in Part I of this book.

Some Basic Yoga Postures

The yoga postures which follow are arranged in a progressive sequence so that one sets up or provides a counterpose for another. In looking at some of these illustrated poses it may seem to you that the formal yoga poses themselves are physically easier to perform than some of the warm-ups for them. Such may in fact be the case with certain of the poses, but be aware that putting your body in a particular position is just one aspect of doing yoga. An essential but invisible aspect to these postures is the inward focusing of your awareness on your internal state as it is colored moment to moment by shifting sensations, emotions and thoughts while you enter into and hold the posture for 20-60 seconds. Yoga practice in this sense becomes a time of formal training in consciousness. The mental aspect is oftentimes more challenging than the physical. While it is not talked about in the description of these poses, never lose sight of the fact that it is at the heart of each one.

The Mountain

1. Standing with your feet parallel and hip-width apart, rock gently back and forth until you find your point of stable balance. Then press the soles of your feet downward.

2. Tighten the muscles of the gluteus folds where the buttock muscles meet the upper thighs; the kneecaps are automatically lifted when the buttocks are tightened. *This is called "bringing up the squeeze" and will be referred to often in these illustrations.*

3. Press the crown of your head away from your shoulders to elongate the spine.

4. From their position at your sides, bring your hands slowly upward, rotating your palms up to face one another as they come into position directly over your head. Extend your fingertips as far upward as you can.

5. Expand your chest and breathe deeply.

6. Slowly lower your arms to your sides, rotating your palms downward.

Benefits

  —develops concentration, poise, groundedness
  —expresses confidence, stability, endurance
  —improves circulation and respiration
  —increases body heat and energizes body

Precautions

  —weak knees: avoid long holding times
  —high blood pressure, heart conditions, menstruation,
    pregnancy during first three months or if problems arise

Contraindications

  —recent or chronic injury or inflammation of knees

Half Moon

1. Standing with your feet parallel and hip-width apart, find your point of balance on the balls of your feet and press the soles of your feet downward.

2. Bring up the squeeze.

3. Press the crown of your head away from your shoulders.

4. Raise your hands overhead, placing your two index fingers together in a steeple position and interlacing the other fingers. Press your fingertips away from your shoulders, relaxing the shoulder muscles.

5. Press your right foot downward as you press your right hip out to the side. Allow the pressing to extend your torso and arms to the left. Lean neither forward nor backward, but sideways.

6. To release the posture, press the sole of your inside foot downward and allow your body to return to the center. Repeat the posture to the other side.

Benefits

—provides alternate stretching and contraction, toning
  and strengthening of the intercostal, lateral and dorsal
  muscles
—increases flexibility of the spine
—expresses balance and flexibility

Precautions and Contraindications

—same as for the Mountain

**Reminder: be aware of what is going on in your body as
you do each posture.**

The Warrior

1. Repeat steps 1-5 as for the Mountain.

2. Take a large step forward, bending your leading knee and sinking into the posture. To avoid knee strain, be sure that your leading knee is in direct alignment above your foot.

3. Press your back hipbone forward and your back heel downward.

4. To release the posture, bring your back foot forward up alongside your front foot, and slowly lower your arms to your sides.

   Repeat the pose with the other leg forward.

Benefits

—strengthens the feet, ankles, knees, thighs, hip joints, back, arms, shoulders and neck
—stretches and strengthens the inner thigh muscles
—stimulates digestion and helps relieve constipation
—expresses confidence and fortitude

Precautions and Contraindication

—same as for the Mountain and Half Moon

The Triangle

1. Standing with your feet wide apart (about the length of one of your legs), turn the toes of your right foot out to the right and the heel of your left foot just slightly to the left. Your right heel is in line with your left instep.

2. Press the soles of your feet downward and bring up the squeeze.

3. Press your right hipbone forward as though you were between two panes of glass to hold your hips in alignment with one another.

4. Raise your hands up to shoulder level.

5. Press your left hip to the left and press out through the fingertips of the right hand.

6. Maintaining your extension, rotate your right hand down to your right leg and your left hand overhead. Press your fingertips away from your shoulders. The objective is not to touch the ground, but to stretch the torso and open the chest.

7. Rotate your head to gaze toward your raised hand, and rotate your chest upward to bring your torso into alignment with your right leg and arms. Breathe deeply and regularly while in the pose.

8. To release, press the soles of your feet downward and come back into position with your hands raised at shoulder level. Alter the position of your feet to repeat in the other direction.

Benefits

—develops concentration, strength, groundedness
—provides alternate flexing and relaxing of the sides of the body and proper placement of the bones and muscles of the hips
—expresses balance, poise, openness, yearning

Precautions and Contraindications

—same as preceding postures, with the additional note that for weak back muscles, bring the lower hand high enough on the leg to avoid too much compression on the lower rib cage; use the squeeze to avoid back strain

The Cobra

1. From a position on your stomach, place your hands palms down beneath your shoulders with your elbows close to your sides.

2. Bring up the squeeze and press your pubic bone and feet downward, allowing your upper body to lift in response to the pressing. Apply no pressure to the palms of your hands. To this point, your lower back muscles are doing the work.

3. Press the crown of your head away from your shoulders.

4. When you feel established in the position, press your palms downward, allowing your torso to come off the ground from the belly button upward. Hold that position for a moment, breathing deeply.

5. Press your palms downward again to allow your torso to lift off the ground from your pubic bone upward. Keep your elbows in, close to your sides, and expand your chest with your head slightly raised.

6. Release the pressure on your palms and gradually release the squeeze as your body returns to the starting position.

Benefits

- —strengthens wrists, arms, shoulders, and back muscles
- —stretches and strengthens abdominal muscles
- —irrigates the kidneys
- —aligns the spinal column
- —helps relieve menstrual disorders as well as the back and abdominal pain that can accompany menstruation and menopause

Precautions

- —weak back muscles: to strengthen, bring up the squeeze with minimal lifting upward

Contraindications

- —pregnancy (after third month)
- —recent abdominal surgery or abdominal inflammation
- —recent or chronic back injury or inflammation

Reminder: in addition to their physical benefits, the postures are a focusing technique for the mind.

Head Toward Knee

1. Sit erect with one leg outstretched, the other bent in toward the body so that the heel fits into the crotch and the sole of the foot presses against the inside of the thigh.

2. Press the crown of your head away from your shoulders and straighten your spine.

3. Extend your fingertips overhead and press them away from your shoulders. Press the heel of your extended leg away from your hip.

4. Slightly lift your tailbone and allow the lifting to extend your torso out over the extended leg. Bend forward from your hips, extending your arms out along the leg and relaxing into an easy stretch for 30 seconds.

5. Find the developmental phase of the stretch by slowly bending forward a little further. A very slight distance in your bend may be all that is needed to reach the developmental phase. Hold it for another 30 seconds.

Variations: if it is helpful, use a towel around the bottom of your extended foot to assist you in doing this stretch. Or, place the foot of your extended leg flat on the floor with your knee bent. Bring your head to your bent knee and slowly slide your extended foot forward, straightening your leg to the extent you are able.

Do not worry about how far you can go; everyone is different. You may find one side more flexible than the other. Work toward equalization. A stretch done on one side is always balanced by a similar stretch on the other side.

Benefits

    —provides comprehensive stretch to entire backside of body
    —irrigates and decongests the kidneys
    —increases flexibility in spine and hips
    —stretches muscles, ligaments and nerves in back of the
    legs
    —massages and oxygenates abdominal organs

Precautions

    —weak or stiff back muscles: do not extend arms overhead
    —stiffness in hips, sciatica or knee injury: use cushions
    under one or both knees
    —constipation: practice carefully, avoiding long holding
    —pregnancy: use a towel and avoid constricting the belly

Contraindications

    —recent chronic back, hip, knee or leg injury or inflammation

The Boat

1. Lie on your belly with your arms at your sides, palms facing downward.

2. Bring up the squeeze, pressing your pubic bone downward and lifting your torso, hands and feet.

3. Interlace your fingers behind your back, pressing your fingers toward your feet and opening your chest. Hold briefly.

4. Maintaining your lift, release your interlaced fingers and slowly extend your arms in front of you.

5. Press the crown of your head away from your shoulders and straight ahead, not looking up.

6. Press the tips of your toes away from your hips and press out through your fingertips.

7. Bring your arms slowly back to your sides and relax.

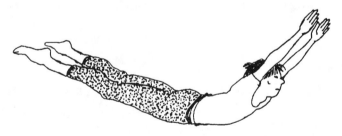

Benefits

   —strengthens back muscles
   —irrigates kidneys with fresh blood supply
   —revitalizes endocrine system
   —stimulates nervous system

—aligns spinal column
—tones and strengthens buttocks, thighs, legs

Precautions

—weak back muscles: to strengthen, bring up squeeze with minimal lifting

Contraindications

—pregnancy (after third month)
—recent abdominal surgery or inflammation
—recent or chronic back injury or inflammation

The Child

1. Sit on your heels.

2. Press the crown of your head away from your shoulders.

3. Lift your tailbone and allow your torso to come forward, with your forehead resting on the floor and your arms at your sides.

Variation: place a cushion over your heels and sit on the cushion. Place another cushion on the floor in front of you and allow your forehead to rest on it in the forward bent position.

 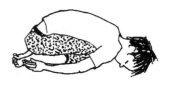

Benefits

—provides counterstretch for backward bending postures
—increases flexibility in hips and knees
—massages and stimulates internal organs
—stimulates digestion and elimination
—relieves intestinal gas, constipation and hemorrhoids
—calms mind and emotions

Precautions

—constipation: avoid long holding
—sensitivity in knees: use folded blanket under knees

—pregnancy: spread knees apart, optional cushion under forehead and buttocks
—unmedicated high blood pressure: place a cushion under forehead

Contraindications

—recent or chronic injury or inflammation in the knees
—varicose veins

Reminder: use your breath as an anchor for your attention.

The Bridge

1. Lie on your back with your arms at your sides, palms facing downward. Bend your knees, bringing the soles of your feet close to your buttocks.

2. Press the soles of your feet downward and your pubic bone upward, bringing up the squeeze.

3. Interlace your fingers and press your hands toward your feet, walking your shoulder blades closer together.

4. Open and expand your chest.

5. Keep your knees located in a line directly above your ankles; do not allow them to extend out over your ankles.

6. Release your hands and allow your spine to roll down, vertabra by vertabra.

Benefits

—helps regulate functioning of thyroid gland
—brings elasticity to spinal column
—stretches abdominal muscles
—strengthens buttocks, thighs, legs

Precautions

—to strengthen weak back muscles, minimal lifting of pelvis
—pregnancy (last trimester): avoid if posture inhibits breathing

Contraindications

—recent or chronic back injury or inflammation

The Half Shoulderstand

1. From a position on your back, bend your knees and lift your legs up overhead, bringing your hands up to support your lower back and hips.

2. Draw your elbows in under your body so that your arms and elbows, not the back of your neck, are taking the weight of your body.

3. Hold the posture for at least a minute to allow blood to flow freely to heart and brain.

4. To release the posture, bring your hands to the ground and press your palms downward as you roll your vertebrae down one by one. Or, bring your knees toward your chest and allow your hands to slide down your legs as you roll down.

Variation: You can enter this posture from the bridge pose by bringing your palms up to support your hips and lifting your legs one at a time, keeping your knees relaxed.

Benefits

—improves flow of blood to brain; may relieve some
headaches

—increased blood flow to neck; helps normalize function of
thyroid

—encourages diaphragmatic breathing, helping to relieve
asthma and respiratory problems

—improves venous circulation, allowing blood from legs
and trunk to flow to heart without strain

Precautions

—cervical and shoulder strain: practice carefully

—heavy or pregnant: practice carefully, pressing soles of
feet against a wall to bring yourself into the posture

Contraindications

—menstruation, unmedicated high or low blood pressure

—chronic nasal, sinus, or thyroid disorders

—detached retina, glaucoma, or any infection or inflammation of the eyes and ears

The Fish

1. Lie on your back with your legs straight and your feet together. Extend your arms underneath your body with your hands resting palms down and your elbows as close together as possible under your body.

2. Press your heels away from your hips, tilt your pelvis forward, and press your buttocks downward, lifting your torso and pressing out through the chest.

3. With your weight distributed between your elbows and your tailbone, allow the crown of your head to roll backward and rest lightly on the floor.

4. To release, press your buttocks firmly downward and lift your head from the floor, gently allowing your back to come down onto the floor.

Benefits

—provides counterstretch for Shoulderstand
—opens the chest area, expanding the upper lobes of the lungs
—helps alleviate asthma and respiratory complaints
—stretches the front and contracts the back of the neck
—stretches solar plexus and abdomen, releases stiffness in shoulders

Precautions

—weak back, neck muscles: use cushion under upper back with additional optional prop under neck or head

Contraindications

—recent or chronic back or neck injury or inflammation

The Forward Bend

1. Extend both legs in a sitting position. If you have difficulty sitting up straight in this position, place a cushion under your tailbone to tilt your spine slightly forward.

2. Press the crown of your head away from your shoulders and extend your fingertips overhead, inhaling deeply as you bring your arms up.

3. Press your heels away from your legs or, if the backs of your legs are too tight, just relax your legs.

4. Lift your tailbone slightly and allow the lifting to extend your torso over your outstretched legs. Stretch forward from the hips without forcing.

5. Bring your arms to your calves, ankles, toes or feet as you are able and relax into the stretch.
   Variation: place a towel around your feet and pull yourself gently forward.

Benefits

—stretches entire backside of body from heels to back of neck
—lengthens spinal column
—stretches muscles, ligaments, nerves in back of legs; can help relieve certain cases of sciatica
—increases circulation of blood throughout body

Precautions

—weak or stiff back muscles: do not raise arms above head; keep back straight and avoid rounding the spine; use a towel around feet and cushion under hips
—sciatica: practice carefully, using cushions under hips and knees to avoid excessive strain
—constipation: avoid long holding
—pregnancy: use a towel around feet and avoid constricting belly

Contraindications

—recent or chronic back injury or inflammation

Reminder: apply the principles of easy and developmental stretching to all the postures.

The Spinal Twist

1. From a seated position with your legs extended, draw your right foot up close to your body with your knee pointing upward.

2. Cross your right foot over your left leg, place the sole of the foot on the ground near the knee.

3. Take your right knee in the elbow crook of your right arm and draw your chest close to your right thigh, straightening your back.

4. Extend your left arm directly in front of you at eye level and slowly begin to sweep your arm to the left on a level arc, twisting your spine to the left and following the movement of your left hand with your eyes as you rotate your torso to the left as far as you can.

5. Bring your left hand down and place it palm down on the floor at the base of your spine, supporting your back erect with your left arm. Hold the posture and breathe deeply.

6. To release, extend your left arm once again to eye level and rotate it back toward the right until you are facing fully forward. Repeat on the opposite side.

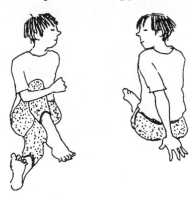

Benefits

    —maintains flexibility in spine
    —corrects deviation in the spinal column
    —removes stiffness from shoulders and neck
    —massages internal organs, increasing blood circulation
    —stimulates digestive process

Precautions

    —weak back muscles: use cushion under both buttocks to
    help keep spine erect; use knee down twist (see warm-up
    exercises) as an alternative

Contraindications

    —recent or chronic back injury or inflammation

The Symbol of Yoga (Head Beneath the Heart)

1. Sit on your heels.

2. Elongate your spine and press the crown of your head away from your shoulders.

3. Bring your hands behind your back, interlacing your fingers. (If this is difficult, grasp a towel behind you, allowing some space between your hands.)

4. Press your knuckles down toward the floor, elongating your arms.

5. Squeeze your shoulder blades together and expand your chest.

6. Lift your tailbone slightly, allowing the lifting to extend your torso forward over your knees. Leading with your chest out and your head up, gradually come down and allow your forehead to rest on the ground.

7. Bring your arms up erect behind and above you, pressing your little fingers toward the floor in front of you.

Variation: from this position, come up onto the crown of your head.

8. To release, press your shins downward and drop your tailbone slightly, coming to an upright seated position. Unclasp your hands, allowing them to float upward and eventually come to rest on your lap.

Benefits

—deeply tranquilizes the whole system, calming mind and
body
—relieves shoulder tension
—improves peristalsis, aiding elimination and relieving
intestinal gas
—massages internal organs and stimulates digestion

Precautions (same as for Child's Pose)

Contraindications

—recent or chronic injury or inflammation in knees, back,
shoulders, or abdomen; varicose veins

**Reminder: mentally "track" the sensations arising in
your body.**

The Sun Salutation

1. Standing with your feet parallel and hip width apart, bring your palms together in front of your chest. Bring up the squeeze. Exhale.

2. Inhale, raising your arms overhead and arch backward from the waist.

3. Exhale, bending forward at the waist and releasing the squeeze as your torso continues downward. Bring your fingertips or your palms to the floor next to your feet.

4. Inhale, bending your left knee and extending your right foot back. Press through the heel of the back foot and the crown of the head.

5. Exhale, bringing your front foot back next to the back foot, keeping your legs straight and pressing your heels towards the floor.

6. Retain the breath, bend your knees and lower knees, chest and chin to the ground.

7. Inhale, pushing chin and chest forward along the ground and up, bending upper half of body as in a cobra position.

8. Exhale, raising your hips and pressing your heels toward the floor with legs straight.

9. Inhale, bending your right leg and bringing your right foot forward with a lunging motion to locate it in the space between your hands.

10. Exhale, bringing your left foot forward and placing it alongside your right.

11. Inhale, slowly coming up with arms raised overhead and arching backwards.

12. Exhale, lowering hands to prayer position at your chest.

Repeat, leading with the left leg back.

1 EXHALE

2 INHALE

3 EXHALE

4 INHALE

5 EXHALE

6 RETAIN

7 INHALE

8 EXHALE

9 INHALE

10 EXHALE

11 INHALE

12 EXHALE

Benefits

- —provides an excellent sequence for stretching and invigorating the whole body; there are twelve different spinal positions
- —develops concentration, coordination, balance and poise
- —stimulates the digestive system by alternately stretching and compressing the abdominal region and massaging internal organs
- —increases cardiac activity and blood circulation
- —ventilates the lungs, oxygenates the blood and removes carbon dioxide from the respiratory tract
- —stimulates activity of the endocrine glands

Precautions

- —high blood pressure, heart conditions, menstruation, pregnancy: practice carefully without long holding times
- —weak back muscles: do not bend forward or come back from the forward bend position with arms overhead; limit the degree of backward arching, using the squeeze to protect the lower back
- —keep the knee in line with the ankle in the lunge position and avoid long holding times

Contraindications

- —recent or chronic injury or inflammation of back or knees
- —unmedicated high blood pressure

The Relax Pose

1. Lie on your back with your feet turned out and about two feet apart. Place your hands at your sides with the palms up.

2. Close your eyes and relax your whole body, fixing your attention on your deep and slow breathing. Remain in this position for several minutes.

3. Begin to move your fingers and toes, bringing your feet together. Stretch your arms overhead on the floor and elongate your right side, pressing out in opposite directions with your right fingers and toes. Hold a controlled stretched for five seconds, then relax and repeat on the left side. Each time you stretch, gently pull in your abdominal muscles to make the middle of your body thin.

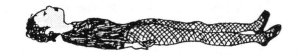

Benefits
—it feels really good
—stretches arms, shoulders, spine, abdominals, intercostal muscles of rib cage, feet, and ankles
—an excellent, easy stretch to do first thing in the morning while still in bed

Every session of yoga should end with the relax pose. It is as important as any of the stretching postures, and in a sense more important, because the point is to calm the wandering mind, which St. Theresa called "the fool in the house," so as to be ready for prayer.

From the relax position, move directly to your chair, prayer bench, or cushion for meditation.

Instructions for Meditation

Find a comfortable, upright position in which you are relaxed but alert, with your eyes lightly closed. Remain as still as possible.

Silently, begin to say interiorly a single word or phrase selected from the context of Christian faith. Listen to it as you say it gently but continuously with faith and love.

Do not think or imagine anything, spiritual or otherwise. If thoughts and images come and your attention strays, as soon as you become aware of this, return to saying your word.

Meditate each morning and evening for twenty to thirty minutes.

Notes

Introduction

1. David J. O'Brien, *Isaac Hecker: An American Catholic* (Mahwah, NJ: Paulist Press, 1992), p. 26.

2. *Ibid.*

3. See Bill Moyers, *Healing and the Mind* (New York: Doubleday, 1993), pp. 115-143.

4. "Canadians Feeling the Time Crunch: StatsCan," *The Montreal Gazette*, Saturday, April 24, 1993, p. 10.

5. "Job Stress Knows No Borders," *The Montreal Gazette*, Tuesday, March 23, 1993, p. 1.

6. Bill Moyers, *Healing and the Mind*, p. 139.

7. Thomas Ryan, *Disciplines for Christian Living: Interfaith Perspectives* (Mahwah, NJ: Paulist, 1993).

1. Meditation: Breaking Through to the Real

1. Henry David Thoreau, *Walden and Other Writings*, ed. Joseph Wood Krutch (New York: Bantam, 1962), p. 102.

2. Thomas Merton, *Contemplative Prayer* (New York: Image Doubleday, 1971), p. 79.

3. Mary Jo Meadow, "Some Understandings About Meditation Practice," paper distributed by Resources for Ecumenical Spirituality, PO Box 6, Mankato, MN, 56002-0006.

4. Anthony de Mello, *Sadhana: A Way to God* (New York: Image Books, 1984), pp. 29-31.

2. What Makes for *Christian* Meditation?

1. Swami Satyananda Saraswati, *Sure Ways to Self Realization* (Bihar, India: Sharda Press, 1980), pp. 169-170.

2. See Ken Wilber's discussion of the perennial philosophy in chapter 5 of *Grace and Grit* (Boston: Shambhala, 1991), to which I am indebted here.

3. *Ibid.* p. 79.

4. Edward Stevens, *Spiritual Technologies* (Mahwah, NJ: Paulist Press, 1990), p. 155.

5. *Ibid.* p. 158.

6. Joseph Cardinal Ratzinger, "Letter to the bishops of the Catholic Church on some aspects of Christian Meditation," in *L'Osservatore Romano*, 2 January 1990, pp. 8-10, 12. See Ama Samy, S.J., "Can a Christian Practice Zen, Yoga, or TM?" *Review for Religious* (Vol. 50, No. 4, July/August 1991), pp. 535-544, for an exposition of the weaknesses of the Vatican document and an assertion that it does not go far enough.

7. *Ibid.* No. 15, p. 9.

8. See chapter one, "The Meaning of Discipline for Christian Living," in my *Disciplines for Christian Living* (Mahwah, NJ: Paulist 1993).

9. See the series of articles on the cross of Christ in *The Word Among Us* (July 1992), pp. 2-21, to which I am indebted in this section.

3. Historical Highlights in the Practice of Christian Meditation

1. M. Basil Pennington, O.C.S.O., *Centering Prayer: Renewing an Ancient Christian Prayer Form* (New York: Doubleday, 1980), p. 31.

2. *The Philokalia*, Vol. 1, trans. G.E. Palmer, Philip Sherrard, and Kallistos Ware (London and Boston: Faber and Faber, 1979).

3. *The Way of a Pilgrim*, trans. R.M. French (New York: Seabury Press, 1965).

4. See *John Cassian: Conferences*, trans. Colm Luibheid, (Mahwah, NJ: Paulist, 1985), pp. 132-138 for the unedited teaching of Cassian on the use of a sacred word or phrase in prayer.

5. *The Cloud of Unknowing and the Book of Privy Counselling* (New York: Image Books, 1973), p. 56.

6. Pennington, *Centering Prayer*, p. 13.

7. Thomas Keating, O.C.S.O.: *Finding Grace at the Center* (Petersham, MA: St. Bede Publications, 1978), with Basil Pennington and Thomas Clarke; *The Heart of the World: An Introduction to Contemplative Christianity* (New York: Crossroad, 1981); *Open Mind, Open Heart* (New York: Amity House, 1986). M. Basil Pennington, O.C.S.O.: see footnote 1 as well as *Daily We Touch Him: Practical Religious Experiences* (New York: Image Books, 1977);

Centered Living (New York: Image Book, 1986); *Call to the Center* (New York: Doubleday Image, 1990).

8. John of the Cross, *The Collected Works of St John of the Cross*, trans. Kieran Kavanaugh, O.C.D., and Otilio Rodriguez, O.C.D. (Washington, DC: ICS Publications, 1979), p. 140; *The Ascent of Mount Carmel*, Book Two, chapter 13, No. 2.

9. Pat Windsor, "Father Thomas Keating Brings Contemplation Out of the Cloister," *St. Anthony Messenger*, (February 1992), p. 14.

10. Two books on Dom John Main's life and teachings are Niel McKenty's *In the Stillness Dancing* (Montreal: Novalis, 1992) and *John Main by Those Who Knew Him*, Paul Harris, ed. (Novalis, 1991). John Main's direct teaching is contained in *Word into Silence* (Mahwah, NJ: Paulist, 1981); *Christian Meditation: The Gethsemane Talks* (Benedictine Priory, 1983); *Moment of Christ* (New York: Crossroad, 1984); *Letters from the Heart* (New York: Crossroad, 1984); *The Present Christ* (New York: Crossroad, 1986); *The Heart of Creation* (Darton, Longman, and Todd, 1988); *The Way of Unknowing* (London: Darton, Longman and Todd, 1989); *Community of Love* (Darton, Longman and Todd, 1990); and *Word Made Flesh* (Darton, Longman, and Todd, 1993).

11. Books by Laurence Freeman, O.S.B.: *The Light Within: The Inner Path of Meditation* (New York: Crossroad, 1987); *The Selfless Self* (London: Darton, Longman and Todd, 1989).

12. *Christian Meditation Newsletter*, April 1991, p. 1. For various testimonies by members of these groups, see *Christian Meditation by Those Who Practice It*, Paul Harris, ed. (Denville, NJ: Dimension Books, 1993).

4. Is Contemplative Prayer for Everyone?

1. William H. Shannon, "Contemplative Prayer," in the *New Dictionary of Catholic Spirituality* (Collegeville, MN: The Liturgical Press, 1993), pp. 209-210.

2. William McNamara, O.C.D., *The Human Adventure: The Art of Contemplative Living* (Warwick, NY: Amity House, 1974).

3. George Maloney, S.J., *Inscape: God at the Heart of Matter* (Denville, NJ: Dimension Books, 1978).

4. Shannon, "Contemplative Prayer," pp. 210-211.

5. *Ibid.* p. 211.

6. *Symeon the New Theologian: The Discourses* trans. C.J. Catanzaro (Mahwah, NJ: Paulist, 1980).

7. James A. Wiseman, O.S.B., "Mysticism," in the *New Dictionary of Catholic Spirituality* (Collegeville, MN: The Liturgical Press, 1993), pp. 681-689.

8. David Steindl-Rost, *Gratefulness: The Heart of Prayer* (Mahwah, NJ: Paulist, 1984), p. 86.

9. James J. Bacik, "Contemporary Spirituality," in the *New Dictionary of Catholic Spirituality* (Collegeville, MN: The Liturgical Press, 1993), p. 225.

10. C. Stevens, "Thomas Merton: Profile in Memoriam," *American Benedictine Review* (20:1, 1969), p. 8.

11. Thomas Merton, *Spiritual Direction* (Collegeville, MN: The Liturgical Press, 1960), p. 94.

12. Thomas Merton, *New Seeds of Contemplation* (New York: New Directions, 1972), p. 1.

13. See Thomas Merton, *Contemplation in a World of Action* (New York: Doubleday Image Books, 1973), p. 94.

14. Thomas Merton, *Contemplative Prayer* (New York: Doubleday Image, 1971), pp. 39, 29.

15. Paul Pearson, "Everyone Is Called to Contemplation: Thomas Merton on Prayer," *Priests and People*, Vol. 5, No. 6 (June 1991), pp. 220-223.

16. Merton, *New Seeds*, pp. 168-169.

17. Merton, *Contemplative Prayer*, p. 83.

18. Thomas Merton, *The Waters of Siloe* (New York: HBJ, 1979), p. 361.

19. Merton, *Contemplative Prayer*, p. 82.

20. Merton, *Contemplation in a World of Action*, p. 176.

21. Harvey D. Egan, S.J., *Ignatius Loyola the Mystic* (Wilmington, DE: Michel Glazier, 1987), pp. 32-55.

22. *Ibid.* pp. 121-126.

23. *Ibid.* p. 121.

24. Harvey D. Egan, S.J., "Affirmative Way," in the *New Dictionary of Catholic Spirituality* (Collegeville, MN: The Liturgical Press, 1993), pp. 16-17.

25. Harvey D. Egan, S.J., "Ignatian Spirituality," *New Dictionary of Catholic Spirituality* (Collegeville, MN: The Liturgical Press 1993), p. 528.

26. *Ibid.* p. 523.

27. As quoted in the introduction to *The Collected Works of John of the Cross*, trans. Kieran Kavanaugh, O.C.D., and Otilio Rodriguez, O.C.D. (Washington, DC: ICS Publications, 1979), p. 35.

28. *Ibid.* pp. 156-159; *Ascent*, Bk II, ch. 17.

29. *Ibid.* p. 148; *Ascent*, Bk II, ch. 15, No. 1.

30. *Ibid.* pp. 140-141; *Ascent*, Bk II, ch. 13, No. 16.

31. *Ibid.* p. 149; *Ascent*, Bk II ch. 15, No. 5.

32. *Ibid.* p. 318; *Dark Night*, Bk I, ch. 10, No. 6.

33. *Ibid.* p. 440; *Spiritual Canticle*, stanza 7, No. 10.

34. *Ibid.* p. 138; *Ascent*, Bk II, ch. 12, No. 5.

35. *Ibid.* p. 317; *Dark Night*, Bk I, ch. 10, No. 1.

36. Merton, *Contemplative Prayer*, pp. 84, 85.

37. *Ibid.*

38. *Ibid.* pp. 418-419; *Spiritual Canticle*, stanza 1, Nos. 7, 8.

39. Thomas Merton, *No Man Is an Island* (New York: HBJ, 1955), p. 61.

40. Keith R. Barron, OCDS, "Quietism," *New Dictionary of Catholic Spirituality* (Collegeville, MN: The Liturgical Press, 1993), p. 803.

41. Shannon, "Contemplative Prayer," p. 213.

Ignatius, for example, was twice jailed—once for two months—under suspicion of being involved with a pietistic movement which claimed the direct and constant inspiration of the Holy Spirit. The investigators found no error in what Ignatius and his companions taught; nevertheless, the subjects on which they were allowed to speak were significantly curtailed.

42. Kenneth C. Russell, "Mystical Theology," *New Dictionary of Catholic Spirituality* (Collegeville, MN: The Liturgical Press, 1993), p. 681.

5. A Method for the Journey: The Use of a Sacred Word

1. *The Collected Works of John of the Cross*, trans. Kieran Kavanaugh, O.C.D., and Otilio Rodriguez, O.C.D. (Washington, DC: ICS Publications, 1979), p. 218, *Ascent* Bk III, ch. 2, No. 13.

2. *Ibid.*, p. 303, *Dark Night* Bk I, ch. 3, No. 3.

3. Thomas Matus, *Yoga and the Jesus Prayer Tradition* (Mahwah, NJ: Paulist, 1984), pp. 44-45.

4. Basil Pennington, *Centering Prayer* (New York: Doubleday, 1980), p. 200. Elsewhere: "This emphasis on the word, and especially the insistence on saying it without ceasing, is not present in Centering Prayer. It may well happen, especially for beginners, that they will be using their word almost constantly as they continually find themselves back in reflective awareness. But the whole emphasis in Centering Prayer is on the Presence, on the Lord our God in the Center of our being, known by faith and reached by love. The word in Centering Prayer is a love word, and it is used only when it is needed to support the love . . . . The

difference in Centering Prayer lies in the fact that we use the word simply to return to the Presence, to return to God at the Center of our being . . . . I want to make it very clear that in drawing a comparison between Father John Main's method and Centering Prayer, I do not want in any way to be critical of his teaching. I think it is excellent. The Lord leads each of us in different ways. For some, Father's very simple method will be the way. For others, it will be Centering Prayer. And others still, in the Divine leading, will find for themselves something of a mixture that will work. But . . . there is value in being clear in our teaching" (*Centered Living*, New York: Image Books, 1986, pp. 62-64). Also, Keating: "There are forms of Christian prayer similar to mantric practice in the Hindu tradition that consist of repeating the sacred word continuously. This is not the method of centering prayer. In this practice, you only return to the sacred word when you notice you are thinking some other thought. As you become more comfortable with this prayer, you begin to find yourself beyond the word in a place of interior peace. Then you see that there is a level of attention that is beyond the sacred word. The sacred word is a pointer and you have reached that to which it is pointing. Until you have that experience, you must continue to go back to the sacred word in order to reaffirm your intention when you notice you are thinking of something else . . . . The method of centering prayer is not concentrative but receptive. While both methods are excellent and aim at the same goal, they are not the same and produce different effects in the psyche. In centering prayer, the use of the sacred word is designed to foster the receptive attitude"—*Open Mind, Open Heart* (New York: Amity House, 1986), pp. 48, 50. "Its use or presence (the sacred word) will vary from one period of prayer to the next, according to circumstances. You need great flexibility in using it. The principle is always to use it to go toward greater peace, silence, and beyond. But when one is in peace, silence, and beyond, forget it" (*ibid*. p. 119).

5. Henri Le Saux, O.S.B. (Abhishiktananda), *Prayer* (London: SPCK, 1967), pp. 52-53.

6. Corona Mary, *Towards God-Consciousness* (Tiruchirapalli, So. India: Jegamatha Ashram, 1990), pp. 100-101.

7. Timothy S. Ware, *The Orthodox Church* (London: Penguin, 1963), pp. 170-171.

6. Practical Questions: Time, Place, Frequency, Posture, Breathing

1. As quoted in Basil Pennington, O.C.S.O., *Centering Prayer* (New York: Doubleday, 1980), p. 37.

2. Teresa of Avila, *The Interior Castle* (Mahwah, NJ: Paulist, 1979), p. 166.

3. Andrew Foley, Lecture #11 in the Christian Meditation Foundation (56 Windsor Road, Brookline, MA. 02146) series of talks, given on Dec. 13, 1989.

4. C.S. Lewis, *The Screwtape Letters and Screwtape Prepares a Toast* (New York: Macmillan, 1962), p. 20.

5. Igumen Chariton of Valamo, *The Art of Prayer: An Orthodox Anthology*, trans. E. Kadloubovsky and E.M. Palmer (London: Faber and Faber, 1966), p. 103.

6. *Ibid.* pp. 96-97.

7. Saraswati, *Sure Ways to Self Realization* (Bihar, India: Sharba Press, 1980), p. 91.

8. Eknath Easwaren, *The Mantram Handbook* (Petaluma, CA: Nilgiri Press, 1977), p. 76.

9. Igumen Chariton, *The Art of Prayer*, pp. 104-105.

10. Laurence Freeman, O.S.B., at a colloquium on "The Prayer of Christ in the Life of a Priest," held October 18-20, 1987, at Villa Marguerita, Montreal, Quebec. See also, John Main, *Moment of Christ* (New York: Crossroad, 1984), p. 1.

11. Pennington, *Centering Prayer*, p. 55.

12. Daniel Goleman, "A Slow, Methodical Calming of the Mind," *The New York Times Magazine* (March 21, 1993), p. 42.

13. *Ibid.*

7. Dealing with Distractions

1. Philip St. Romain, *Kundalini Energy and Christian Spirituality* (New York: Crossroad, 1991), pp. 62-63.

2. As quoted in "Meditation and Psychology," an unpublished paper by Marie A. Foley, The Christian Meditation Foundation, Brookline, MA., pp. 3-4.

3. *Ibid.* p. 5. In particular cases, a person may benefit from some help in dealing with these surfacing traces of deeply embedded positive or negative experiences by talking with one who understands these dynamics and how they work psychologically.

4. Thomas Keating, O.C.S.O., *Open Mind, Open Heart* (New York: Amity House, 1986), pp. 15-16.

5. See chapter 9, "The Unloading of the Unconscious," in Keating's *Open Mind, Open Heart* to which I am indebted.

6. *The Collected Works of St. John of the Cross*, trans. Kieran Kavanaugh, O.C.D., and Otilio Rodriguez, O.C.D. (Washington, DC: ICS Publications, 1979), p. 122, or, *The Ascent of Mount Carmel*, Bk II, ch. 7, No. 5.

7. Thomas Merton, *Contemplative Prayer* (New York: Doubleday, Image Books, 1969), p. 76.

8. As quoted in Merton, *ibid.* p. 100.

9. *Collected Works*, p. 365, or, *Dark Night,* Bk II, ch. 16, No. 7.

10. Teresa of Avila, *Interior Castle* (Mahwah, NJ: Paulist, 1979), p. 70.

11. Eknath Easwaren, *The Bhagavad Gita for Daily Living*, Vol. 2 (Petaluma, CA: Nilgiri Press, 1979), pp. 198-199.

8. Learning To Let Go

1. As quoted in Basil Pennington, *Centering Prayer* (New York: Doubleday, 1980), p. 38.

2. John Main, O.S.B., *The Way of Unknowing* (London: Darton, Longman and Todd, 1989), p. 19.

3. Thomas Merton, *Contemplative Prayer* (New York: Doubleday, Image Books, 1969), pp. 94-95.

4. *Ibid.* p. 90.

5. *Ibid.* p. 37.

6. *Ibid.* pp. 69-70.

9. The Kingdom of God Is Among You

1. Evelyn Underhill, *The Spiritual Life* (London: Mowbray, 1984), p. 20.

2. Edward Hays, *In Pursuit of the Great White Rabbit* (Forest of Peace Books, 1990), pp. 10-11.

3. Thomas Merton, *Conjectures of a Guilty Bystander* (New York: Doubleday Image Books, 1966), p. 158.

10. The Bridging of East and West

1. *Spaceship Earth* (New York: Columbia University Press, 1966), p. 16.

2. See especially *The Marriage of East and West* (Springfield, IL: Templegate Publishers, 1982).

3. *Ibid.* p. 150.

4. John Tully Carmody and Denise Lardner Carmody, *Catholic Spirituality and the History of Religions* (Mahwah, NJ: Paulist Press, 1991), p. 157.

5. William H. Shannon, "Intuition," *The New Dictionary of Catholic Spirituality*, Michael Downey, ed. (Collegeville, MN: The Liturgical Press, 1993), p. 555.

6. F.E. Crowe, "Intuition," *The New Catholic Encyclopedia* (New York: McGraw-Hill, 1967), pp. 598-600.

7. As quoted from *New Seeds of Contemplation* (New York: New Directions, 1962), p. 267 in Shannon, "Intuition," p. 555.

8. Edward Stevens, *Spiritual Technologies* (Mahwah, NJ: Paulist, 1990), pp. 150-151.

9. Denise Lardner Carmody and John Tully Carmody, *Peace and Justice in the Scriptures of the World's Religions* (Mahwah, NJ: Paulist Press, 1988), p. 8.

10. Thomas Merton, "Christian Culture Needs Oriental Wisdom," *Catholic World* (May 1962), p. 49.

11. Thomas Merton, *Seeds of Destruction* (New York: Macmillan, 1967), pp. 182-188.

12. Michael Amaladoss, S.J., "Rationales for Dialogues with World Religions," *Origins*, Vol. 19, No. 35 (February 1, 1990), p. 574.

13. *Ibid.* pp. 574-575.

11. The Aim and Origin of Yoga

1. Pantajali, *How to Know God: The Yoga Aphorisms of Pantajali*, Swami Prabhavananda and Christopher Isherwood, trans. (New York: Penguin Books, 1969).

2. Swami Satyananda Saraswati, *Sure Ways to Self Realization* (Bihar, India: Sharga Press, 1980), p. 61.

3. Jacques Dupuis, S.J., *Jesus Christ at the Encounter of World Religions* (MaryKnoll, NY: Orbis Books, 1991), pp. 34-35.

4. Thomas Matus, *Yoga and the Jesus Prayer Tradition* (Mahwah, NJ: Paulist, 1984), p. 17.

5. Denise L. and John T. Carmody, *Eastern Ways to the Center* (Belmont, CA: Wadsworth, 1983), pp. 20-22.

6. Matus, *Yoga and the Jesus Prayer Tradition*, pp. 20-21.

7. Nancy Roth, *A New Christian Yoga* (Cambridge, MA: Cowley Publications, 1989) p. 22.

8. Carmody and Carmody, *Eastern Ways to the Center* pp. 20-25.

9. James Funderburk, *Science Studies Yoga* (California: Himalayan International Institute of Yoga Science and Philosophy, 1977), pp. iv-ix.

12. The Heart of Yoga Practice

1. B.K.S. Iyengar, *Light on the Yoga Sutras of Patanjali* (San Francisco, CA: The Aquarian Press, 1993), p. 46.

2. Yogi Amrit Desai, *Meditation-in-Motion*, Book II (Lenox, MA: Kripalu Yoga Fellowship), pp. 1-5.

3. Yogi Amrit Desai, "Kripalu Yoga: A Metaphor for Life," course handout from the Kripalu Yoga Institute, Lenox, MA.

13. Yoga and Christian Faith

1. *Dominum et Vivificantem* (On the Holy Spirit in the Life of the Church and the World) (Vatican City: 1986), p. 50.

2. See chapter six, "The Doctrine of the Incarnation: Human and Cosmic Considerations" in Dermot A. Lane, *Christ at the Center* (Mahwah, NJ: Paulist Press, 1991), pp. 130-158.

3. Francis Baur, *Life in Abundance: A Contemporary Christian Spirituality* (Mahwah, NJ: Paulist, 1983), pp. 84-85.

4. Tilden Edwards, *Living in the Presence* (San Francisco: Harper, 1987), p. 18.

5. *Ibid.* p. 17.

6. *Ibid.* p. 18.

7. Louis Hughes, O.P., *Body, Mind and Spirit* (Mystic, CT: Twenty-Third Publications, 1991), pp. 26, 150-151.

8. Joseph Cardinal Ratzinger, "Letter to Bishops of the Catholic Church on Some Aspects of Christian Meditation," in *L'Osservatore Romano*, 2 (January 1990), No. 16, p. 9.

9. *Ibid.* Nos. 27-28, p. 10.

10. Edwards, *Living in the Presence*, pp. 18-19.

11. Hughes, O.P., *Body, Mind, and Spirit*, pp. 42-50.

12. Nancy Roth, *A New Christian Yoga* (Cambridge, MA: Cowley Publications, 1991), p. 104.

13. *Ibid.* p. 35.

14. Notions Strange to Christian Ears

1. Walter Kaspar, "Reincarnation vs. Resurrection," *L'Osservatore Romano* (April 16, 1990), p. 6.

2. Christoph Schoenborn, "Reincarnation vs. Resurrection," *L'Osservatore Romano* (April 16, 1990), p. 7.

3. The question of karma is very complex. The simplest definition of the law of karma is that choices have consequences. The following passage from one of Ken Wilbur's books amply demonstrates the nuances and complexity of teaching on

karma: "According to Hinduism and Buddhism, your present circumstances are the results of thoughts and actions from a previous life, and your present thoughts and actions will affect, not your present life, but your next life, your next incarnation. The Buddhists say that in your previous life you are simply reading a book that you wrote in a previous life; and what you are doing now will not come to fruition until your next life. In neither case does your present thoughts create your present reality. Now I personally don't happen to believe that particular view of karma. It's a rather primitive notion subsequently refined (and largely abandoned) by the higher schools of Buddhism, where it is recognized that not everything that happens to you is the result of your own past actions. As Namkhai Norbu, master of Dzogchen Budddhism (generally regarded as the pinnacle of Buddhist teaching), explains: 'There are illnesses produced due to karma, or the previous conditions of the individual. But there are also illnesses generated by energies that come from others, from the outside. And there are illnesses that are provoked by provisional causes, such as food or other combinations of circumstances. And there are illnesses generated by accident. Then there are all kinds of illnesses linked with the environment.' —*Grace and Grit* (Boston, MA: Shambhala, 1991), p. 265.

4. Reender Kranenborg, "Christianity and Reincarnation," *Dialogue and Syncretism*, Jerald Fort et al., ed. (Grand Rapids, MI: Wm. B. Eerdmans Publishing Co., 1989), pp. 176-177.

5. Schoenborn, "Reincarnation vs. Resurrection," p. 7.

6. Kranenborg, "Christianity and Reincarnation," p. 181.

7. Alan Schreck, "Reincarnation All Over Again," New Covenant (May 1990), p. 36.

8. Hans Küng, *Christianity and the World Religions* (Garden City, NY: Doubleday, 1986), p. 238.

9. *Ibid.* pp. 234-235.

10. *Ibid.* pp. 238-239.

11. As quoted in Schoenborn, "Reincarnation vs. Resurrection," p. 8.

12. Gerard O'Collins, S.J., and Edward Farrugia, S.J., *A Concise Dictionary of Theology* (Mahwah, NJ: Paulist, 1991), p. 197.

13. Jim Arraj, "A Christian Explanation of Kundalini," unpublished paper, p. 5.

14. Schoenborn, "Reincarnation vs. Resurrection," p. 7.

15. Arraj, "A Christian Explanation," pp. 5, 6.

16. The definitions are largely given in Philip St. Romain, *Kundalini Energy and Christian Spirituality* (New York: Crossroad, 1991), pp. 11-12.

17. Dr. Lee Sannella, M.D., *The Kundalini Experience* (Lower Lake, CA: Integral Publishing, 1987).

18. Philip St. Romain, *Kundalini Energy and Christian Spirituality* (New York: Crossroad, 1991).

19. *Ibid.* p. 78.

20. *Ibid.* p. 103.

21. *Ibid.* pp. 45-46.

22. *Ibid.* pp. 100-101.

23. *Ibid.* p. 128.

24. *Ibid.* p. 106.

25. *Ibid.* p. 104.

26. *Ibid.* p. 100.

27. *Ibid.* p. 110. St. Roman cites a wide variety of extraordinary mystical phenomena observed among saints which has been associated with kundalini. Sts. Philip Neri and Paul of the Cross experienced intense heat that caused great discomfort. St. Macarius, St. Peter Alcantara, and St. Rose of Lima went long periods without sleep. St. Ignatius Loyola, St. Philip Neri, St. Francis de Sales, St. Charles Borromeo and St. John Vianney had experiences of inner light or mystical aureoles (halos or auras of light around their bodies which were sometimes visible to other people). St. Thérèse of Lisieux experienced spontaneous *asanas* or bodily contortions, and St. Teresa of Avila the temporary paralyses of limbs. St. Clement, St. Francis of Assisi, St. Anthony of Padua, St. Francis of Xavier, St. Anthony Claret and St. Alphonsus Ligouri were noted for bilocating. "Kundalini does not explain bilocation of the physical body, but it can account for the energy that empowers the astral body to leave the physical body and roam about where it may be seen by those with inner vision" (p. 113).

28. *Ibid.* p. 90.

29. *Ibid.* p. 98.

15. How Yoga Can Help a Christian Pray

1. John Garsuch, *An Invitation to the Spiritual Journey* (Mahwah, NJ: Paulist, 1990), pp. 70-72.

2. Brother Lawrence of the Resurrection, *The Practice of the Presence of God*, trans. John J. Delaney (Garden City, NY: Doubleday Image, 1977), p. 132.

3. J.M. Dechanet, O.S.B., *Christian Yoga*, Roland Hindmarsh, trans. (London: Burns and Oates, 1960), pp. 83-85.

4. André Van Lysebeth, *Yoga Self-Taught* (New York: Barnes and Noble, 1971), p. 77.

5. *Ibid.* pp. 71-72.

6. Walter Gibson, *The Key to Yoga* (Ottenheimer Publishers, 1962), p. 103.

7. Dr. Marcus Bach, "Introduction," in Swami Vishnudevananda, *The Complete Illustrated Book of Yoga* (New York: The Julian Press, Inc., 1960), vii.

8. Swami Vishnudevananda, *ibid.* pp. 47-50.

9. *Ibid.*

10. Lysebeth, *Yoga Self-Taught, op. cit.* p. 28.

11. Desmond Dunne, *Yoga Made Easy* (New York: Award Books–Prentice-Hall, 1966), pp. 136-138.

12. Dean Ornish, M.D., *Dr. Dean Ornish's Program for Reversing Heart Disease* (New York: Random House, 1990), p. 164.

13. *Ibid.*

14. Dunne, *Yoga Made Easy*, pp. 66, 73.

15. Vishnudevananda, *The Complete Illustrated Book of Yoga*, p. 235.

16. *Ibid.* pp. 235-237.

17. Nancy Roth, *New Christian Yoga* (Cambridge, MA: Cowley Publications, 1991), p. 29.

18. Edward Stevens, *Spiritual Technologies* (Mahwah, NJ: Paulist Press, 1990), p. 38.

19. As quoted in Ruben L.F. Habito, *Healing Breath* (New York: Orbis, 1993), p. 43. For a different translation, see *Collected Works of St. John of the Cross*, tr. Kieran Kavanaugh, O.C.D. (Washington, DC: Institute of Carmelite Studies, 1991), pp. 622-623.

16. Holistic Benefits

1. Swami Satyananda Saraswati, *Sure Ways to Self Realization* (Bihar, India: Sharga Press, 1983), p. 67.

2. Dean Ornish, M.D., *Dr. Dean Ornish's Program for Reversing Heart Disease* (New York: Random House, 1990), p. 141.

3. *Ibid.* pp. 141-142.

4. Bruce A. Baldwin, "Unplug Yourself," *US Air Magazine* (April 1993), pp. 16-20.

5. *Ibid.* p. 20.

6. Ornish, *Dr. Dean Ornish's Program*, p. 140.

7. Swami Vishnudevananda, *The Complete Illustrated Book of Yoga* (New York: Julian Press, Inc., 1960), pp. 53-55.

8. Desmond, Dunne, *Yoga Made Easy* (New York: Award Books–Prentice-Hall, 1966), p. 135.

9. Ina Marx, *Yoga and Common Sense* (New York: Lancer, 1970), p. 103.

10. J.M. Dechanet, O.S.B., *Yoga in Ten Lessons* (New York: Simon and Schuster, 1965), pp. 89-91.

17. Theological Reflections from the Christian East

1. Gregory Palamas: *The Triads*, Nicholas Gendle, trans. (Mahwah, NJ: Paulist, 1983), pp. 57-70.

2. John Meyendorff, *St. Gregory Palamas and Orthodox Spirituality* (Crestwood, NY: St. Vladimir's Seminary Press), pp. 59-60.

3. Thomas Matus, *Yoga and the Jesus Prayer Tradition* (Mahwah, NJ: Paulist, 1984), p. 94.

4. George A. Maloney, *Prayer of the Heart* (Notre Dame, IN: Notre Dame, 1981), pp. 50-51.

5. As quoted in *Speaking of Silence*, ed. Susan Walker (Mahwah, NJ: Paulist, 1987), pp. 52-53.

18. Jesus Christ at the Encounter of World Religions

1. Glen Hinson, "Ecumenical Spirituality," *Ecumenical Trends* (July/August 1991), Vol. 20, No. 7, p. 102.

2. Jacques Dupuis, S.J., *Jesus Christ at the Encounter of World Religions* (Maryknoll, NY: Orbis Books, 1991), p. 124.

3. *Ibid.* p. 167.

4. *Ibid.* pp. 140-141.

5. *Ibid.*

6. *Ibid.* p. 144.

7. Frederick W. Norris, "Christianity and Interfaith Dialogue," *Ecumenical Trends* (April 1993), p. 59.

8. Dupuis, *Jesus Christ*, p. 176.

9. *Ibid.* p. 177.

10. Frank Whaling, *Christian Theology and World Religions: A Global Approach* (London: Marshall Pickering, 1986), p. 94.

11. Dupuis, *Jesus Christ*, p. 151.

12. *Ibid.* p. 110.

13. *Ibid.* p. 109.

14. *Ibid.* p. 110.

15. Norris, "Interfaith Dialogue," p. 61.

16. Dupuis, *Jesus Christ*, pp. 93-94.

17. *Ibid.* p. 204.

18. Thomas Matus, *Yoga and the Jesus Prayer Tradition* (Mahwah, NJ: Paulist Press, 1984), pp. 154-155.

19. Dupuis, *Jesus Christ.* p. 151.

20. *Ibid.* pp. 228, 241.

21. *Ibid.* p. 241.

22. *Ibid.* p. 239.

23. *Ibid.* pp. 101, 150.

Appendix I

1. Andre Van Lysebeth, *Yoga Self-Taught* (New York: Barnes and Noble, 1971), p. 87.

Appendix II

1. Dean Ornish, M.D., *Dr. Dean Ornish's Program for Reversing Heart Disease* (New York: Random House, 1990), p. 170.

Appendix III

1. Bob Anderson, *Stretching* (Bolinas, CA: Shelter Publications, 1980).

2. *Ibid.* p. 61.

Appendix V

1. For a more detailed development of this approach to yoga than the brief synopsis provided here, see Yogi Amrit Desai, *Kripalu Yoga: Meditation-in-Motion* (Lenox, MA: Kripalu Publications, 1990), and *Kripalu Yoga: Meditation-in-Motion, Book II, Focusing Inward* (*ibid.* 1992).

I am indebted in this section to the Kripalu Teacher Training materials from which I have derived much help in providing clear and concise instructions to accompany the various posture illustrations as well as the listings of benefits, precautions and contraindications.

Other books by Thomas Ryan

Fasting Rediscovered: A Guide to Health and Wholeness for Your Body-Spirit

Tales of Christian Unity

Wellness, Spirituality and Sports

A Survival Guide for Ecumenically-Minded Christians

Disciplines for Christian Living: Interfaith Perspectives